Calling

Calling

ESSAYS ON TEACHING
IN THE MOTHER TONGUE

Gail B. Griffin

Trilogy Books
Pasadena, California

Publisher's Cataloging in Publication

Griffin, Gail B.
    Calling: essays on teaching in the mother tongue / Gail B. Griffin.
    p. cm.
    Includes bibliographical references.
    ISBN 0-9623879-2-4

    1. Women college teachers—United States. 2. Women college teachers—United States—Biography. I. Title.

LB2332.3.G5 1992   378.12092
                              QBI92-507

Library of Congress Catalog Card Number: 91-068032

pour les pucelles

We are grateful to the following poets, publishers, and copyright holders for permission to reprint material in this volume:

"Penelope Writes" from *Antarctic Traveller* by Katha Pollitt. Copyright © 1981 by Katha Pollitt. Reprinted by permission of Alfred A. Knopf Inc.

From *Miss Weeton: Journal of a Governess*, ed. Edward Hall. Copyright © 1936 by Edward Hall. Reprinted by permission of Oxford University Press.

"february 13, 1980," "friends come," "in populated," "the light that came," "mother, i am," and "to Joan" from *Two-Headed Woman* by Lucille Clifton. Copyright © 1980 by the University of Massachusetts Press. Reprinted by permission of Curtis Brown Ltd.

"Poetry, II: Chicago" from *Your Native Land, Your Life* by Adrienne Rich. Copyright © 1986 by W.W. Norton & Co. Reprinted by permission of the publisher.

"Voices" and "Aspects of Eve" from *AM/PM: New and Selected Poems* by Linda Pastan. Copyright © 1982 by W.W. Norton & Co. Reprinted by permission of the author and publisher.

"Wise Man" from *The Moon as Seen as a Slice of Pineapple* by Conrad Hilberry. Copyright © 1984 by Conrad Hillberry. Reprinted by permission of the author.

A version of "Alma Mater" first appeared in *Profession 90* (New York: MLA, 1990): 37-42.

Thanks also to the Kalamazoo College Archives for the cover photograph: The Gaynor Club. Kalamazoo College, 1914.

Contents

Introduction

This is a book about living as a feminist woman in an academic institution. Much has been written about the status of academic women, teachers and students; about women's studies; about feminist pedagogy. Not much has been written about the daily, lived reality of women who work within institutions dedicated to the Life of the Mind—itself historically a gendered concept. One thinks of Virginia Woolf's comparison of the domed roof of the British Museum to a large bald head.

A feminist professor lives inside that head. Such a life has its privileges, its protections. Such a position can also afford an excellent vantage point, for watching girls becoming women, boys becoming men. Living inside the Head can also give rise to a unique and severe kind of alienation. And that is the point when such a life breaks open.

Women are, historically, quite recent immigrants to the academic groves; we are still anomalies, regardless of our numbers, in the sense that western academic tradition is grounded in male notions of reality and knowledge, including the notion that all that is female must be excised from the world of intellect. Yet a woman teaching is surely in her oldest element, doing classic women's work—raising the young. We are thus in a wonderfully ambiguous position, in place and out of place, marginal and central. In our daily encounters, conversations, decisions, obligations, we are tangled in the most basic, most profound feminist issues. These days, hounded by the P.C. bogey, we hear on all sides that we have "won," that we are dominating the academic world, wreaking bloody vengeance, causing, as it were, a cerebral hemorrhage within the great male academic Head. Yet the feminist women I know don't feel or act like avenging Amazons. They feel besieged, conflicted, frustrated, and exhausted. Their lived reality is sharply at odds with the way it is described publicly. Their feminism is a daily act of faith.

This book was growing in my head for years before one word made it onto paper. It is at once a theoretical tome and a collection of stories, a portrait of a place and also a self-portrait. In trying to preserve, in these essays, a constant interplay between anecdote and analysis, living and reading, experience and theory, I have sought to explore feminism as it exists for me: dynamic, mundane, practical, and personal; a way of living more than a school of thought; a process more than a product; a tool much more than a solution.

In almost all cases, the names of students and colleagues have been changed to protect the innocent—and the guilty, and the rest of us who wander somewhere in between. For helping this book come to fruition, I want to thank most of all its "star," Kalamazoo College. A friend and colleague there asked me if this project was going to be an expose; I answered that it was probably more of a love letter. Finally, I think it's both.

I'm grateful to the Institute for Research on Women at Douglass College, Rutgers University, for giving me a room of my own in which most of these essays were first drafted, and to the Ragdale Foundation, where I worked on others. They were revised into a book on Marco Island, Florida, where Regina Bruno and Kate Warner so generously gave me a paradisical retreat from winter and the rest of my life. Among the manuscript's first readers, I want to thank Bob Maust for having to put it down and walk around the room, and Joycelyn Moody, for reading it behind my back and letting me know what it said to her.

Finally, I thank my mother, Barbara Hamel, who made it impossible for me not to become One of Those; and Diane Seuss-Brakeman, whose answering voice informs and encourages my calling.

Kalamazoo, November 1991

Part One

THE FORTUNATE FALL

1

The Fortunate Fall

mother i have managed to unlearn
my lessons. i am left
in otherness.
                    —*Lucille Clifton*[1]

Gee, Toto . . .

December 22, 1976, the seventeenth anniversary of my father's death.
Snow on I94. *I want this day over. I want to be heading back in the other
direction, toward Ann Arbor. I want my mom. I want a drink. What I don't
want is this job.*

*Of course I want this job. All fifth-year graduate students want a job, not
to mention a bona fide tenure-track job.*

That went without saying. Except that hardly anything else was
ever said around the windowless subterranean corridors of Wilson
Hall, the home of the English Department of the University of Virginia.
Those first-floor hallways described a perfect square, around and
around which we wandered all day, like numb trained rats awaiting
electroshock, checking to see who was in their offices, who was in the
lounge. With peers, we stopped to commiserate or brag, depending
upon who we were and who they were, about dissertations, faculty
attention or lack thereof, job possibilities. With faculty, we invented
business to warrant stopping to say how well the dissertation was
going but how worried we were about the Williams thing or the Penn
State deal. Our lives that year amounted to an unrelenting PR campaign to keep ourselves in the forefront of the great minds whose
recommendation, dropped casually into a phone receiver or a martini
glass at a conference or the last paragraph of a letter, could mean
salvation. We circled—or rather, squared—that infinite, confining corridor like hungry dogs around a heavily guarded dump.

I had spent my adolescence worshipping the Beatles. I was spending my twenties worshipping these new stars. Love, love me do.

Life had narrowed gradually and irrevocably to this point. We had come five years earlier with B.A.'s in English. We loved Keats and Williams, Spenser and Tennyson, Nabokov and Faulkner, whose loquacious, mendacious ghost loomed almost as large on that campus as that of Mr. Jefferson himself. Some of us harbored an illicit passion for Bronte or Woolf. We were of an age. We compared stories of the Strike of May '70. That first fall we were there, Nixon was reelected and Watergate was a murmur growing louder. There were a lot of us that fall, and we had to establish ourselves fast. Some of us vanquished others of us at those early parties by dropping the names of literary critics or of faculty Eminences under consideration as dissertation directors four years down the pike. An exalted few devastated the remainder by mentioning that they'd already published.

After a year, we were winnowed out. Many departed, M.A. in hand. Many simply fell away, silent. The rest of us pushed on, relieved to have made the first cut. By the second year we were identified by field—"She's a medievalist." The wiser of us were cultivating Eminences like mad, having sniffed out reputations and psyched out departmental politics. By the third year we were known by prospective dissertation topic or by the name of the Eminence to whom, if we were lucky, we already belonged, like vassals. In the fourth year, we vanished—"reading for orals." Most of our conversation at parties and in the graduate student lounge took the form of endless more-or-less educated wagers as to whom we'd "get" for each segment of that tripartite trial-by-discourse: genre, period, author. Neurotic, agoraphobic days surrounded by books, legal pads, cigarettes, coffee—a real Paper Chase, devoid of any illusion that these would someday be the Good Old Days. Once the great watershed of Orals had been navigated, we glanced back in fleeting, silent horror at those who capsized, and then we forged on down toward the big enchilada, the dissertation. It was like a marriage. To secure a dissertation director was a process resembling elaborate courtship, ending in proposal, acceptance, commitment, vows, and general rejoicing. But this romance was of the chivalric variety, where one party remains dependent, insecure, lovesick, living vicariously and parasitically upon the day-to-day responses, moods, signs, and vagaries of the Beloved Eminence. The birth of the two-hundred-page Child was not the primary concern, except to those legendary ghosts who had been around, writing, for seven, eight, nine years. For us, the consummation devoutly to be wished was the Job. For this, one thing was needful: a good chapter, finished and approved by the time the MLA job list came down from Sinai in mid-October.

This holy writ became the unmoving point on which we focussed until we were cross-eyed. I remember clearly holding it in my hands, opening it, reading through. There were that year exactly two institutions of higher learning in the United States of America which asked for my specialization, Victorian literature. Both of these institutions dismissed my application in record time. Ah, but that was only the beginning, for I'd sent out some eighty letters, typed by hand, each different, each tailoring myself to the specifications of the job description. What you want, baby, I got it. I became a shape-changer, an academic chameleon. My meager bread—the carefully concocted c.v., the various cover letters—was upon the waters, and I waited hopefully, and then, as the autumn waned, desperately, for a big fish to bite. For me, as for everyone else except the genuine stars and the healthy, sane few, this was a referendum on everything we were.

I don't want this job. I don't. Maybe when I get home tonight, there'll be a message from Penn State. God, I hate this. I'm not coming back to Michigan to some godforsaken four-year school with a name only a comedian could love. I'm not. I don't want this job.

In one of my circuits of the first-floor corridor that year, I stopped to see the department chair, on whom I had a huge crush composed of equal parts daughterly adoration, dependency on his power and influence, genuine liking, and his nice beard. That day he held out a slip of paper. Kalamazoo College in Michigan had written him a private letter. They'd be advertising in MLA, but they were soliciting the best departments in advance to garner the names of likely prospects. Because we shared a Michigan connection, and perhaps because I'd hovered with adequate frequency, taste, and pitifulness outside his office door, he'd thought of me. "Do you want me to contact them?"

Of course I did. You didn't pass anything up, a job being a job and November being November. But I wasn't going to take it. I was going East. I was going to a real University. I was going somewhere someone had heard of.

The chair of the department at Kalamazoo, discovering that I was a Michigander who would be in Ann Arbor for Christmas, cheerily suggested that I come on over for an informal preliminary get-together with just the English department.

I find the campus, sitting neatly on a hill on the west side of town. I drive in the Lovell Street side, around the parking lot behind some buildings. Suddenly the drive curves to the left and the central quadrangle opens like some wonderful painting. I stop in front of a historical marker and look up the hill, through two flanks of red and white Georgian brick buildings, to the chapel that stands at the highest point, watching over it all, its tall bell tower rising from its left side in some kind of salute or blessing. A walkway snakes across the center of the quad, but there are few signs of life this close to Christmas. The snow is falling in fat, wet flakes. I read the marker: "founded 1833 . . . first institution in Michigan offering college-level instruction . . . special honor in teaching of the sciences." So the English department probably sucks. But the place is at least respectable. God knows it looks the part. Archetypal College. But without the formidable austerity of the archetypal Lawn that Mr. Jefferson had laid out for his Academical Village of Young Gentlemen. Here the buildings look at one another, and the chapel glances down benevolently upon it all, unlike the breathtaking Rotunda, gleaming in its white solitude like Shelley's Mont Blanc.

I drive out the other side of the quad and down the brick pavement of Academy Street to a gas station, where I phone the English department to announce myself. I am directed back up Academy Street to Humphrey House, a fat old reddish brown brick mansion covered with ivy— like brown wires in December, but probably pretty in spring— and gargoyles and stone railings. It sits on a small rise of its own, across Academy from the quad. Somebody's home, obviously, once upon a time. I park behind the building, fight the wind to the front door, and enter in a gust of snow, despairing for my hair but noticing in passing the wrought ironwork around the door, where two deer move through William Morris tendrils and vines. The work of a nineteenth-century imagination. The heavy door shuts behind me and I push my hair out of my face to see the chair of the department awaiting me, smiling. We shake hands. I wait while he goes to the foot of the stairs and yells, "She's here!" Low voices, footsteps. Then down they come, one by one. Six men. Not one under fifty. Six of them. My god. I'm the only woman here.

And the woman saw that she was naked, and knew not where to hide herself.

Later, a member of the department tells me that "if I'm interested," I can meet with some of the women faculty in a lounge in the Student Union. He sounds like he doesn't expect me to be interested. "I'd love to." I am surprised by the eagerness in my voice.

Opening the massive wooden doors into the lounge, I hear female voices and see twenty or so women standing, sitting, talking, laughing. Relief washes over me. I smile, shake hands all around, sit down, and breathe. I have never had this experience before.

Carry Me Back

Spring, 1977. So OK, I'm going to Kalamazoo. Beggars can't be choosers. In the interim, there is the Dissertation. It concerns autobiographies by four Eminent Victorians, all men. I have a Director, too, a man who, happily, believes that the purpose of a dissertation is to get finished.

I have become friendly with an untenured Assistant Professor named Alice, who is a Victorianist as well. At first she scared me to death. She was tall, thin, quiet, closed. As if there were something she was not saying, biting back. But my officemate is her closest friend there, so I have come to know her. Behind that impassive, guarded surface lies warmth, gentleness, authenticity—rare commodities around here. I begin to feel relief around her, as if I'm waking up from a troublous dream. My course work is over, but I ask to audit her Victorian Novel course.

Alice constantly frets about her teaching, another rarity. The class is large. She moves to the front of the room purposefully, powerfully. She is this strong, intense presence, articulate and responsive. It is as if this course were her primary concern in life. Outside class, she seems to like to talk to me about Dickens and Trollope and Eliot. Her love of them is unadulterated with the ubiquitous irony and effete wit we have all mastered here. Watching her in class, I think, "This is what I want to be." It is the first time I have said this to myself.

In four years of college and five years of graduate school, she is my sole female professor. And I'm not even taking the course for credit.

Like other junior faculty, Alice has an administrative job. These departmental duties serve a twofold purpose, I come to see: they are hoops through which junior faculty jump to prove their potential as colleagues, and they alleviate the workload weighing down the Eminences, who have better things to do. Alice is Assistant Director of Something. The Director has just published a volume of poetry and is off on his third book tour. Meanwhile, she is approaching tenure and desperately seeking a publisher for her own book, teaching her classes, directing dissertations, sitting on oral exams, and getting married.

I'm not shocked, of course, when she's denied tenure, but I'm heartsick for her. And I'm having an additional reaction that surprises me: contempt for the club that doesn't want Alice as a member. The grapevine has it that at the gathering of Eminences where the vote was taken, it was said that, in addition to lacking the requisite published volume, Alice was too emotional. Cool, self-possessed Alice? What will become of histrionic me in this world I'm working so hard to join? Alice is approached about taking some kind of legal action, but declines. Her husband is hired at a college nearby, and they move to a house in the country.

During my last year, I go there sometimes for the weekend, when the stench of boxwood and the drone of cicadas overwhelm me. Her home is relaxed, quiet, peaceful, and so is she. I believe her when she swears to me that she's glad it happened. At first she is very careful of what she says about the department, since I am still officially a student; gradually, though, she loosens up and we cackle together. When I'm walking down the dirt roads with Alice, watching horses run, the sun fondling the hills, Virginia becomes almost beautiful again. The gods decline into the twilight, at least temporarily.

Summer, 1977. If I finish the Opus by August, I can have $500 added to my base salary and a bump up from Instructor to Assistant Professor. Motivated less by these inducements than by a burning desire to close this chapter of my life, I work like a fiend through this hellish summer. Endless 100-degree days, broken by late-afternoon thunderstorms.

Louise, the departmental star, has nabbed not only that Grail of Grails, the Yale Job, but an attractive young assistant professor to boot. Talk about your brass ring.

I turn in the final, approved, defended copy of the dissertation, pack three cats and the rest of my life in the back of my Toyota wagon, and drive west on 250, up over Rockfish Gap and down into the Valley. Carry me out of ole Virginny. I wish I were going somewhere besides Kalamazoo, Michigan. But I'm going. I'm going to teach, I'm a professor. And I'm going somewhere.

A Gal in Kalamazoo

you might as well answer the door, my child,
the truth is furiously knocking.

—Lucille Clifton[2]

In the 1820s, a twenty-one-year-old woman named Harriet Noble emigrated with her family from New York State to the wilds of southeastern Michigan. In a letter home, she described the incongruous spectacle of herself breaking stones and hauling logs to build her new home:

> I suppose most of my lady friends would think a woman quite out of 'her legitimate sphere' in turning mason, but I was not at all particular what kind of labor I performed, so we were only comfortable and provided with the necessaries of life... The logs which I alone rolled in, would surprise anyone who has never been put to the test of necessity, which compels people to do what under other circumstances they would not have thought possible.[3]

Necessity, the mother not only of invention, but of transformation.

Women came "west" sometimes eagerly, sometimes grudgingly; sometimes in fear, sometimes in hope; sometimes of their own volition, sometimes at the behest of a husband or father. They found terrible obstacles and restrictions; they found unprecedented liberty. And often, like Harriet Noble, they found new, astonishing versions of themselves.

✹❀✹

That first year. Clear air in the lungs. Waking up. Hard, bright, real things. Real voices, close to me, not muffled and far away as if I were underwater. People smiling, so interested, so encouraging.

I am still sure I'm going to leave after two or three years. I also feel oddly as if I've come home.

Expository Prose comprises half my teaching load. Exploratory Prose, the students innocently misname it, or Suppository Prose, which seems wonderfully apt to me. That first morning in that first Expos class, my first entrance into the room as a professor. I greet everyone and launch into the spiel—"this will almost certainly not be the most interesting course you'll take in your college careers, but it will almost certainly be the most important." This always gets them. They're all as new at this as I am; they sit quietly, intent on me. Especially a dark young man in the front row, who leans toward me, chin in hand, elbow on knee, brow furrowed.

I finally run out of breath and pause for questions. His hand shoots up. "You don't have your doctorate, do you?"

He's wrong: The catalogue went to press before the final certification came through from Virginia.

He's right: What the hell am I doing up here? Who am I to profess? He has smelled it, sniffed me out: an imposter.

Female English majors slip into my office to confide how glad they are I'm here. An intense young woman comes in to announce that the Women's Rights Organization is being revitalized and to ask if I will be its faculty advisor. In actuality I have replaced a man of retirement age, but I am often introduced as "Gail Griffin, who took Barb's job." Barb was the last in a long line of temporary women. I am the first one on a tenure track. When I meet people, they say, "Well. So you're the woman in the English department."
This I cannot deny. I am.

The faculty women close around me. They buoy me along. They catch me. They wise me up. They provide points of reference that I have not needed before. Or have I? I think of Alice a lot.

I often feel inept. In a committee meeting I make a point that is wholly ignored. A few minutes later a man makes the identical point and it becomes a topic of discussion. I tell this story later to two other women, who burst into laughter. "Ah, yes," one of them nods sagely. "The old Echo Syndrome."

I become particularly close to an anthropologist who is forever providing me with studies and theories to corroborate my observations and impressions. Sometimes the theories are original. One day she tells me her new theory of gender and work. Men, she says, define their jobs as their jobs are defined. Their model is the football field, where everyone has his assigned task. Women, she says, have a different model— the kitchen, where your job is whatever needs doing.
Well, of course. What other way is there to look at your job? You do what needs to be done, right?
Yeah, she says. And you get real tired.

A women's studies reading group forms. Our first selection, at the suggestion of a man in the psychology department, is Jean Baker Miller's *Toward a New Psychology of Women*. The night before we are to meet, I turn the last page, close the book, look up, and think, "My God. I thought it was just me."

On occasional Fridays the women faculty and administrators have TGIF's at someone's home. I begin to look forward to them with almost childlike anticipation. I can rely on the relief that settles over me as I walk in. I can hear the raucous laughter before I reach the front door. I can see the tension flying away, out the windows.

Some of the men drink together on Fridays too, at a local bar. I join them when they do. One Friday I face conflicting TGIF's. I try to make it to both. I feel torn, tense. I don't understand this, and it annoys me.

Some of the men drill me about the women's TGIF's with a degree of suspicion that completely confounds me. Sometimes they warn me of the dangers of separatism.

By spring quarter, when I walk into Karen's living room, or Jean's, I am conscious of performing a political act.

❈❈❈❈

Teaching is also learning. Teach what
you need to learn.
                    —*Audre Lorde*[4]

They told me when I interviewed that I could teach my Women and Literature course "if I wanted to." Doubtless hoping I wouldn't. I do. Given the departmental plum, the senior seminar, I decide to do it on Virginia Woolf. The students scarf it all up like starvelings.

I see them as a long line outside my door. Freshwomen with painstakingly arranged hair, perfect make-up, squeaky voices. Self-possessed senior women heading for law school. Poets in black tights. Feminists in fatigues and subversive T-shirts. They've come to ask about graduate schools. They've come to ask about a problem with a boyfriend. They've come to tell me they've been raped. They've come to tell me they're pregnant. They've come to tell me they're coming out. They've come to ask about black women writers. They've come to tell me that Dr. X has made a joke about gang rape in class. They've come to tell me that Dr. Y doesn't think that eating disorders is really a significant topic for a research paper.

They've come to tell me how they got here. They've come to ask me how I got here. And I, for the first time, begin to think about it.

They are by and large the daughters of privilege, white, suburban or rural. They get cars and trips abroad, and they have access to good clothes whether they wear them or not. I was one of them, so I know them. Of course, they do not see themselves as privileged. And as daughters, they aren't. The see themselves as struggling. They are. They always come for the same reason. They are looking for a way to grow up instead of down. They are looking for a viable way to live female. They are looking for information they don't even know they need. What was hidden from me remains hidden from them.

I am beset by a lot of abstractions. Political, ideology, feminist, radical. Even women's studies is an abstraction. Reality is these girlwomen. They are facts. Their need is my fuel. I have something they can use. At this point, "women's studies" is a diary of daily instances, problems, discoveries. "Feminism" comes down to pragmatism. All of it is information I must have—not only to make sense of my own life, but to give to them.

> *The movement is exactly what the word suggests,*
> *a motion of the mind.*
>   —*Toni Cade Bambara*[5]

One of Those

One night during that first year, I am home in Ann Arbor, at my parents' table. I am sharing with my mother the remainder of the wine and an account of what I am learning. She listens intently, somewhat sadly. Suddenly she says, "Oh, Gail, you're not becoming One of Those, are you?"

In her eyes as she says this, there is a wonderful emotional melange. There is fear. There is a little awe. There is also a strange subverbal comprehension, as if she knew that this would happen, that it was inevitable.

I mull over her question for a moment, and then say, "Yes, I guess I am."

2

Fair Arcadian Hill

or

"Yes, There Really Is . . . "

Welcome to Kamp Kalamazoo

When these dear scenes are left behind,
No fortune can subdue
The chords of love that closely bind
Our hearts to thee, Kazoo.
Each tree upon thy fair Arcadian hill
Is dear to us for aye;
Dark storms may come, cold blasts may chill.
But friendship e'er will stay.[1]

Honest, that really is the second verse of the Alma Mater. The lyrics are the brainchild of an esteemed member of the History Department who, in the twenties, was obviously seized with a paroxysm of that all-too-authentic brand of institutional love that can speak its name only in cliche, archaism, and syntax heroically deformed for the sake of appalling rhyme.

I have just typed the lyrics from memory.

꧁꧂

I never thought I'd stay long enough for that. In fact, when this little musical white elephant came to my attention along about my second year at Kalamazoo, it struck me as a perfect anthem for such a place: a bad parody of an inherently ridiculous genre. It reeked of midwestern, small-college provincialism. At the time, the chamber of commerce had just hit upon a clever way to exploit the city's extraordinary name, through T-shirts, bumperstickers, and buttons broadcasting the response to the question residents are constantly asked: "Yes, There Really Is A Kalamazoo!"

I had my doubts. I gave myself two years, max—the length of my initial contract.

Quite a piece of work I was then. A classic case of the alienation in which one distorts and denigrates oneself in order to sustain a learned allegiance to a privileged system. Academe, like any other establishment, teaches its apprentices not merely a body of materials and skills but a set of values, a sense of what counts and what doesn't. I was a very good student. Ergo, I came to Kalamazoo and saw what its original white settlers saw: wilderness.

There were no graduate students, so life revolved around eighteen-to-twenty-one-year-olds. The community numbered less than two thousand; my high school student body was four thousand. The intimacy, the familiarity, struck me first, making me squirm—in part because I responded to it. Everyone in the faculty and administration knew everyone else—their histories, their family problems, their eccentricities. They told endless stories about each other. Departmental boundaries, so sacrosanct where I came from, dissolved, at least socially and in many respects intellectually. Not many people were known to publish with any frequency, and then mainly articles, not books. They were all very friendly to and respectful of me, seemingly eager to have me in their midst, impressed by the U.Va. seal. In an interesting variation on a theme by Groucho Marx, I considered what it said about them that they were so glad to have me.

The faculty discussed students with astonishing familiarity. Coming from an educational background in which being one of three hundred students in a lecture hall was unremarkable, I kept reminding myself that a big class here was thirty people. If a student were in academic trouble, you would hear very quickly about family problems or social behavior or track record in someone else's class. The benign neglect, the laissez-faire distance to which I was accustomed was nowhere to be found. The faculty's interventionism, their involvement in their students' lives, their very knowledgeability about the students seemed to me paternalistic (oddly, since if this kind of nurturance is parental, it is maternal) and claustrophobic. The students themselves were a motley and interesting crew. On the whole, I liked them: a degree of Detroit-suburb insularity, but an encouraging proliferation of beards, wraparound skirts, tie-dyed shirts, long hair, marijuana smoke, alienated artistic types, political activists. After the five-year parade of Docksiders, Shetland sweaters, and Oxford shirts in Charlottesville, where the word "preppy" never gained much currency because it is essentially synonymous with "normal," this human landscape came as a relief.

I quickly learned that the students' distinctiveness and eccentricity were fed by the unique—and I mean it—academic organization of the College, an ingenious, Byzantine, early-sixties development known as the "K Plan." It sneaks up on the students, whose first year resembles that of any other college student—three quarters on campus, summer off. As sophomores, they are on campus in the fall and winter, but then gone in the spring, pursuing a Career Development internship. They return for the summer and then leave in the fall for six to nine months overseas on Foreign Study, the College's primary claim to fame, for better or worse, a completely endowed program which sends 85% of the student body all over the world. They come back in the spring or summer and then, in either the fall or winter, depending upon the major department, they vanish once more to complete a Senior Individualized Project—research, internship, creative work. They return to finish out the senior year and then are gone for good, except for those who fall behind in this wild steeplechase and remain for the summer to finish some requirement or other. They are called Super Seniors. And what I have just described covers only the "A-Plan," the most common option.

Since the great leap of faith taken by trustees, faculty, and administration in moving to the plan, it has become the Ground of All Being, driving the entire institution. The special language spawned by the Plan was part of what rankled during my first year. A private jargon, insular, like the secret tongues of children: C.D., S.I.P. (from whence a verb, "sipping"), Deviant (one who does not follow the Plan), Rising Junior or Senior (one's status during a summer quarter preceding the indicated year). People are spoken of as being "off" or "on," since everyone's whereabouts must be calculated in any given quarter (including those of faculty members, who might be off-campus in any given quarter and may not have the same off-quarter two years running).

To complicate matters further, the daily class schedule is a diabolical masterpiece, so that what is called an "eight o'clock class" meets from 8:00 to 9:00 on Mondays, Wednesdays, and Fridays, but from 8:00 to 9:40 on Tuesdays; "nine o'clocks" meet from 9:00 to 10:00 Mondays, Wednesdays, and Fridays, but from 8:00 to 9:40 on Thursdays; "ten o'clocks" meet only on Tuesdays and Thursdays, from 9:50 to 11:50; and "eleven o'clocks" meet from 10:00 to 11:40 on Mondays and Wednesdays, but only from 11:00 to 12:00 on Fridays. I am not making this up. I could go on into the afternoon hours, but usually this suffices to render first-year students (and faculty) childlike and whimpering.

The Plan impressed me, and I met seniors with an astonishing array of experiences behind them. Yet something in the *peculiarity* of all this made me impatient, ill at ease in this odd little world, solipsistic and self-referential, anomalous in the wide academic world. I felt like Alice at the Tea Party, failing to understand the references, knowing the guy next to me was really a dormouse, and wanting to tell everybody to wake up. The whole place reminded me repeatedly of summer camp, so it came as no surprise that the bookstore sold a T-shirt reading, "Welcome to Kamp Kalamazoo!"

And the camp-like rituals of the place, the tacit pressure to participate! People collaborated so as not to schedule evening events against one another. Everyone actually attended the opening fall convocation—and graduation, too, I was told. What's more, on such occasions faculty wore academic regalia, for God's sake. For me, this lack of properly sophisticated academic cynicism was summed up in the institution of Chapel. Required Friday Chapel was a thing of the near enough past to make me nervous. It survived as an ecumenical common hour at 10:00 a.m. on Fridays—and that is why "eleven o'clocks" don't meet until eleven on that day: Nothing is scheduled in that time slot. This seemed to me the epitome of the whole place's claustrophobic protectiveness, its disregard for laissez-faire individualism and secular humanism. Not to mention that such community consensus would be impossible at a real University. This Chapel phenomenon was, for me, one sure indicator that I was nowhere near the academic fast lane.

Except that when I first walked into Stetson Chapel (to hear a visiting speaker, not one of the Friday Chapel services, which I boycotted for a year or so), my heart stopped, and then beat and beat. Stetson Chapel is spare, plain, cream-colored, with tall, clear windows around the chancel and along the sides, through which are light and leaves. At the time, the only color came from dark green velvet cushions in the pews. There are two aisles—something in the odd absence of a center aisle intrigued me, as did the absence of an altar; I didn't know much about the American Baptists. Huge pillars along the aisles reach up to the roof. There is no religious imagery anywhere, little of anything to break the quiet ivory expanse. To the right of the building, as you face it, the bell tower rises into the trees. In those days an amplified tape of a carillon called the campus to Chapel. Though I knew it for a technological reproduction, the sound of bells rippling through Friday morning air always yanked at something in me. I began looking forward to occasions that drew me to this building, the quiet, unelaborated statement at the heart of this little campus; an unadorned, light-swept place, less a church than a meetinghouse somehow alluding to a heritage that eluded me, waiting.

A Usable Past

In the first half of the last century, one tributary of the great westward expansion was the so-called Second Great Awakening, the evangelical movement that swept the eastern Protestant churches and sent their missionaries into the forests and plains of what was known sweepingly as "the West." Often intellectual, progressive, and reformist in spirit, these emissaries numbered among their first concerns the building of schools —institutes, seminaries, and colleges that flowered between 1830 and 1860 in settlements-cum-towns throughout Michigan, Ohio, Indiana, Illinois, Iowa, Minnesota, and beyond. When the great universities existed only on paper and the land-grant schools were decades away, these little denominational proto-colleges proliferated in towns and cities that still today are generally small, unlikely, out-of-the-way places: Granville, Gambier, Yellow Springs, Greencastle, Crawfordsville, Grinnell, Albion . . .

In 1833, a Vermonter named Caleb Eldred and another easterner, Baptist minister Thomas Merrill, joined forces to launch the first institution of higher learning in Michigan, which would not even achieve statehood for four more years. Their site was Bronson, in the southwestern corner of the state, on the coach road between Detroit and Chicago. Their sense of the singularity of their project, as well as perhaps their vision of its importance, was reflected in its original name: the Michigan and Huron Institute, taken from the two Inland Seas between which it was planted. Its first building was completed in 1836, the year the town changed its name to Kalamazoo, the word the earliest residents had used to describe the local river, which appeared like "water that boils in a pot." The name must not have bothered the town then. Now it is something of an embarrassing burden to some, a cherished eccentricity to the rest of us. The yearbook is still *The Boiling Pot*, the literary magazine *The Cauldron*.

Two years later, in 1838, the state legislature opened the Kalamazoo Branch of the University of Michigan. The latter was still mostly a concept and would not open actual doors in Ann Arbor until 1841. The Branches, of which there were eight, were designed to stand "between the common schools and the University"[2] as a species of prep school, bringing Michigan's sons to a common academic level at which the University would take over. But additionally, their charters stipulated three other purposes: to train common-school teachers for the state, to offer agricultural and technical training at at least one Branch, and to afford education to young women through adjunct seminaries and "female departments."

In 1839, seeing the impracticality of two competing institutions in so small a town, the Baptist Institute and the state Branch merged, in what seems a marriage of convenience but was to prove a testy union of church and state. For fifteen years the Branch (the Baptists relinquished the name in return for continuing power to choose the Principal) thrived and made something of a name for itself, and in 1855 the Michigan legislature granted it a charter—the first private college chartered in the state—as Kalamazoo College.

In my first years there, I became gradually, vaguely aware of this history, sort of by osmosis. My interest was catalyzed one day while reading Eleanor Flexner's study of the suffrage movement, *Century of Struggle.* I began to notice the frequency with which people and developments central to the nineteenth-century women's movement emerged not in the "civilized" east but in the outposts of the West. Oklahoma was the first state to enfranchise women, as I'd learned to my astonishment back in 1968 in the Capitol rotunda on my senior trip to Washington. Oklahoma also boasted the first female justice on record, Esther Morris. Susanna Medora Salter of Argonia, Kansas, was the first female mayor in the country. Lucy Stone and her sister-in-law, Antoinette Brown Blackwell (also the first woman ordained as a Christian minister), were Oberlin graduates, and Antoinette's sister, Elizabeth Blackwell, became the first academically trained female physician by surviving a nightmare of harassment at the Geneva College of Medicine in western New York State. Carrie Chapman Catt graduated from Iowa State College and, closer to home, Anna Howard Shaw from Albion. Women obtained university educations first by prying open the doors of the great midwestern universities in the late 1850s and 1860s. And Flexner concludes, "By 1865, the higher education of women had made little progress except in the Middle West."[3] Surely, I thought, there is a connection between this phenomenon and the fact that most of the feminist energy in this country at the time was coming from its heartland.

This small scholarly episode was, for me, revolutionary—and representative, repeated time after time in the lives of female scholars who stumble into the story-within-the-story, the obscured saga that suddenly brings history home, endowing the institutions within which they operate with new significance, as products which they have had a hand in making, as bastions which have excluded them, and often as both—hence our tenuous relations to "our" institutions.

Today, when the history of women's higher education in the United States is treated, the discussion usually touches down briefly at Oberlin, dwells lovingly on the Seven Sisters, and forges on to the integration of the state universities and thence forward into the new century and the long wait for the Yales and Harvards (and University of Virginias) to cave in to the monstrous regiment of women pounding at the door. While the bravery and vision of those who launched the Seven Sisters are undeniable, their mission unique and critical in the project of liberating women, I sometimes suspect that the dominance in contemporary histories of Mt. Holyoke, Vassar, and Smith reflects contemporary feminist concerns. They afford such convenient metaphoric rooms of our own. But 150 years ago, in fact, many educational feminists saw coeducation, rather than separate institutions, as the more radical and ultimately more desirable goal. To their everlasting credit, feminist educators often spoke, in terms very like our own, of integration with the goal of transformation of male institutions, rather than the mere subsuming of women into unchanged dominant traditions. This is not to say that the women's colleges were not in themselves revolutionary; they played a central role in transforming Ladyhood to Womanhood as the century waned. But the women's education movement was multifaceted, and one of its arguments held that intellectual progress for women (and the social progress incumbent upon it) would come most directly through coeducation—because it would bring women into unprecedented intellectual and social contact with men, because it would ensure for women the most rigorous curricula and standards, and because the male institutions, for better or worse, were the privileged and prestigious ones.

Coeducation, for various reasons, was a western phenomenon.[4] And decades before the highly publicized battles to open the universities, the groundwork was being laid at those tiny colleges dotting the midwestern landscape. To study their histories with a woman's eye is to unearth a subtle, desultory, and devious text revealing the subterranean progress of women's education beyond anomalies like Smith, Oberlin, and Antioch. The real story of coeducation in the West is one of advance by hook or by crook, integration via the back door and the windows, pragmatic adjustments, gradual accommodation to and compromise with "frontier" necessity. Its settings are towns where financial exigency precluded totally separate institutions for men and women. It describes female departments, female seminaries, coordinate female institutions overlapping and slowly merging with male colleges. It tells of legislatures establishing "Normal Departments" or "Normal Schools" open to women only in order to stock the state's or territory's primary and secondary schools with teachers. Oftener than not, coeducation simply evolved as shared space gave way to shared curricula and faculty and then to equality in the granting of degrees, the final prize. If something holds all the diverse threads together, it is that women rushed into the marginal academic territory allotted them and then shaped themselves into a flying wedge to push further toward the center.

I've discovered that every story of every little college like Kalamazoo reveals a foremother—a dean or principal or teacher, some woman of extraordinary gifts, power, and persistence who presides over some chapter of the institution's life and whose portrait appears somewhere on campus. At Kalamazoo her portrait hangs publicly now, but when I found her for myself it was sheltered in the College archives. Her name was Lucinda Hinsdale Stone. A brilliant, free-thinking girl, youngest of twelve children of a Vermont family, she was deeply seared by local gossip and ridicule surrounding her ambition to learn Greek—a simple enough intellectual interest, but highly symbolic in academic history, where Greek was the secret tongue of male academic tradition. She spoke once or twice of wanting to go to college—and then, in the wake of the resounding laughter, fell silent. Denied any prospect of a career, she, like many of her sisters, married one, in the shape of one of her teachers, James Andrus Blinn Stone, a Baptist minister, and came west with him when he was called to the Principalship of the Kalamazoo Branch. But in accord with its charter, the Branch had established a Female Department, and Lucinda Stone became its Principal.

She and her husband seem to have worked out one of those dynamic nineteenth-century marriages in which two people engaged in the same life-consuming work create an invincible, charismatic force that sweeps people and institutions into its vortex, moving the world around it largely by sheer power of personality. The Stones increased enrollment exponentially and made a name for their little school. And from the outset they quietly, gleefully fostered coeducation wherever and however they could. Very much people of their time, they believed that the relentless evolutionary progress of the race was drawing Woman ever closer to her finest hour, wherein educational, social, and political emancipation would free her gifts to the betterment of the species. Together the Stones presided over the Branch through its reincarnation as Kalamazoo College and for eight years afterward, until they were literally, and viciously, driven from office in 1863 by a reactionary and explicitly antifeminist movement in the local Baptist hierarchy.

In the twenty years of the joint Stone administration, Mrs. Stone took her Female Department into the realm of legend, raising enough money to build it an impressive new edifice as the campus moved gradually from Bronson Park, downtown, westward toward the hill on which the College now sits. She and her husband also accumulated enough prestige to draw to this oddly named city a stunning array of notables. I knew about Emerson's visit; only in my pursuit of this other story did I discover that Elizabeth Cady Stanton, Frederick and Helen Douglass, and Sojourner Truth had all disembarked at Kalamazoo, all stayed at the Stones' house on the hill, some yards from my office in Humphrey House. "We were," wrote Mrs. Stone, "openly anti-slavery in thought and acknowledged women suffragists, as were most of those who filled the lecture platform of those days, and toward the private hotel on the hill people of this kind drifted."[5]

After the fall in 1863, Lucinda went on teaching women—in her own private academy, on eight study trips to Europe and the Middle East, and in the plethora of women's clubs she fostered in Michigan, through which she came to national recognition and a central role in the National Federation of Women's Clubs. Entirely ignorant of this last phenomenon, I turned down another path, into the history of the women's club movement, learned what it accomplished for older women, isolated in their homes and in their ignorance, and the dimensions of women's educational history shifted once again for me. I also discovered that the admission of women to the University of Michigan in 1870—considered then and now a landmark decision—meant the admission of one Madelon Stockwell, Lucinda's protege, who applied to the University in order to study Greek. It was pressure exerted upon the regents by Lucinda and James Stone for fifteen years before that finally made it possible for Madelon to take her entrance exam, in which she was asked to translate Ismene's speech from Sophocles' *Antigone*: "But it behooves us in the first place to consider this, that we are by nature women, so not able to contend with men . . ." Madelon called this "an instance of the irony of fate"[6] when she wrote of it to her mentor. Again I imagine the slow smile on the face of the woman who had passed on to her the secret, the occult art, of translating the forbidden tongue.

Part of the character of my mind—a feature which I used to regard as typically feminine and therefore embarrassing—is that I come to ideas and realms of knowledge most quickly and eagerly through biography, a lived life. So it was that Lucinda Stone became my attendant spirit, my guide to the heart of my chosen profession and to the heart of the institution that had chosen me. My research conspired with my daily life at the College to give me an odd new sense of the significance of what I was doing and where I was doing it. I seemed to be moving in two time zones at once. And my words, my steps seem to echo down corridors stretching more than a century behind me.

A Gender Gap

In an article called "Expansion and Exclusion: A History of Women in American Higher Education," Patricia Albjerg Graham notes that between the mid-nineteenth century and the mid-twentieth, a change in the ethos of higher learning occurred, one that reflected the emergence of the leviathan university as the representative American educational institution. Generalism gave way to specialization, teaching to research, so that the generation of "new" knowledge superseded the transmission of heritage. The old-style professor who had embodied that general cultural heritage was overtaken in the evolutionary march by the new disciplinary expert, loyalty deeply rooted in an ever-narrowing academic field, in contrast to his predecessor's loyalty to the institution itself. And the nineteenth-century pedagogue's concern for the student's "character"—by which was meant something like what we tend now to refer to as "the whole student"—gave way to the modern professor's concern with the training of the student's capacities in a given field or skill in preparation for a professional role.[7]

In that first year at Kalamazoo, wandering around the campus half-contemptuous, half-tantalized, my culture shock was in some ways the result of having landed in an academic outpost of the nineteenth century. The progressive features of the K-Plan aside, Kalamazoo, like many of its sister schools, is indeed an anomaly, an evolutionary vestige, a wondrous dinosaur. Very basically, it is undergirded by those values of the last century, though they survive by no means intact, unchanged, or confirmed by general consensus. Examined against the gigantic shadows of the multiversities, colleges like Kalamazoo by and large require their faculty to be generalists (hence their inferior reputation amongst their peers, regardless of their reputation as teachers or thinkers). I teach my "specialty," Victorian literature, once every other year. Teaching has traditionally taken clear precedence over research in our communal discourse and evaluation procedures. Institutional loyalty and involvement—that summer-camp quality that disturbed me—are profound. And for the most part, such colleges take greater cognizance and care of the student's "character" than do universities, though this may be a function as much of size as of values. The late twentieth century impinges enough so that there is at least a constant battle between the forces for professional preparation at any cost and the forces for a well-rounded education for life, but the latter philosophy dominates our public and private discourse.

A corollary of Graham's argument, of course, is that those nineteenth-century educational values also happen to overlap with traditional female values. Schoolmarms, like most women workers, are generalists, lacking the luxury of overspecialization and also usually viewing their work and its relation to the world in a holistic way. Every housewife is a highly accomplished generalist. Where the "researcher," that lonely, solipsistic figure in lab or library stack, is male, the "teacher" is a woman, and the woman so often is some form of teacher that nineteenth-century pioneers in education deemed teaching her natural vocation. Teaching, of course, is communal, other-directed, service-oriented, parental. *Loyalty* to a discipline or to one's own project at the expense of the institution violates the traditional female imperative of concern for the group, especially when the "institution" is no abstraction but a concrete small community of people dependent upon one another—rather like a family, to use our most overworked metaphor at Kalamazoo. And the care for the "whole student"—well, of course, that's nurturance.

I have noticed over the years an uneasy, subliminal recognition among faculty and administrative colleagues that in some obscure way many of Kalamazoo's values are tinged with femaleness. Sometimes it emerges in comments that our student "stars" are usually women. Sometimes I see it in male discomfort when the "nurturant" aspects of the pedagogical role are encouraged, or even discussed; or in defensive, reactionary tributes to the virtues of disciplinary depth, departmental loyalty, "hard knowledge," and a pitiless male deity called Rigor. A few years back I spotted it when an incoming class broke down 60% female, skewing our usual gender balance for the first time since World War II. (Up through the fifties there was an acknowledged, carefully preserved policy of maintaining a male majority—for the sake of social life, I'm told. Lowered supply and hence increased demand for the female minority would keep the boys in line.) Beneath the genuine concern about attrition and other campus-life ramifications was a certain queasiness about the danger of becoming perceived as a "girls' school." Which is to say, in the symbolic language of gendered thinking, academically unmanly, vaguely homosexual. In fact, that particular subtext has surfaced in recent faculty anxiety over the emergence of homosexuality from the closet as a campus issue. In any case, I have no doubt that at least a healthy handful of my male colleagues, and some of the women, would feel considerably more comfortable at a more intellectually virile spot in academe. Without doubt, Kalamazoo has sissy tendencies. And that certainty, of course, lay at the root of the uneasiness afflicting the junior member/sole woman in the English Department when she arrived in 1977, having learned her lessons well.

In part, this academic machismo is a reaction to the hard times besetting small private colleges, and Kalamazoo has seen its share. Such colleges are in profound identity crisis, seeking markets, seeking, I think more importantly, a way either to shed the nineteenth century for good and appeal directly to the junior technocrats marching out of high schools, or to refurbish those old values, selling them expertly to an age which hungers for them, knowingly or not, in an educational market where they are a rare commodity whose stock may well be going up.

Lately, at Kalamazoo, I wonder which road it is that we are taking. Loyalty to the traditional values of liberal arts colleges seems strong, but recently its strength has been enhanced by its alliance with the reactionary conservative academic movement whose figurehead is Allan Bloom and whose nostalgia privileges precisely the most masculinist elements of educational tradition in the last century and earlier: essentially hierarchical concepts of significance, value, and quality enshrined in canons that dilute and simplify pieces of human experience and exile the rest. Flanked by Bloom & Co. on one side and the Technocrats on the other, a genuinely liberal, and liberating, education is hard beset.

Yet I somehow persist in thinking that if it has a chance of surviving anywhere, it may be at a place like Kalamazoo. In my most passionate ravings against the encroachment of atomistic, deadening robots and white patriarchal ghosts, I often realize, with a jolt, the degree to which personal principal has fused with "institutional loyalty." And I wonder how I ever came to this.

You Get What You Need

I laugh at all the faculty stories now, familiar as family stories. And just as we internalize family incidents that occurred before our birth, I am sometimes aghast to realize that I'm telling a story about something that happened at the College five years before my arrival. I am careful never to plan an event in conflict with another, and I know just whom to call to find out what I want to know, about a student or anything else. I toss off the strange jargon as if I'd been speaking it all my life, and I must remind myself to translate for foreigners. I gossip and commiserate around the faculty table at lunch, embroil myself in internal intrigues and crises. I show up for every convocation after fetching my very own regalia from the closet in my office. And I never schedule anything for 10:00 on Friday morning. The chapel tower has a ring of eight huge brass bells, cast in Whitechapel Foundry, London, where the Liberty Bell was cast. The soprano bell, all four hundred pounds of her, is inscribed for Lucinda Stone.

I try consciously to sustain a degree of the outsider's perspective against being wholly chewed, swallowed, and digested by the place. I am the first to descry, and decry, its limitations—the self-importance, the claustrophobia, the gossip, the oppressive weight of campus opinion, the particular kind of conservatism peculiar to small colleges, the various chauvinisms. But I think I may be a lost cause.

Often when a student is distraught at some one of life's betrayals, I toss off the only words of wisdom I ever gathered at Mick Jagger's knee: "You can't always get what you want, but if you try sometime, you might find you get what you need." What is it I needed that Kalamazoo provided? I needed, first of all, some gently corrosive force to erode the shell I'd accreted in the course of my graduate education. It crumbled surprisingly quickly, and behold, there I was after all. I responded like crazy to a place that seemed to need and value the things I had and, at heart, valued. I needed to know again that education was fundamentally about people talking to one another, and I found them. I also needed a small pond in which to be a big fish, as my dissertation director had astutely told me. I swam around happily and made a few waves in the process. After years of tension and uncomprehended alienation, I needed to belong, and quickly found that I did.

But there was more to this belonging. I needed a tradition in which to root my doings, my believings, as a teacher and as a woman. My own academic upbringing had given me precious little soil for that. I found it in the College's complex, sometimes contradictory past, which included both Lucinda Stone and the reactionaries who threw her out, and in its equally complex and contradictory present. And finally, I needed a sense of vocation, of being called to something. I had begun to find it at Virginia, the first time I stepped into a classroom. Now, at Kalamazoo, I was positively overwhelmed by the sense of a call for me, a space, several spaces, that I could and must fill, and important things that I might become.

One thing that I became was a feminist. I suppose that might have happened anywhere, for my time was certainly ripe for that particular evolutionary spurt—indeed, it was probably overdue. But in part Kalamazoo unwittingly nursed the viper in its bosom through its values, its history, its ambience of general tolerance and encouragement, and its sturdy coterie of like-minded faculty, staff, and students. Yet of course, in another sense, my feminism was honed in friction with an institution which is, like any other, run by men via male structures, perpetuating an androcentric cultural heritage. So regardless of, because of, and in spite of Kalamazoo, I became a feminist.

My gradual coming to belong to Kalamazoo was inseparable from my coming to feminism, which seems now to define a large chunk of the role I vaguely sensed was waiting for me there. Yet to be a woman is fundamentally not to belong to most institutions, and if feminism is a kind of conscious womanhood, then to be a feminist is to be perpetually aware of that marginality; indeed, it means on some level to choose it, to resist full belonging.

Which conundrum serves to explain why I and thousands of other women live in such tension with the institutional structures in which we operate. Some women, feminist and not, never feel the tension or resolve it for themselves. Some feminists claim their alienation absolutely, so that the college becomes a place of employment, nothing more. For me, and I suspect for the majority of us, neither path is possible. The one is a lie, the other a kind of compartmentalization which most women, born integrators, find impossible and unhealthy. So we navigate as we can. We feel deeply valued and brutally exploited, usually within the same day. We know how much we know that could make a difference and how little we can do. We have spoken the academic tongue for thirty or forty years, taught it for ten or twenty, yet we speak and are not heard, or are heard and dismissed. We are beloved of our students and denied the respect we watch them lay at the feet of our bearded colleagues. Having learned that academe is about conservation of heritage, we work to excavate and conserve our own and are belittled. Having learned that academe is about the courageous, unfettered examination of all established truths, we courageously examine established truths and are called political ideologues, fraudulent academicians. Having learned that academe is about imagination, possibility, the probing of the unknown, we imagine, posit, and probe and are called radical or, what's sometimes even more damning, "not serious."

Sometimes the tension is creative, sometimes merely tense. One day it seems we really have transformed "our" institutions; the next day it's quite clear that we've been had, swallowed whole. From one day to the next, we get by. With a little help from our friends.

3

Alma Mater

The Oldest Profession

In truth, woman's oldest profession is teaching. Or rather, it is her oldest occupation; it became her profession only in the last century, under conditions fraught with paradox. The feminization of teaching came about in a culture whose dominant ethos, where gender was concerned, rested heavily on the belief that women were mentally limited and primitive creatures. It was not simply that their minds were inferior to those of men; it was that in the larger Victorian concept of the human species, men *were* the head, women the heart—or, in an alternate construction, the vile body. The alternatives depended in large part upon class and race. In either case, women had a symbolic function to perform having nothing whatever to do with the mind—in fact, inherently opposed to it. The Good Woman, the Heartwoman, was enshrined in the middle-class home. But absolutely central to her symbolic and practical function was the icon of motherhood and her supposedly inherent disposition to supervise the development of children. And this made her a natural-born teacher.

Thus was the Cult of True Womanhood hoisted on its own petard: Behind the Angel in the House stood a genuine woman whose work in large portion consisted of teaching. This was the cunning argument seized by proponents of the opening both of universities and of the teaching profession to women. This argument, plus a mammoth demographic problem called Redundant Women, a vast American frontier demanding teachers, and the irresistible attractions of a pool of very cheap labor, gave middle-class women their first viable, respectable profession. They proceeded to enter it in droves, and, true to form, the male teachers moved up the ladder into administration and professorships and large salaries. In only a short time the stereotype of the schoolmarm was fully current. And from then on, little girls were counseled that if the mythical prince did not show up to redeem them, they could always teach.

Teaching, our last resort, our fall-back. Along with nursing, the most traditional of female occupations; thus it was that the likes of Catherine Beecher and Florence Nightingale were able to turn them into professions. Yet how tenuous, how uneasy, how problematic still is our presence in academe, especially at what are called the higher levels. In this world built so firmly on rigid concepts of authority—scholarly, administrative, pedagogical—we are impostors, pretending to an authority that in fact, in the external world, we do not have. We are alien elements who, through history's loopholes, have managed to infiltrate what is arguably the most powerful profession in the world: the profession of manipulating ideas and messing around with the heads of children.

There is an undeniable, understandable thrill in entering the academic world as a woman. I remember it clearly—the rush of power, the sense of liberation from student serfdom, the pride in one's obvious accomplishments and in taking one's place in the procession of the sons of educated men, to use Woolf's classic phrase, the long black line stretching back into the dim medieval past. For a woman there is the thrill of being, by virtue of one's appointment, taken for an authority, though the thrill is mitigated by that persistent little voice whispering that you are a fraud and will be found out sooner or later. But if you work like a dog and behave yourself, maybe you can forestall exposure.

After that honeymoon period, if you settle in for the long haul (also known as the tenure track) at a single institution, there comes a period of readjustment. You stop being grateful that they've taken you in and start wondering just what it is that you're doing here. In other words, you begin to define your relationship to your place of employment. Doubtless every young instructor or assistant professor goes through this realignment. But for a woman it has an additional dimension. For in situating herself consciously within an academic institution, she is analyzing and negotiating her position within academe itself, determining her relation to its assumptions and traditions, its ceremonies and values, most of which originated not only without her and despite her but in overt opposition to her, thus constructing the intellectual and philosophical undergirding for her oppression.

I hasten to amend: "Some women." Some women actually entertain such reflections while standing in the long black line before commencement, looking around at her colleagues in their costumes. The woman two places ahead in line may only be fumbling with her stole, which was fashioned to attach to a man's shirt button, or bobby-pinning her mortarboard into place.

A Portrait in the Attic

The only recourse is the attic, as Jane Eyre well knew. You may not own the house, but in the attic are old dress forms, brittle letters tied with blue ribbon, scrapbooks of fading daguerreotypes that testify to a woman's presence—your great-aunt, your great-grandmother, some woman you need to know about who has waited generations to speak to you.

I found her by means of what is at once a haphazard and supremely appropriate route. Shortly after I arrived at Kalamazoo, I devised an Expository Prose assignment that proved very successful. I asked the students to research some aspect of the College itself—programs, history, architecture, people. They enjoyed it and the papers were among the least painful of the quarter. And each time, a handful of the students discovered the Archives—a college's attic.

Along about my second or third year on the faculty, a young man produced a paper recounting a scandal that had ripped through the College in 1863. The first president, James Stone, and his reputedly remarkable wife Lucinda, head of something quaintly (and, I thought, faintly zoologically) entitled the Female Department, had run the place in tandem for twenty years with astonishing success. Then, for reasons obscured by time, President Stone became the object of a concerted smear campaign on the part of the Baptist trustees, culminating in charges of sexual liaisons with female students. Mrs. Stone was charged with, among other travesties, polluting the curriculum with French novels, Byron, and German philosophy, reading popular periodicals, and promoting feminism. In November of 1863, the dynamic duo tendered their resignations.

By this point in my student's paper, I was engrossed. But the kicker lay ahead: In protest, three-quarters of the student body withdrew from the College. I reread the sentence, checked the footnote, read it again, and finally asked the author if he was sure he'd read his source correctly. He promised he had. He got a decent grade and I determined to check this incredible statistic. As a green assistant professor, I drooled at the thought of such a dramatic demonstration of student devotion. Who were these people, and what power elicited this degree of loyalty? And what was a Female Department? And above all, who was this woman, whose name I had never heard, whose portrait hung on no College wall, and whose radical tendencies, if my student was correct, had run her afoul of the Fathers?

I found her a year or so later. I mentioned her to the director of the library, who said, "Oh, haven't you seen our portrait of her?" She led me downstairs to the attic, as it were, unlocked the door, and ushered me in. My eyes swept the walls—the shelves of old yearbooks and newspapers, the old photos and awards. Suddenly I turned to look behind me, and there she was. The portrait shows her at mid-century, in her thirties or early forties, her dark, shiny hair brushed back and falling in Elizabeth Barrett Browning ringlets around her ears. She is seated, looking up from a book on which her hand rests. Hers is a finely carved face, handsome rather than pretty, not the least bit delicate. Her large grey eyes are gentle and grave. They look like they have seen a great deal and are ready for more. Her wide, eloquent mouth turns up ever so slightly at the corners, as if she knows something about you. The face just radiates intelligence and power. It is lovely, engaging, but it is the face of someone I should not wish to try to fool and certainly should not like to have for an enemy. The director left me alone with her and for about fifteen minutes I did nothing but look back at her, suffused with the slightly eerie feeling that rather than having come down here to find her, I had been drawn down here to where she waited for me.

In 1982 I procured a quarter's leave to find out who she was. In the three frantic months allotted me, I found out nearly all there is to know about her. The weariness of leaving a library at 5 p.m., eyes bleary, head swimming, fingers dusty—I hadn't known that since graduate school. But this was different, not an assignment but a quest. I had those quiet thrills known to biographers—the days I pieced together a small mystery or matched up event and date; the days I received letters from her descendants, providing information and wishing me godspeed; the day I deciphered the scrawl of the aged, nearly blind Elizabeth Cady Stanton, writing to Lucinda about politics, health, their families; the day I decided to transgress the injunction of a label asking me to handle only the xerox copy and instead took softly in my fingers a brittle, yellowed sheet, typewritten, beginning, "My Dear Mrs. Stone," and signed "Susan B. Anthony." And there were those days when the century between us thinned to a near-permeable membrane: when her eclectic, welcoming spirit, incorporating works by and about women into her teaching and writing, seemed to shed a blessing on our young, besieged women's studies program; or when the reactionary conservatism that drove her from her College seemed a breath away from what was sweeping Reagan's America in 1983.

More importantly, though, Lucinda Stone became my point of entry into my own professional and intellectual life, in three significant ways. First, she led me into the history of American women. Each of her involvements, her correspondents, her causes led me ignorantly but eagerly down a new road, scrambling to unearth the context that would give these things significance—the abolition movement, the women's club movement, the Women's Building at the World's Fair, municipal suffrage movements, and above all the history of women's education. Second, she led me to rethink the question of historical importance. What I had always heard of Lucinda from old-timers on campus was that she was "ahead of her time." (A former president of the College had avowed that she was "the best man who ever led the institution.") I discovered, on the contrary, that she was very much of her time, that extraordinary as she was, she was one of multitudes of women occupied in the same struggles, from whom she drew her strength. I came to see that her ordinariness and extraordinariness do not conflict, and I came to understand that to relegate her to a ghetto of anomalies is to diminish her, the thousands of women with whom she worked, and the work they did. Enshrining visible, accomplished women in history as "exceptional" is one means by which the whole fabric of women's history is kept dark. Through this realization I arrived at a new understanding of the relation between the individual and history, the single and the collective, the remarkable and the mundane, that has soaked into all my thinking and teaching.

And finally, she led me into my profession. My most important discovery in search of Lucinda came at the very beginning of my search. Not knowing where to start, I was prompted by some pre-science or presence, maybe the portrait itself, to begin at home, in our archives, with a slim volume commemorating an event in May of 1883: the reunion in Kalamazoo of three hundred former pupils of the Stones from the years before 1863. The volume consists mostly of transcribed speeches made on that occasion. So my second glimpse of Lucinda, under the watchful eyes of that portrait, came through the eyes of her students, her "girls," the alumnae of the Female Department. That is to say, I knew her first as a teacher.

Reading panegyric upon paean, I was boggled. My specialty being Victorian prose, the stylistic excesses were familiar to me. But these women, in their fifties and sixties at the time of the reunion, spoke of their former teacher with an intensity and reverence whose genuineness seared through the words themselves and through the years since they were spoken—one hundred years exactly.

"I can recall now," said one alumna, "so vividly, your every tone and gesture, when after the morning reading, you would often try to impress upon us some truth that had just seemed to strike you."[1] Said another, "Even the dullest of us did not hesitate to bring our thoughts to you, sure of as careful consideration as if we had been your equal." This humble soul went on: "We remember how tenderly you led us, making us know our ignorance not so much by anything you said, as by our own quickened sense of comparison. Somehow you had the power of divining the best there was in us, and the tact to bring it out."[2] Among the most illustrious alums gathered that day was Alice Boise Wood, whose father taught at the University of Michigan and snuck her into classrooms as an auditor in the 1850s, before Mrs. Stone's other pupil was officially admitted. So Mrs. Wood spoke from a position of unusual educational privilege: "No instructor—and I came under many both in Michigan and Chicago Universities—ever so deeply impressed upon me the necessity, and also the possibility of progressive accomplishment, of constant enlargement, as you taught it to me. And you taught that lesson by the best of all methods—an ever present example."[3]

Throughout these testimonials, I noticed, a certain metaphor recurred. "Your great Mother love," said one of the women, "large enough to take in all of us girls, with all our faults and failings, in our eyes surrounds your face with a circle of light."[4] And again: "We must thank our Alma Mater—our dear Mrs. Stone—for the impulse toward the good, the true, and the beautiful she gave us; with the firm principle she aimed and fixed in our youthful minds; that life was in earnest, and women had a place to fill, a work to do, as well as men; under God's guidance she must act well her part. . . we are all Mrs. Stone's 'girls'. . . and to the end, we and our children shall 'rise up and call her blessed.'"[5]

I should get such evaluations.

Sifting through other sources, I kept running across the same metaphor. When Lucinda Stone died in 1900, the *Kalamazoo Gazette* quoted another old pupil, describing her classroom: "It appeared like a lot of girls having a friendly talk with their mother, yet never was teaching more effective."[6] Another student's memory preserved a remarkable picture of her, seated at the front of the classroom, hearing recitations, with her third son, Jim, on her lap and the family dog, Prince, at her feet.

That image lodged firmly in my imagination throughout the months of my research: the academic Madonna, in a circle of light; Mother and Child—and Dog. A group of eager girls surrounding her, self-doubtful but inspirited, en*couraged* to take themselves seriously, to prepare for a future, to value their minds, to live worthy lives. A kind of Sapphic academy in the midst of an academy that denied them a real place, centered on a woman who was daily, incarnate proof of the existence of that chimeric, unnatural phenomenon, a Female Mind. A lot of girls having a friendly talk with their mother. Yet never was teaching more effective.

Quite a picture. It might come straight out of a terrible Victorian genre painting except that it is also an icon of tremendous power. It is a beautiful image, but it troubled me. What, really, would I do with evaluations like that? Would I indeed be thrilled, or would I be embarrassed? How would I feel about the provost or the personnel committee reading them: "Your great mother love." "Our dear Alma Mater." "How tenderly you led us." "Divining the best that was in us." No pretense that she was one of the boys, no comparison with her husband or any other man on the faculty. But neither any suggestion that this entirely female ideal of pedagogy was somehow a lesser quantity. No embarrassment whatever about the presence of Mother in the classroom, as if it were the most natural thing in the world. Yet never was teaching more effective.

Family Portrait

mother: 1. a female that has borne an offspring.
2. a female who has adopted a child or otherwise established a maternal relationship with another person.
3. a creative or environmental source: "Religion is the mother of the sciences."
4. a woman having some of the responsibilities of a mother: *a house mother.*
5. qualities attributed to a mother, such as the capacity to love: *a baby that appealed to the mother in her* [or, for that matter, "your great Mother love . . . "].
6. an affectionate, familiar term for addressing an elderly woman.

father: 1. a male parent.
2. a male who functions in a paternal capacity with regard to another; especially, a man who adopts a child.
3. any male ancestor; especially, the founder of a line of descent; a forefather.

4. a man who creates, founds, or originates something: "George Stevenson has been called the father of railways."

5. Capital. a) God. b) the first member of the Trinity.

6. Any elderly or venerable man.

(The American Heritage Dictionary)

To know itself, a culture has only to turn to its dictionaries.

The initial definitions correspond. The second are close, though there is that interesting discrepancy between a "paternal capacity" and a "maternal relationship." The third "mother" corresponds to the fourth "father," with another striking difference: the male creative source is human and individual; the female is an abstract force or idea. The fourth and fifth "mothers" are distinguished by their "responsibilities" and "qualities"; the third "father" rests on historical status. There are apparently no female ancestors, no foremothers. The fifth "father"—well, he's unique. The sixth mother and father are similarly aged, though one gets affection, the other veneration.

"To father" is to beget biologically, to inject successful sperm. "To mother" has almost nothing to do with childbirth; it is to sustain a relationship of a certain kind. To father is an act; to mother, a process. Dictionary fatherhood is status, identity. Dictionary motherhood is a composite of qualities, roles, and responsibilities. The father is a being, the mother a force.

Alma Mater: from the Latin, "nourishing mother."

The Motherheart

Lucinda Stone did not intend to teach when she came west with her husband in 1842. Indeed, she was pregnant with their second son and anticipated making a home for the new principal of the school. But there sat the Female Department, mandated by state law, wanting a director. She thus happened into teaching at precisely the point in American history when Catherine Beecher was promoting the training of women to teach in the "west" and the profession was being feminized. Lucinda Stone came to take teaching in grave earnest as women's work, an almost mythically heroic vocation requiring superior skill and careful training and retraining. Its particular rigors for female teachers, who were mostly underpaid, overworked, undertrained, unreasonably constrained and regulated, were the object of her deepest, angriest concern. With that distinctively Victorian evolutionary ideal of life as a process "of progressive accomplishment, of constant enlargement," she wrote that "A teacher's life, of all lives, must be a growing one."[7] Women could not grow under present conditions, but must wither and shrink. She wrote of seeing a disproportionate number of former teachers in female mental institutions. And what became of their progeny? A starving mother cannot nurture strong children, after all. It is characteristic of Lucinda Stone that the metaphor of the teacher *in loco parentis*, instead of demeaning the profession, enhanced its seriousness for her. "Surely," she wrote, "there is no responsibility like that of a teacher, except that of a parent . . ."[8] The professions were not simply analogous, but kindred in spirit. If she assumed the demeanor and attitude of a mother in her classroom, it had little to do with sentimental reverence and everything to do with responsibility, commitment, and relationship to the minds and hearts within her sphere of influence—that circle of light.

This I began to understand one day when, reading through some of her writings, one sentence yanked me up short: "The motherheart must be at the center of all true teaching."[9]

So it was not a mere accident of gender, I thought, nor a fond analogy on the part of her devoted "girls." It was a consciously adopted maternal ideal of pedagogy. In a century when even most feminists employed the generic male in speech and writing (though I think she is the first person on record to use the word "freshwoman"), Lucinda Stone, describing her profession, adopts a generic female reference, unqualified: not "all women's teaching" or "all teaching of girls" but "all true teaching," period, must be informed by the maternal spirit. Did this woman comprehend what she was saying?

Perhaps it was merely a slip, or a function of the predominantly female audience to whom she was writing. Perhaps.

A maternal ideal of pedagogy discomforted me for a long time. Only in part was my discomfort a function of ingrained notions of academic seriousness, which is to say maleness, based on nine years of tutelage by father-professors. As a junior faculty member I was spending a great deal of time, and I saw my female colleagues spending a great deal of time, wrestling with the pressure from their students and sometimes their colleagues to play Academic Mommy—to do the housework, kiss the hurts and make them better, forgive everything, take on the wretched refuse, emotional and psychic, of academic life, play intercessor and softy. Struggling to resist this stereotypical trap, many academic women overcompensate and become as tough, distant, compartmentalized as Professor Kingsfield on a bad day. In a culture that idealizes Motherhood but holds real mothers in contempt, women know only too well how near impossible it is to enact Mother but elicit the respect accorded to Father. My own tendencies bending strongly in the motherly direction, I was doubly leery of maternal pedagogy, and doubly awed by Lucinda Stone's apparent ability to bring it off with neither internal conflict nor external loss of respect.

Except the whiff of surprise in that initial conjunction: "*Yet* never was teaching more effective," as if, in a maternal classroom, one would expect it not to be.

The Mother and Child Reunion

One night in June of the year I discovered Lucinda, I was sitting with a friend on the porch of the first house I owned in Kalamazoo, a little blue bungalow I had bought, essentially, for the porch, on whose railing you could prop your feet, which is what we were doing at the moment. It was exam week. I was very tired.

A week earlier that porch had been sanctified, in a sense, by an extraordinary ceremony. A student who had been for four years at the center of campus feminism had been hit by a car while riding her bike. After a week in a coma, she was dead, a week before she was to graduate. I happened to be at the hospital at the time, along with many other young women, her friends. As I left, I whispered to one of them, "If anybody needs someplace to go, I'll be home." A woman colleague and I repaired to my porch, sad and quiet. Then, one by one, cars began to pull up in front. The porch filled with ten, fifteen women, crying, laughing, holding each other, talking, silent. They stayed on into the night.

That was the end of another long spring quarter. Now, with commencement a day or so away, I had announced to all implicated parties that today was the last day I would accept papers. As my friend and I sipped and talked, watching evening fall gently, the phone was ringing every five minutes, pulling me up out of my wicker rocker and into the house to hear a panicky or exhausted voice assure me that It was coming, It was on its way. Occasionally a car pulled up, disgorging a bedraggled, unwashed body bearing a set of white stapled pages and a long stream-of-consciousness having to do with the current tally of sleepless hours, the tests yet to come, the possible weak points and potential strengths of the product in my hands. "Good," I murmured. "I'm glad that part worked out. No, I'm sure it will be fine. Yes, that sounds OK to me. I hope the chem test goes well. And please try to get some sleep. And listen, eat something tonight, OK? I mean protein."

Finally, a blessed hiatus, during which my friend turned slowly to me and said, "Weren't you lamenting the other day that you don't have any kids?"

My tired chuckle was half despair, half resignation. Academic motherhood at that point felt sometimes like somebody else's old housedress that fit too tightly or too loosely, sometimes like a garment that suited me well but that I was ashamed to wear in public. The problem was that I had bought the same dry goods that everybody else had been buying. I had made an error similar to that of the Victorians who mistook the sentimental icon, the angelic madonna, for the real thing: the woman who expressed her commitment to younger people in her care (and thus to the future in her keeping) in the form of teaching. I wonder at the power of such icons to replace reality and then to begin to recreate it. I had only to sweep the cobwebs and gauze away and look at my own mother to realize that Motherhood is neither winged and haloed nor necessarily haggard and self-abnegating. The heart is, after all, first and foremost a muscle. And the motherheart, uncorrupted, unsentimentalized, is a vital organ.

Since that time, when Lucinda and her "girls" first bequeathed to me that unabashed image of the maternal professor that both attracted and repelled me, it has evolved in my imagination through two subsequent stages. From a sort of fated role that had certain strengths, it grew into a way of conceiving the teacher-student relation that partook more of possibilities and problems than of known forms, obligations, and traps. It became potential rather than defined, active more than reactive.

And the longer I have taught, and the longer I have observed contemporary higher education, the stronger has become my conviction that Lucinda was right: The motherheart must be at the center of all true teaching. This means more than the simplistic addition of traditionally female ingredients to the academic stew—a dash of empathy, a handful of concern for the student's "personal problems." Nel Noddings has written, "It is time for the voice of the mother to be heard in education."[10] She means by this, I think, not merely that more women ought to pipe up, or even that there ought to be more women to make their voices heard. She means that a different voice must be heard, speaking from the pedagogy of centuries of motherhood. It must speak against tendencies toward ever greater specialization, compartmentalization of students and subject matter, and competition enthroned as a deity. It must speak for an immersion in process against an obsession with product, for education as superior to training. And, to borrow Carol Gilligan's terminology as I have just borrowed her title, it must speak in the most unsentimental and serious way for an ethic of care and en-courage-ment whose aim is to teach not subjects but people and whose larger goal is to create an environment where human beings can grow in and toward the fullness of themselves.

And the point is not simply to make this voice audible through increasing the critical mass of women on faculties. First, that guarantees little; second, it is exploitive of women and harmful to students if women are relied upon to humanize the fathers' institutions as always. The point is for the fathers to start learning to speak in the voice of the mother as well. For some it comes easy, as foreign languages do to certain people. For others, it will require listening carefully, shaping the mouth in uncomfortable new ways, over and over, until they are competent and then fluent, not only in the other tongue, but in the reality beneath it. What feminists have said about the necessity of role transformations in parenting applies equally to those who act, still, for better or worse, *in loco parentis*. The academic family, too, must be shaken and transformed.

Two years after my encounter with Lucinda, I was given an annual award presented by the student government association at Kalamazoo to a faculty member for involvement in "student life," that grand abstraction, that administratively demarcated Bantustan for everything that has no place in the classroom. It happened that the president of Student Commission that year was a good friend of mine, whom I've always suspected of throwing the election. In presenting the award to me, she handed me a large, furled poster. I unrolled it to discover a print of an especially beautiful Mary Cassatt mother-and-child. A two-year-old sits on its mother's lap with that look children get just when sulk and whine are about to explode into wail. The mother bends over the child, whispering, consoling, promising, her face obscured. Yet she is a formidable presence, massive and enclosing. "It's beautiful," I told her later. "I love it." The student sighed. "I drove *all over* this city looking for a Cassatt. Nobody had it. I just had to find one for you. It shows what you do for us." And then she added hastily, "In the best sense."

I laughed. "Of course. In the best sense."

Translations from the Mother Tongue

I will never get evaluations like Lucinda's. I'm still not at all sure that I want them. They smack of a cult of personality that, if entirely healthy and necessary for young women in Lucinda's day, seems dangerous in light of what I have observed of the deification of professors. To exchange gods for goddesses is no revolution. If one of my "girls" saw my face surrounded with a circle of light, I would wonder what chemical in her system produced it. Through quarter after harrowing quarter of student evaluations, year after year, I have fought to retain my belief that however persistently one's thoughts drift to libel actions or suicide, evaluations always contain general truth of a valuable sort. And even at a distance of a century, Lucinda's strike me as useful repositories of student wisdom about inspired teaching.

"You would often try to impress upon us some truth that had just seemed to strike you." That is, the willingness to be alive and personally present before one's students, the resistance to retreat behind a facade of professorial abstraction and transcendence. The vulnerability to observation that allows students to see one under the immediate influence of ideas, as one wishes them to be. (Just recently, after a summary lecture on *Frankenstein*, a student said, shaking his head, "You always make it seem like you just thought of this stuff last night because of what we said in class yesterday." His skepticism revealed to me how pervasive is their disbelief that we ever make new discoveries or, even more incredible, that these insights might arise because of what they, the students, had said.)

"Sure of as careful consideration as if we had been your equal." The genuine respect that is worlds away from the inauthentic pretense that students know as much as you do or the false, condescending comraderie that denies differences in age or experience. The equality that has to do not with degrees of learning or intelligence, but with the deeper integrity of selves and minds. The respect for another's reality, the struggle to understand the point where someone else is standing in the world.

"How tenderly you led us." The leadership of care rather than command.

"The power of divining the best that was in us." The highly cultivated vision and hard work that collaborate to discern in a student some worthy source of pride in herself or himself. The skill to imagine versions of the student that the student cannot yet see.

"And the tact to bring it out." To bring something out ("to educe," the root of "education"), not to hammer something in.

"The necessity, and also the possibility of progressive accomplishment, of constant enlargement." Education as process, not product. A process of getting bigger, not smaller, having room for more, becoming inclusive, not exclusive.

"Your every tone and gesture." "The best of all methods—an ever present example." To cultivate (rather than weed out) the human element in teaching; to know that ideas are embodied most powerfully in people. To accept that you teach as much by what you are as by what you assign or lecture on, and to avoid assiduously letting that knowledge culminate in heroic arrogance and tempting cults of pedagogical personality.

"That life was in earnest." To communicate that one's "subject matter" is always life and that the goal of one's course is more than knowledge. To encourage a seriousness that may often laugh but always rejects the meretricious, the hollow, the superficial.

"And women had a place to fill, a work to do, as well as men." To refuse to allow any myth, any lie, any poisonous tradition to persuade any student of her or his unimportance or subordination.

"Your great Mother love." Fundamentally, the commitment to the values of life, growth, and creativity, cultivated and perpetuated through the human bond between teacher and student. The passion in watching something grow distinct and strong while knowing that it was once and always will be part of you. The Motherknowledge of another being depending on you for sustenance so that it may become itself.

A Woman in My Head

We think back through our mothers, if we are women.

—Virginia Woolf

Woolf's syntax here has always intrigued me. That conditional clause hooked on at the end—was she merely clarifying her pronoun? "We think back through our mothers, if 'we' equals 'women.'" Or is it a qualification in another sense, a test, a thrown gauntlet: "We think back through our mothers, if we are really women." She was right: We are not really women until we have done that subversive research, unearthed that alternate family tree.

I found Lucinda's portrait and recognized some kind of family resemblance, some relationship. In many ways it was the process of investigating that relationship that made me a woman—in my head. Much else was going on in my head and my life that made that process possible and necessary at that time; but I, who had never had a female professor, needed that specific figure, especially now that I was trying to be one myself. Patriarchal tradition told me that my womanhood did not belong in the classroom. Liberal tradition said it was irrelevant. But I was finding it impossible to leave my womanhood outside the door—or the syllabus. It was a truly practical matter: to find a way to be, a way to live, in my profession, as myself. Lucinda Stone was one of the women who taught me how to do it, and by "the best of all methods—an ever present example."

She never knew the campus of the Kalamazoo College where I work. None of the present buildings was standing in her lifetime. When she left, wounded and bitter, in 1863, only one building stood atop the hill where the campus now sits. At the bottom of that hill, where she built with her own sweat and a lot of her own money a splendid edifice for her thriving Female Department in the late 1850s, there is now a wholly mediocre restaurant. I have a photo of her portrait in my office, for times of need. But the portrait itself now hangs in a formal dining room at the college. Often when I am seated at some dinner there, my eyes and attention wander to her face again. I often wonder what she'd think of me, whether I've created out of whole cloth the foremother the dictionary denies me, dyed to match my own philosophical wardrobe. Then I run the words through my mind again, the actual words that do not lie. I look around the room at my assembled colleagues and wonder what she'd make of them. And I remember that in 1863 she was driven out, she whom her students, in a splendid confusion of person and institution, called Alma Mater.

> mother, i have worn your name like a shield . . .
> i put on a dress called woman for this day
> but i am not grown away from you
> whatever I say.
>
> —Lucille Clifton[11]

4

A Rite of Passage

The table was a large one, but the three
were all crowded together at one corner of
it. "No room, no room!" they cried out
when they saw Alice coming. "There's plenty
of room!" said Alice, indignantly, and she
sat down in a large arm-chair at one end of
the table.

   "Have some wine," the March Hare said,
in an encouraging tone.

   Alice looked all round the table, but
there was nothing on it but tea. "I don't
see any wine," she remarked.

   "There isn't any," said the March Hare.

   "Then it wasn't very civil for you to
offer it," said Alice, angrily.

   "It wasn't very civil of you to sit
down without being invited," said the March
Hare.

   "I didn't know it was your table,"
said Alice; "it's laid for a great many more
than three." [1]

Academe is a highly ritualistic, symbol-riddled world. Some of the rituals and symbols are very public, very conspicuous. Others are quieter. One such is the passing of a new course. As an addition to the curriculum, the meat-and-potatoes of ivied halls, this event, however frequent, however common, is an occasion heavy with significance. For it means that some body of material is officially legitimized for admission into the Canon, the Body of Knowledge, that which we construct as knowable, teachable, and more important, worth knowing, worth teaching. This is particularly so at a small institution with meager financial and human resources and a consequently small curriculum. Every course counts. Frills are few. Luxury courses are minimal.

Sometimes the new course represents a new person: "Well, basically, we're proposing this course because our new young colleague, Erasmus More, did his dissertation on the subject of medieval travel literature." Sometimes the course represents a new development in the field; discussions of such innovations are generally entertainingly brief, as the assembled committee bows in unison to Expertise. If the development overlaps with something they know about, there is likely to be more talk, especially if the part they know about is suspect. Sometimes the new course reflects the social or geopolitical scene: courses in Islam resurfaced in our religion department when "hostage" and "Jihad" and "Shiite" worked their way into common American parlance. I tend to like those innovations, supporting as they do my idea that academe sometimes really does turn its lights upon events and issues of the hour. Sometimes the new course results from student interest, though only if their interest is blessed by their academic parents. If the students petition for a course in macrobiotic diets, their request is likely to fall on amused ears. When black students in the sixties petitioned for courses in African American culture, the administration responded with two familiar refrains: In the first place, we do not have the expertise on the faculty to cover such courses. (This is called the Vicious Circle Argument.) In the second, such courses would not be Objective, but rather Political. (This is called the Argument from Intellectual Rigor. Privately, faculty members add another poisonous adjective: Popular, a word which means both "widely liked" and "of the common people" and thus clearly denotes that which has no place in academe.)

One learns these rules, these categories, this vocabulary quickly as a young professor. It is part of the rite of passage. Sometimes the rite of passage gets all mixed up with the trial by fire.

My minor in college was history. For me the past has always been a source of solace. This has especially been so in the area of women's history. When I began to study the story of coeducation, I found a context in which my experience with women's studies suddenly made a great deal more sense. Given what women had to do to make it physically through the doors of academe, I no longer marvelled at what they were enduring to make it into the curriculum.

Shortly after I arrived at Kalamazoo in 1977, the Women's Interest Group rose from the ashes of the old Women's Rights Organization—the difference in the tenor of the names representing pretty accurately the difference between 1972 and 1978. The impact of "WIG," as it quickly became known, was considerable. They launched regular Wednesday-night symposia and Thursday dinner discussions. Their ambition and their audience outdid those of any other student group. For about two months in 1980 a splinter group called SOAR—Sisters Organized in Amazon Rage—embarrassed practically everybody it didn't outrage, and then disappeared by common consent, with only residual hard feelings among the Sisters and their sisters. WIG rolled along, serving one function of which its participants were generally ignorant: It formed a grass-roots base for those of us interested in generating women's studies at Kalamazoo.

In 1979 the president, who like most presidents liked to be able to say that his college was keeping up, created an ad-hoc women's studies committee charged with surveying the curriculum to determine needs in women's studies and proposing new courses. A group of us—teaching faculty, the research librarian, the assistant director of the Career Development Center, three or four WIG students—went to work, chaired by the director of media services, also our representative to the Great Lakes Colleges Association's Women's Studies Program. This was an invaluable network then as now to a struggling feminist impulse on a small campus, providing a kind of gestalt for its twelve components, an alternate affiliation for faculty needing strength in numbers.

I found myself among the group almost as a matter of course. To be truthful, I had given the issue of women's studies little prolonged thought, but it made me nervous. At that point I was teaching a freshman seminar in "Women and Literature," attending conferences, reading Moers and Showalter and Rich and Miller, being excited by the body of knowledge and riddled by doubt. Even as a student I had dismissed contemptuously arguments for curricular relevance. Oh, I was a good conservative intellectual. I firmly believed that academe should be above politics. I thought courses on women writers were, if not absolutely pernicious, then certainly problematic—I stress that I thought so while teaching such a course. Yet there was this energy in me moving in this new direction. Sensing this energy, the feminist faculty at Kalamazoo snapped me up.

So in the fall of 1979 we duly did our survey of the faculty as to the presence of women's studies in our curriculum (which might have been ascertained by a cursory glance through the catalogue, but process is process). We constructed an elaborate and painstakingly worded questionnaire to elicit information. The returned questionnaires—very few—ran the proverbial gamut, from "Hey, maybe it's time for me to work up that Liberation Theology course I've been thinking about" through "Science has no gender" and "I do not teach political courses" to "I resent being asked to complete this document." The "positive" responses tended to assure us that the revolution was well underway; they were already teaching Queen Victoria and Abigail Adams and Emily Dickinson.

We counted up the handful of courses where women's studies was genuinely present and saw a core cluster: "Women in Cross-Cultural Perspective" was in place in anthropology, and we decided that it would serve well as the entry-level course, the introduction to women's studies. It covered important basics, and the cross-cultural approach was philosophically sound and congruent with the outlook of a college that sends 85% of its students overseas and had just launched an International Studies Program. I would turn my freshman seminar "Women and Literature" into a regular course open to all students and rechristened "Literature of Women." "Liberation Theology" would be offered periodically, and there were history courses dealing with the suffrage movement, sociology courses including sex roles, and "Twentieth-Century Art" taught by a woman who knew and liked women's work. There was the sporadic "Psychology of Women" course, whose appearance depended on which woman was currently occupying the revolving-door Developmental slot in the psych department. The off-campus components of our program could be assets: The sophomore Career Development Internship and the Senior Individualized Project afforded nice, firmly established vehicles for independent research or experiential learning of the kind that other women's studies programs had to struggle to bring into the curriculum.

We also surveyed the student body as to whether they felt additional courses in women's studies to be necessary and, if so, what the content of those courses ought to be. Education is a wonderful thing: Several students said they also did not want their courses politicized. Those who were interested mentioned women's history, women's "roles," women's arts.

So, we asked, what do we really need? What is missing, we concluded, is a capstone—a seminar for upper-level students that will pull the small program together and also cover territory neglected elsewhere. And for the next year we concentrated on developing this paragon of a course. Even in our own deliberations that course began to swell to slightly mythic proportions. And the time from its conception through its gestation to its birth turned out to be a rite of passage in my own life, a genuine coming of age. I emerged . . . well, cooked. Well done. Tempered, in the very fullest sense of the word.

This Season of the Witch in my professional life must have felt as significant to me then as now, for recently I discovered that I kept a record, a hastily recorded chronicle. When I wrote it, I remember, its theme was the convulsions and convolutions of academic politics trying to deal with the dreaded Political. Reading it now, I see that more than anything else, it is about me.

※ऽ(※)ॳ

October, 1980

A solid year of stalemate, deadlock, frustration, confusion over multiple goals and priorities. On top of it all lie the impossibilities of calendar, curriculum, staffing, problems we sort through again and again.

One immense a priori problem: How can we cover what the course needs to cover when no one of us has that expertise? There's that word again. Another sizable difficulty: How are we to finagle release time for one of us to teach a new course not within our home departments?

And then, suddenly, a break in the weather. In the midst of another of those women's studies committee meetings where I am weighing the alternatives of a quick exit versus femicide, Karen suddenly, quietly, describes a course. A marvelous course, a unicorn of a course, a unique, daring, imaginative course, a course that does it all.

Basically, it is a one-unit course, but stretched over three quarters. During two of the quarters, the students would take it as an overload; during the third, they would take only two other courses. The first quarter would deal with historic feminist texts—Wollstonecraft, Mill, de Beauvoir, etc. The second will turn to the social sciences—psychological, sociological, and political perspectives on gender. The third will explore the arts—not women's literature, but ideas and imagery of gender. We will team-teach the course. I will be nominally in charge of the first unit, Karen of the third, three social scientists of the second. The expertise issue is solved. The release-time issue is negated. The coverage issue is settled.

Has this wonder sprung fully armed from Karen's brain? Or has she been nursing it secretly for weeks, months? A calm but quickening silence falls over the smelly faculty lounge where we meet. It is as if a bright wind has swept through, waking us. A subcommittee leaps into existence. We adjourn. I feel like singing.

November, 1980

The subcommittee meets several times over lunch. The snarls in this course of ours are commensurate to its originality and appeal. Integrity and coherence will be problems in a course stretching over three quarters, encompassing five different instructors and diverse material. Are we aiming too high, trying for the Ultimate Women's Studies Course? Faculty and students alike will at some point be doing the course as an overload, which is anathema at Kalamazoo. Team-teaching itself presents a host of problems. The course cannot count for departmental credit; where will the credit go? Where will the course be listed? We don't fall into the usual categories here. Will its ineligibility to fulfill any graduation requirement deter enrollment? How about the barrier of a three-quarter commitment? If it is designed as an upper-level capstone seminar, how will the clientele be admitted? What if a student jumps ship after one quarter? &tc., &tc., &tc.

But we whip the sucker into shape with gratifying speed, voicing and solving problems almost simultaneously. There is a *will* among us. The enthusiasm of accomplishment is bracing after the constipated irritability of the last months. The next step is the Educational Policies Committee, which approves all new courses before they are sent to the whole faculty at a monthly meeting for final approval. We decide to shoot for EPC passage before the end of the fall quarter, as a couple of us, including me, are off campus in the winter and want to be around to shepherd our little prodigy through the corridors of power.

Courses ordinarily come to the EPC from departments. This one will come from the vaguely recollected presidential edict and an ad-hoc committee of renegades. In other words, it is illegitimate, a bastard course. It lacks legal parents. So we decide we'd better run it by a couple important potential allies: the registrar, a remarkable and powerful woman who will instantly see all administrative difficulties in the course; and the provost, who wants to know what we're up to. This is not merely any old new course. This is a new idea. His support is critical.

Later that month

The registrar eagerly helps Karen clear out the swarm of bugs in our baby and Karen returns to us with a neat, airtight package. A group of us goes to the provost, who, to my delight, loves it. Thinks it's "nifty." He loves innovation and thinks his faculty somewhat stodgy. "They demand innovation," he tells me, "but when you offer it to them, they scream bloody murder." It's true, of course; what we all want is our own particular pet innovations; other people's are treasonous.

We decide to propose the course on a trial basis, for one year only, to be reviewed by EPC. The provost asks good questions, the ultimate of which is, "Whose name is on this course? Who oversees the course as a whole?"

Everyone looks at me.

Even later that month

Karen writes up a lengthy, articulate course description and a rationale—two EPC requisites. We devise reading lists. And we send our foundling to the chair of EPC, who sents it on to the New Course Subcommitee. The chair of that group is a guy who could argue his way through a minefield in toe shoes. I wonder what he'll do with this. The other two members are congenial friends of the cause. "Fellow travellers," as it were.

My image startles me.

Early December, 1980

EPC meets at 10 a.m. in the library. By this time everyone on the committee has seen a copy of the course description, and the New Course Subcommittee is formally proposing its approval by the full committee. This will require two "readings"—this week and next. The ad-hoc women's studies committee is fully present. I am very tense. I know I look grim and tight. I am terrified by such confrontations with Authority. Together, I tell myself, we are armed for any and all opposition, any and all questions. What I cannot handle, I remind myself, someone else can.

To my amazement, there is not only no fire, there is no smoke. Three people ask administrative and structural questions, and then there is silence. Karen acknowledges that the committee will want to think about the course before the final reading and vote, and that we are all happy to be consulted with questions. Silence again. Someone then says, "Since there seems to be no disagreement, why wait?" A vote is taken. The course passes unanimously.

I walk out, nonplussed, let down. Premature ejaculation. Did something in me relish the anticipated, dreaded battle? Or is it that that silence didn't sound right to me?

On December 18th, having bored through mountains of finals and papers and calculated grades and turned them in and arranged a house- and cat-sitter, I board a plane for Oregon, to spend Christmas with my brother's family.

January, 1981

I call Karen from Portland to arrange for her to pick me up at the airport when I come home. "Well, I'm glad you're coming back," she says, "but I'm not sure you want to come back." Huh? "The shit has hit the old fan." Huh? "The course. It's biting the dust."

She tells me they decided to take the course to the faculty at the January meeting, upcoming this Monday. This is a month earlier than I'd anticipated. Well, I'd be back anyway. That ain't all, says Karen. The course proposal, distributed to the entire faculty before the meeting, had hit the mailboxes on Tuesday of last week. On Friday it was followed by a four-page memo from a man in my department, the leading conservative on the faculty. Saying what? I query. "Oh, just wait," laughs Karen, darkly. "Wait 'til you see it."

They have yanked the course from the agenda for Monday. They have also called a special faculty meeting for February 3rd.

> *"Your hair wants cutting," said the*
> *Hatter. . .*
> *"You shouldn't make personal remarks,"*
> *said Alice, with some severity; "it's very*
> *rude."*
> *The Hatter opened his eyes very wide*
> *on hearing this; but all he said was,*
> *"Why is a raven like a writing desk?"*[2]

January 31, 1981

I return to Kalamazoo. Karen doesn't want to talk about it. "Go read your mail," she says. "There's another missive. He's been very prolific of late."

February 2, 1981

I sneak into my office—nominally "off campus," I am trying to avoid students, secretaries, colleagues. I sift through my mail to find the memo, dated January 9th, halfway down the mountain of paper on my desk.

The preamble distinguishes women's studies as a unique educational issue, since it is related to no identifiable discipline (and disciplinarity is central to the Liberal Arts Tradition) and is supported by no consensus of opinion. The author assumes, acid tongue in cheek, that the Educational Policy Committee can back this proposal with hundreds of hours of debate and hundreds of pages of documentation to justify this radical deviation from our intellectual tradition. There ensue seven "questions" which, notwithstanding the said assumptions, the author deems critical to raise once more. First, what exactly is this women's studies? Second, is it ideological, since after all feminism as a philosophical movement has so obviously failed? Third, is there a body of scholarship undergirding it, apart from the two or three studies generated by the women's movement? Fourth, who is qualified to teach such a course, since one cannot teach John Stuart Mill without a thorough grounding in his historical and philosophical milieu? Fifth, we assume that the course will not be foolish enough to deal in terms like "women's art" or "women's music," since attempts to distinguish such categories have clearly failed. Sixth, what is EPC prepared to do about feminism's attempt to alter our language, our reality, nay even the past itself? And seventh, what about the effect of women's studies on students? Even assuming, as of course we do, that its proponents do not intend to proselytize or evangelize, does the danger not remain that students exposed to the course will become moral relativists, uncritically accepting notions such as tolerance of divergent lifestyles and practices, including homosexuality, child pornography, and incest?

Deep breaths. Hurriedly I dig further down the pile to find #2. This one is directed only to EPC and women's studies committee members. This one is a parody of our published course proposal, including description and rationale. The course, called "Advocacy," extends over four quarters, its units entitled "Should We Change Human Nature," "Old Wine in New Bottles," "Revolution," and "Me and My Search for Identity." The readings include Karl Marx, Jane Fonda, and Mao Tse-Tung, as well as Mary Daly and Noam Chomsky. The rationale for the course includes its potential popularity, its representing for its instructors a holiday from serious scholarship and a chance to teach mediocre writers, and its amenability to non-academics, including satanists, pedophiles, and followers of Pol Pot.

I check the cover of this one to make sure it's for real. Then I rise and close the office door and sit down, head spinning.

For at least fifteen minutes I cannot even begin to sort out my responses. I am very angry. I am flabbergasted. I am insulted, as if I'd been slapped. I am mentally responding to each and every charge, sputtering defensively. A ridiculous waste of energy, but I feel exactly as I did twenty-five years ago when I felt misunderstood by the grown-ups—that desperation, that urgency. I want to phone the author of the memos. I want to scream, "How dare you!" With discomfort I realize that I share his feeling about the EPC cop-out, the silence amounting to cowardice. I want to march into the office of the provost, or the president, waving the memos. I want to sue. I want a hug. I want

Karen and the other women around me. No, I want some man. I want some man, any man on the faculty to walk in right now and say, "I just want you to know I think the course is great." I want the students to tell me again how excited they are about the course. I want a knight in shining regalia. And I want to be one, too.

Somewhere in this morass of response is also a certain odd excitement. Apparently we've done something of a significance beyond what I'd understood. I am embedded, it seems, in a major controversy. The good girl is being very, very bad. I am horrified. I am tantalized.

And I am frightened. I am frightened by the raw anger in the memos. I don't like to make men angry. I am very frightened of angry men. I remember my father's biting sarcasm, his cold contempt—scary. I remember my brother's violent eruptions and disparagements.

I decide I need to go home. I cursorily glance through the remainder of the mail and come upon a fat document, addressed only to me. It is a draft of an article he has written for publication, and his cover memo says that since I am implicated, he figures I should see it. It's nineteen pages long. Essentially it's a narrative version of the first memo, contemptuous, would-be-satirical tone intact. But midway through is a paragraph recounting the author's private conversations with other faculty about this Medusa in their midst. Some, he says, were too wimpy to stand up to us. Others opposed us but fell back on the need for collegial trust, God help us. Several, he says, were only amused, chuckling about these emotional women-without-men (most of us on the committee are single) banding together to strengthen our hatred of men and conspiring to avenge ourselves on the male gender for having rejected us.

Bingo. Now, in addition to everything else, I am paranoid. I see clots of senior male faculty members forming around the campus, laughing at me, vilifying my ideas, my credibility, sneering at my private life. I am an untenured third-year junior faculty member. I am the only woman in this department. All my dealings with this faculty have been bright and friendly. I have been the good daughter here, an object of affection, a source of pride. Now I feel like Regan in *The Exorcist*, suddenly peeing on the living room carpet.

Well, after all, apparently I am guilty of huddling with other harpies around the cauldron, planning the demise of the American family and the corruption of children.

Double, double, toil and trouble.

Later that day

Sometimes, as Mick Jagger said, you get what you need.

A few people seek me out to share their anger and concern, to express support.

I seek out the other women and feel fortified, less paranoid, though most of them are not nearly as upset as I think they ought to be.

I have dinner with Karen. She tells me that after the memos appeared, a man who participated in the silence at the EPC meeting announced that it was "railroaded" through the committee. I hear that internal yelp, that outrage. And then something is released. I see that I have a lot to learn, a row to hoe, and I will need to conserve energy.

February 3, 1981

Good attendance at the Special Faculty Meeting. My stomach is in my throat. But I have in the interim regrouped and recouped. I am more coherent, more solid. Angrier, too.

According to a prepared agenda, the meeting is to open with Linda, the chair of the women's studies committee, reading a statement about women's studies in the consortium and about the president's original charge to the ad-hoc group. Then a man on EPC is to talk about the design and content of the course.

But no sooner has everyone assembled and quieted than the hand that wrote the memos shoots into the air. Addressing the EPC chair, he asks that Linda and Brian yield the floor so that he may make a statement. The silent room falls more silent, draws taut. The chair deliberates briefly and then denies the request to suspend the agenda. I make a mental note to buy him a beer.

The agenda unfolds as planned. Finally the memo-writer gets his chance. Among other things, he discloses that he has been doing a little spadework: He has gone to the library to check out the books on our reading lists and has discovered that not one of us has previously checked out the books. He goes on to detail the dangers and delusions of women's studies as lesbian propaganda and leftist poison. When he finishes, he turns and stalks out.

"Jeez," Karen whispers to me, "I wonder if it ever occurred to him that we own the damned books."

"Or that we read them a long time ago?" I suggest. We smile.

The floor is open for questions of the members of either committee. Karen is asked to distinguish between women's studies and feminism. And damned if she doesn't do it, right before my eyes. The F-word, apparently, is one of the clearer present dangers and will be banished at all costs from these proceedings.

A number of people ask why we need this separate course. So separatism is another lurking monster, I note. Why, they ask, can't we simply include material by and about women in extant courses? Wonderful, I think; when? Integration is emerging as the lesser of two awfuls, I see.

When the meeting concludes, I am a little lost. Where is the poor course now? I'm briefed: It's back in the EPC New Course Subcommittee. Someone in the full committee moved to rescind approval, but the clever EPC chair, who is now getting angry, struck a deal: Approval will stand, but the course will not go to the faculty until the subcommittee has studied it more fully and obtained answers to all the questions that apparently were burning under that silence in December.

I call the provost's office and make an appointment.

February 4, 1981

I am in my office when a student comes by to give me a copy of a petition sent to EPC, asking that the work of the ad-hoc women's studies committee not be permitted to go down the drain. Our crackerjack grapevine seems to be functioning up to par. The memos have leaked and WIG women are worried and angry. Students are always stunned by faculty emotion and discord.

There are not many signatures on the petition. "Could've gotten more," the student explains, "but I kept getting involved in long discussions with people who wanted to talk about women's studies." The hell with signatures, I think; at least somebody's actually talking about women's studies.

A man in my department walks by, toward his office, sees me and turns in at my door. We have not seen each other since I got back. "Listen," he says quietly, almost apologetically. "I'm really appalled by what's going on, the memos and all. That's just . . ." He shakes his head. "I want you to know that doesn't represent the department feeling, not at all."

I want to leap from my chair and throw my arms around his neck. Instead I smile, thank him, and tell him that it means a great deal to hear that. One must try to be a grownup.

February 5, 1981

I'm again in the office when the chair of the New Course Subcommittee charges in, having been, he says, looking for me "everywhere."

He looks a bit worn. He asks if I will "flesh out" the first of the three units of the course, as Karen has done for the others. I agree eagerly. He then reads me a draft of his subcommittee's new report on the course, consisting of responses to six questions about the course in particular and women's studies in general.

"Is women's studies a viable academic area?" (Is this yes-or-no?) He has written in response that only practitioners in a discipline fully understand it, so the faculty should accept the word of those of us involved in women's studies that it is a viable field of study. A masterpiece of academic logic. I also recognize an appeal to Kalamazoo's traditional respect for academic freedom and collegial competence and independence. But I hardly think this monumental begging of the question will do.

Question #2: "Why should we put our energies into this course instead of some other?" He elaborates: "Why not, for instance, a Classics Department?" Well, because I don't know Greek, I guess. And who's asking y'all to put your energies into anything? And, more to the point, is this course really in competition with all conceivable alternative courses in the universe? I feel very tired.

He leaves, looking distinctly like a man who did not want this particular ball in his court yet again. But on his way out he says, between clenched teeth, "I just want to get this thing passed." I have to chuckle. The unforseen benefits of things.

> *"Who are you?" said the Caterpillar.*
> *This was not an encouraging opening*
> *for a conversation. Alice replied, rather*
> *shyly, "I-I hardly know, sir, just at*
> *present—at least, I know who I was when I*
> *got up this morning, but I think I must have*
> *been changed several times since then."*
> *"What do you mean by that?" said the*
> *Caterpillar, sternly. "Explain yourself!"*
> *"I can't explain myself, I'm afraid,*
> *sir," said Alice, "because I'm not myself,*
> *you see."*
> *"I don't see," said the Caterpillar.*
> *"I'm afraid I can't put it more clearly,"*
> *Alice replied, very politely, "for I can't*
> *understand it myself to begin with; and being*
> *so many different sizes in a day is very*
> *confusing."*
> *"It isn't," said the Caterpillar.*

> *"Well, perhaps you haven't found it so*
> *yet," said Alice; "but when you have to turn*
> *into a chrysalis—you will someday, you know —*
> *and then after that into a butterfly, I should*
> *think you'll feel it a little queer, won't you?"*
> *"Not a bit," said the Caterpillar.*
> *"Well, perhaps your feelings may be*
> *different," said Alice; "all I know is, it*
> *would feel very queer to me."*
> *"You!" said the Caterpillar,*
> *contemptuously. "Who are you?"[3]*

February 10, 1981

I meet with the provost at 10:00 a.m. I'm not sure why I'm there in his office. I guess I just want some perspective. Ever one for the positive approach, he launches immediately into strategy, which fires me up. He mentions the possibility of funding the course from his office directly, and I'm vaguely aware that a certain milestone has just been passed—I think again about unforseen benefits.

He tells me that we—I note that he always uses that pronoun—cannot be too defensive; that it does us no good to assert that no course in memory has met with such hostile suspicion or undergone such protracted, repeated scrutiny. I hear the oblique message to me and so I decide to reassure him that I am not going off the deep end. Not only is defensiveness counterproductive, I respond, but the scrutiny is completely legitimate in my view. "This is more than a new course; it's a new idea." I say that my anger has to do with the way scrutiny was initially avoided and then brought righteously to bear as if we, the course's sponsors, had been trying to elude it. I assure him that I am willing and able to face every kind of question, but that the brand of "question" raised in the memos and at the meeting leave me a little speechless. "Obviously," I muse, "we're threatening people on some very deep level."

"Yeah," smiles my boss, "their masculinity."

Masculinity? That seems to me too easy, too superficial. It is what is always said about feminism, and now part of me is interested enough in this uproar to want to get below that, to find out what really is at issue, something bigger, deeper than "masculinity." Unless . . . unless masculinity is bigger and deeper than I'd supposed.

The provost says he thinks the main objection on the part of our more rational opponents is faculty overload—setting a dangerous precedent by allowing a few of us to teach more than the regulation two courses per quarter. We rehearse counterarguments, and then I say that I think that's a smokescreen for the real objection. "Maybe so," he says, "but you gotta face the smokescreen anyway." This is beginning to feel a little like Viet Nam, a jungle in which I'm not sure where or what the enemy is. All bullets count equally. This perturbs me. It puts us in a completely defensive, reactive position. We must respond to everything seriously.

Before I leave, I tell him of the strain this is putting on my relations within the department. I am feeling ill at ease, like the black sheep in the family, the renegade. He says, "I hear what you're saying—and what you're not saying." Oh, God, he thinks I'm talking about tenure, which I'm not. I'm talking about working conditions, environment, climate, relationships. But he wants to talk about tenure. When the provost wishes to talk about one's tenure, one does not change the subject. "Keep talking to him," says the provost of my memo-writing colleague. Easier said than done, I respond. "Try," he says, heavily. "When tenure comes around, it's imperative that you have a unanimous department behind you.

Now, believe it or not, that is a bit of academic reality of which I was ignorant. So it startles me and I feel a small finger of fear on my spine.

I think back to my second retention review, which took place the previous summer—a fairly routine procedure unless one has assaulted a student or snorted coke in class or taken five weeks off, but one that requires the candidate to amass a weighty file documenting her every move for two years since the last review. My problematic colleague was then department chair and therefore required to submit a letter of evaluation. Mostly it said what a good guy I was and how splendidly I was coming along. He had, however, one reservation: my involvement in women's studies. It was, he said, changing my personality. Several people, he averred, had remarked on it.

At the time I had read it, the thought had struck me suddenly: This is how it starts. This really happens, then.

Yet wasn't he right, in a sense? It has certainly changed me. I bet I'm not nearly as much fun. I see differently, I react differently, my energies go in new directions. I think back to the grinning idiot who'd arrived three years before, eager above all to please, dealing with the twelve males in my building as if they were her long-lost father or funny uncles or potential sugar daddies. I shudder.

And now I've changed. I rapidly review recent encounters where I was defensive or short, and I am embarassed. Why can't I relax in an adversarial situation, as they do, these academic men? No matter how overwrought they seem, they are thriving in their element. I clench like a fist, not from anger—which always comes later—but from anxiety. I do not do the language of academic thrust and parry; I cannot bring it off. It unnerves me, threatens me, frightens me. I take what I'm fighting for personally. Women are so personal, right? In this case, I realize, I'm taking it increasingly personally each day. I have been inept in this whole difficult process, and these men have seen a disturbed personality. "Several people have remarked on it." How good he is at that offhand reference to others that wakes the cold snake of paranoia. Though he probably does not do it consciously, I see how tactical it is, yet I feel it working in me, working perfectly.

I am very confused.

"He sees you as a good colleague," the provost is saying, "one he's proud to have and wants to help, but one who's going down the wrong road."

"Yes, I know that. And if I came up for tenure today, I think he'd vote yes." I take a breath. "But the thing is that I'm going on down that road. And I don't know what he's going to think three years from now."

The provost smiles.

As I leave, I make an addendum to myself: I don't know what *I'm* going to think three years from now either. I don't know who I'm going to be. Riding a broomstock over the chapel with one breast lopped off, probably. Where does this end?

Ends. There is a much-quoted, much-misunderstood, much-mocked slogan carved into the stone above one of the entries to Mary Trowbridge House, the oldest dormitory on campus: "The End of Learning is Gracious Living." I do not feel very gracious. The end of learning is in actuality pretty scary.

February 11, 1981

The student newspaper is faithful in its play-by-play of the Women's Studies Crisis. The editor tells me that she has interviewed the chair of EPC, who grumbled about the uproar and then said, off the record, "Before I leave that committee, there is going to be a women's studies course at this college, if it's the last thing I do." I cackle rather wildly.

> *"Come, we shall have some fun now!" thought*
> *Alice. "I'm glad they've begun asking riddles.*
> *I believe I can guess that," she added, aloud.*
> *"Do you mean that you think you can find*
> *out the answer to it?" said the March Hare.*

> *"Exactly so," said Alice.*
> *"Then you should say what you mean," the*
> *March Hare went on.*
> *"I do," Alice hastily replied; "at least*
> *—at least I mean what I say—that's the same*
> *thing, you know."*
> *"Not the same thing a bit!" said the Hatter.*
> *"You might just as well say that 'I see what*
> *I eat' is the same thing as 'I eat what I see'!"[4]*

February 12, 1981

EPC meeting. The provost has told me that during January the course suffered in the committee for the lack of someone knowledgeable about it. Expertise again. So Karen and I attend, in order to demolish any potential excuses this time around.

The subcommittee chair presents his report and then takes questions. They come from every quarter. They move from logistical to pedagogical to theoretical so quickly I am spinning. It feels like volleying solo against twelve players on the opposite side of the net. One missile that shoots toward us repeatedly consists of the question of Ulterior Motive: In short, is this course the flying wedge for a women's studies department/major/concentration (Kalamazoo's version of an interdisciplinary minor)? Karen and I narrate the thinking that led to the proposal. No, that is not what they want. Finally we give them what they do want: an outright disavowal of any master plan for conquest, secession, or dominion.

Sometimes we try for context. We mention what Oberlin or Denison is doing. This turns out to be ineffectual and even deleterious, for the Kalamazoo faculty prides itself on its independence, its disdain of fashion and peer pressure. After all, one of the black marks against women's studies is the threat of the Popular. "Everybody's doing it" carries about as much weight with this faculty as it used to carry with my mother.

Then the Expertise question leaps up again. An intense young man says that we have all been hired with Ph.D.'s in certain fields, and we are in no way competent or certified to teach outside a given field. I desperately want to engage the larger issue here, but I am becoming more tactical by the day: Instead, I explain that it is precisely for this reason that we intend to team-teach the course. But why, he persists, why not just keep women's studies within departmental boundaries, within our areas of training?

Fleetingly I wonder why it is safer to him if we keep it in the house, like a vicious dog. Surely all the theoretical problems he and the rest of them see with women's studies don't evaporate within disciplinary confines. As I have so many times in the past month, I am trying to sniff out the root of all this, the bottom line, but every time I think I'm close, I catch another scent altogether. Is it the validity of interdisciplinary studies that is at issue here, or is it interdisciplinary women's studies that piles insult upon injury to academic tradition? Or is it simpler: If we housed a women's studies course firmly within established departments, it could be dealt with in-house, like a family problem?

We respond that an interdisciplinary approach yields a different kind of understanding. Karen draws an analogy—we have all become adept at analogies. She compares interdisciplinary women's studies to an earlier college experiment with an interdisciplinary Western studies program. A man involved in that project counters: But Western studies has an obvious congruence, which is missing here. His objection gets lost in the ensuing discussion. I step into a pause to ask if we may return to it, for, I say, he has raised a crucial point. Indeed, I am thinking that it might be the bottom line I've been seeking.

And so I launch into another analogy—with American studies, in which we have a small program. We academics, I explain, see a congruence in American experience that justifies a course of study called American studies. On one level, of course, it is a false congruence, since no two Americans have identical experiences, and since the American experience differs along lines of race, geography, class, etc. But on a broader level, scholarship has defined a general, subsuming category of American experience containing its enormous diversity. He nods and I move in for the kill:

"The abundance of literature, most but not all of it emerging in the last fifteen years" (I'm hoping here that they all recall the charge, voiced in the memos and the special meeting, that women's studies lacks a body of literature), "has established a broad congruence in women's experience that likewise contains great diversity." I feel I have said something I have been burning to say for a while, and said it well. There is thoughtful silence in the room. My opponent keeps looking at me, quizzical, skeptical, his head cocked to one side. Finally he speaks: "Is that true?"

Karen's arm drops off the table into her lap. "No, Merrill, she's lying to you." The meeting dissolves in laughter. But, sitting next to her, I feel the anger ripple through her and into me. And I see the ultimate futility of all this. There is no answer good enough for them, definitive enough, in the face of basic unwillingness to believe. Ultimately, what we can do to sell this thing is very limited.

Karen leaves the meeting tight as a fist. I am laughing and invigorated and I have no idea why.

February 20, 1981

Karen hosts a TGIF for women faculty. This is an inspired move. This tradition has not been much observed this year. I am very glad to be there. Our art historian brings her baby daughter. The women's athletic director lectures us on supporting the swim team, and she and I compare prices on running shoes. Eventually the discussion wanders to The Course. One more EPC meeting, reconfirmed approval, and it goes to the faculty on March 2nd. We debate the question of whether this meeting will be bloody. Someone suggests that the opposition has used up its ammunition. Inwardly I doubt this. I have come to expect the worst. Paranoia strikes deep, as Buffalo Springfield used to sing.

Karen mentions having heard that we are promoting lesbianism. Everyone laughs and offers means by which lesbianism might be promoted— billboards, TV ads, bumper stickers. I'm laughing too— I'm laughing a lot these days—but there is a little grey thought lurking in a corner of my mind. What if someone actually brings that one up at the faculty meeting?

Looking around the room, I think that this little crusade has drawn the women together, though I am certain not all of them support either the course or the concept of women's studies. One of the joys has been the sense of alliance manifesting itself in subtle incidents, remarks, smiles to one another, commiserations. There is a loyalty—personal and also primal—that transcends politics.

One of Kalamazoo's considerable advantages for women is the prevalence of women with faculty status in important administrative posts. Never have I appreciated them as much as now. The registrar is a very important person at a small college, especially so at a college whose academic program is a little like a fiendish obstacle course. She is a gruff, constitutionally conservative soul who rules with an iron hand. If you're on her bad side, you can get little accomplished at Kalamazoo College. If she thinks you're all right, she will go through fire for you, find you minute loopholes in rules and regulations, come up with saving solutions at the eleventh hour, make quiet exceptions for you. I have never been certain of her sympathy for women's studies, always sure of her support for women faculty—primal, not exactly feminist, more like pre-feminist, though increasingly I see such bonds as part of the fundamental structure of feminism. She smoothed the way for us early on, before the siege began, as if something about our project catalyzed her innate loyalties, and she began to play the role of guard dog for our brigade. In EPC, where she is an ex-official member, and in the special meeting, she has virtually leapt from her seat to head off red-herring logistical objections. Every knot thrown her way she untied deftly, then smiled conspiratorially at us across the room.

And then there's the library. The director and the research librarian are both women. As I've listened to colleagues elsewhere moan about the politics of accumulating a women's studies collection or sustaining subscriptions to feminist periodicals, my eyes have been opened to the role of the library staff in academic politics. Our senior librarians, male and female, have been just loving this current fracas, especially when some corner of it falls to them. They transmit regular reports about which central figures in the fray come in to look up what information or seek out what texts. When information and resources—the ammunition of academic battles—are needed, they appear with lightning speed.

I head home from Karen's a little drunk and smiling.

February 26, 1981

Final EPC meeting. Vote held off until this week to contracept any new charge of railroading.

I enter the room loaded for bear. But the bear are in absentia, off at a conference someplace. Damn, I think, startling myself by this novel attitude toward confrontation that seems to be evolving in me. Damn. Watch them come back and cry foul, just watch them.

When we come through the agenda to The Course, there is silence. "Come on, folks," I laugh, "I didn't come all this way for THIS." They chortle and relax a bit.

The fact that the course is experimental, with only a year's lease, seems to have attained significant proportions. It lets people off the hook; they can permit their eccentric colleagues to pursue this erratic idea without feeling they've caved in entirely or permanently to the Popular, the Political, the Ideological, the Intellectually Unsound, and all the rest of the armies of night. It also lets them swallow the logistical awkwardness of the course, a somewhat separate issue.

As a result, the discourse has taken a fascinating turn. The emerging message goes something like this: "Well, OK, you've all worked hard on this, so do it. But in a year we *really must see* a proposal for a *regular, one-quarter, one-teacher* course in women's studies." In a rush I realize we've somehow maneuvered them into *demanding* a course in women's studies for permanent adoption into the Kalamazoo College curriculum. Well, OK, guys, if you really want it, we'll see what we can do.

A bullish fellow sitting directly across from me raises the issue of our proposal to interview students for admission into the seminar. He's agin it, and, he says, others are too. He talks around his objection for a while until a supporter of The Course says, "Marv, is your real objection that the interview may be ideological in nature?"

"Yes," he blurts, rather defensively, as if he knows he's moving close to a serious accusation against professional integrity, the kind we don't hear too often at Kalamazoo.

I grab this one, telling him that I had heard this objection and was, frankly, shocked by the suspicion that we would screen students on the basis of their personal beliefs. I repeat what is clearly explained in the course proposal: that the interview was instituted for the purpose of determining the student's academic background and readiness for advanced, independent work and responsibility within a seminar setting. I mention the Senior Honors Seminar at Northwestern, for admission to which I had to apply in writing. And then I start a sentence about a hypothetical student applicant, using the singular. I can see the pronoun coming and I try to warn myself, but before I know it, I've said "she." I see Marv's eyes flicker across the table, and he pounces.

He is "interested, very interested," to hear me use the female pronoun. Someone interjects, "Aw, Marv, she always does that!" and we all laugh, excepting him. He forges ahead: He certainly hopes males will take the course (read "be welcome"). Someone asks him about collegial trust. He keeps on. I try to respond, but he talks straight over me, a verbal bulldozer. I give up and settle into a smile. In the end, we agree to delete reference to the interview, and I thank him for giving us help in getting the course through. This I do effortlessly and half-sincerely.

As I do so, I realize that I have of late, and wherefore I know not, gained a considerably enlarged capacity for conflict and criticism, for appreciating small gains, and for releasing small tensions that formerly would have gnawed at me. In fact, I feel as I do when I'm exercising regularly—waking up the next morning with muscles at once sore and undeniably stronger.

EPC reaffirms its approval of the course by vote.

Monday, March 2, 1981

All my day tends toward 4:00. All morning and early afternoon my mind is leaping ahead. We are getting out the vote, reminding all the women and friendly men to come to the meeting. I am nervously talking to feminist students about the upcoming vote. I have mixed feelings about doing this. I wonder if I am using them, manipulating their ready sympathy and support. Or am I legitimately drawing them into a process in which they are centrally implicated, involved, invested, more than they know? Is it right to heighten their awareness of how political this course is? How political academe is? Is that, in fact, a significant part of the course? Throughout the process, one of the subtexts has been a half-articulate suggestion of illicit and unhealthy complicity between feminist faculty and students—those same girls we are seducing to sapphistry and altered personalities. All I know at this point is that I need them, I need their embraces and good wishes, their anger and concern, which I can indeed manipulate so easily it frightens me.

I have tried very hard through the past week to rein in my Joan of Arc tendencies and an awful proclivity toward thinking of The Course as mine, or worse, as Me. In the endless revaluations and self-critiques that have kept me awake at night—Are they right? Am I an ideologue? What's an ideologue? Am I politicizing the classroom? Is there a coherence to female experience?—I have constantly, neurotically monitored my own motives and objectives. I keep coming back to a simple reality: that there is a significant body of knowledge that students need.

Students' need. No question that there is something gratifying to me in the students' concern about The Course's fate. But there is also real value in it. To feel that one has fought for knowledge, for the privilege of education, is worthy. Their great-grandmothers certainly thought so. They fought. I wish these daughters to feel they have fought for the chance to learn about themselves.

At 4:00 I walk into the amphitheatrical classroom where we congregate on the first Monday of each month. A bunch of Us sit together— a compromise reached after some jocular talk of trying to get all the women to sit in a bloc. The chair of the Faculty Council convenes these meetings and then takes reports from committee chairs. EPC is always first. Its chair—he who vowed that this course would enter the curriculum if it were the last thing he did—briefly introduces The Course. The faculty have received descriptions, rationales, reading lists, clarifying memos ad infinitum. He then describes, tongue gently in cheek, what's gone on since December. The floor is open for discussion. There are a few final statements for and against, some heartfelt. I am all ready to talk, but no one asks me or any of the women's studies committee anything.

Again I hear with bemusement the notion that this hybrid should be released for a year and watched carefully, but that then it will be time for a standard one-quarter course that can work permanently in our curriculum. Shades of Bre'r Rabbit, or Tom Sawyer, or somebody.

The chair calls for a vote. A show of hands, he decides, rather than the potential ambiguity of a voice vote. I am unable to resist turning in my seat to note the hands against. The final vote is 58 in favor, 3 opposed.

> *"At any rate, I'll never go there again!"*
> *said Alice, as she picked her way through the*
> *wood. "It's the stupidest tea-party I ever was*
> *at in all my life!"*
> *Just as she said this she noticed that*
> *one of the trees had a door leading right into*
> *it. "That's very curious!" she thought. "But*
> *everything's curious to-day. I think I may as*
> *well go in at once." And in she went.[5]*

⁂

Our problems, of course, had only just begun. Now we had to teach the damned thing, and that's another story. Suffice it to say that a year later I filed a full report with EPC, proposed a one-quarter seminar in women's studies, saw it through to full faculty approval and appearance in the college catalogue, and have taught it every spring since.

Today, rereading all this, I was a little sad. My own innocence surprised me; I'd forgotten it. Much of the solidarity of the women and men behind The Course has vanished. And I saw how pivotal this chapter was in my evolving sense of myself in relation to the College and to my profession. After this time there was no turning back for me. I had eaten of the apple, and the Garden was permanently closed to me. I was, for good or ill, an outsider on the inside, permanently at odds. Sometimes that feels right, if a little sadly so. Often it feels painful, lonely. I had discovered that I was, without ever having chosen to be, a kind of academic guerrilla.

Some of the big abstract questions surrounding women's studies and feminism I have yet to resolve. But some of the ideas about teaching and learning and the act of knowing that are most central to me now germinated or solidified during that rite of passage. Chief among them is the notion that information is inherently apolitical; it is merely information. Its context—that is, its relation to the tacit assumptions and dominant world view—determines whether or not it is political. Some information gets by scot-free. Other information snags in the net, glows red, explodes.

The episode permanently tinged some relationships in my life, staining some, gilding others. I still feel sometimes, talking to certain colleagues, a buried but live grenade. I still wish this abrasion, this dissonance, were something I could accept and even relish as interesting and healthy rather than disturbing and awkward.

It was another fall. Yet oddly, my dominant feeling in rereading my account of this time is that it rooted me ever more firmly in the College, in the profession. When you fight for something, you acknowledge a vested interest that deepens with the fight. I came out of it committed, not only to the idea for which I was fighting, but to the place where I was doing it.

> *"Now, I'll manage better this time,"*
> *she said to herself, and began by*
> *taking the little golden key, and*
> *unlocking the door that led into the*
> *garden.*[6]

5

Serafina

An Angel in My House

April 13, 1985

Dear Di and Peter (and baby makes three):

It's Saturday afternoon, and I'm supposed to be reading women's studies journals and generally gearing up for another week in the salt mines, but I'd rather write to you because another one of those occurrences has occurred which has no validity until it's communicated to you two (two-and-a-half?). But first . . .

. . . as to the enclosed ovoid items: birthday/anniversary presents from Oaxaca, sold to me at a cafe by a beautiful little girl with lots of Indian blood and entrepreneurial spirit who kept making me deals because I was her "amiga," loading me with more and more onyx eggs, turtles, pigs, elephants. . . . These two items instantly reminded me of you because of their sheer solidity, rich colors, and, of course, symbolism. I figured it's a pretty fertile spring for all three of us, and these were appropriate for birthdays, anniversaries, fetuses, spring solstice, Easter, and affirmations of tough old life in general. The little kids in Oaxaca, so poor, sell this stuff to you every time you sit down or even pause in walking; they carry around boxes full of it, trying to make a peso or two. You can divide these up however you want or keep them community property. Give 'em names. Pet Eggs.

Also enclosed are two new poems, which I wrote after my talk to the Women's Interest Group the other night, when I found myself struggling to articulate two principles: why creative women self-destruct, and why, for women, passion is so alluring, so terrifying.

And also: my list of proposed names for Little X.

I told you, methinks, that I have a great women's studies seminar. But that course is such a struggle for me, every time. I rethink everything, rediscover everything that's saved and damned my life for the past fifteen years. Damned and saved, I should say, in correct order. One of the people in that class is Sera. Pronounced "Sarah." Sera came to my attention last fall when another faculty member called to plead with me to lift the ceiling on my Modern Poetry course in order to let Sera in. A really special person, she said, with a severe writing block. Oh, boy, just what I need—a hard case. But I did it and wasn't sorry, because Sera is the kind of woman you love to love—dark and doe-eyed, shy and unpresuming, talented and interested and serious and willing to work so hard. The writing block is a particularly interesting one: She writes beautiful, brilliant exams and can't finish a paper to save her little soul. C-minuses on the papers, A's on the exams, every time. I've never seen anything like it. I realized immediately that she writes under pressure because she has no choice, but give her two terrifying weeks to prepare a paper on her own, and the freedom, the emptiness, the responsibility for creation are too much. I worked and worked with her, made a little headway by having her try writing the papers in one sitting, as if it were an exam setting. But she kept choosing poems to write about like A. Rich's on Beethoven's Fifth Symphony, and nothing in Sera's experience can connect with that level of feminist insight and rage. And yet she kept choosing those poems.

So when I see her in women's studies this quarter, I'm a little amazed. She didn't seem like the type. Yet there she sat. So we plunge into our first two weeks on Victorian Womanhood, and by yesterday I feel we have a pretty clear understanding of the Angel in the House, the reasons Angelhood was forced upon women, and, what was much harder for the class to understand and accept, the reasons Angelhood appealed to them, the strength and *power* they drew from it, the ways they subverted it. Yesterday we saw slides of Victorian paintings depicting said Angel in her House. After class, as the crowd thins out and everyone wanders out into the warm weather and into their weekends, there stands Sera, eyes swimming with tears.

By this time I've learned a little about Sera's background. When she was eight, her mother gave up and joined a weird, ascetic fundamentalist church. At that point Sera, being the oldest of four, became Functional Mother. Since then, she's been the glue holding the ragged family together. Her father became so depressed that he developed various ailments that have had him in various elite clinics, where they apparently told him the truth—that it's psychosomatic and that he needs to deal with his life. So now he's withdrawn into his bedroom because he can't stand the house with Mama floating around. Sera's brother is hyperactive, troublesome, resentful of her for succeeding in school while he's failed. Her sister takes revenge against Mama's hatred of Our Fallen World by immersing herself in clothes, jewelry, cars, and boys. The youngest brother, eleven, is at sea, scared and confused. Sera feels particular maternal responsibility toward him. Meanwhile, Mama is really off the deep end of a very long dock. Turns off the TV every time somebody switches it on; berates Sera for going to college and learning secular humanism and how to think; berates her for dating and especially for visiting her boyfriend's home (Sera is a virgin still, by her own decision); tries to control her reading by stocking the house with pamphlets entitled "The Hour is at Hand," etc. Worst of all, for Sera, she refuses to see that the family is ripping apart at the seams. Floats around in pure air where human complexity does not enter.

Now Dad has decided to move out, which Sera thinks is a good idea. One problem, however: How does Sera continue to play the role that defines her, that of keeping the family together, if the family is in the process of splitting up? Result: She is splitting up too. Half of her is here, completing a B.A.; the other half is at home, taking care of everyone, mending, smoothing, feeding, bandaging. She is "selfish" to be here at school. And the worst of it is that her father is turning on her and her siblings, accusing them of exacerbating the situation all these years, screaming at her when she, in her perfect, believe me, perfect innocence, tells him that her third course is a women's studies seminar.

So Friday she tells me, big brown eyes shiny with tears, that she doesn't think she's coping too well and needs to talk to "somebody"; do I know anybody in town? I tell her that the one therapist I really trust has moved to Cincinnati and is having a baby (thinking to myself that I'd give anything to get her into a room with you for an hour). I tell her that I'm no professional counselor, but that I'm available as a friend, and her eyes light up. We make a date for Saturday morning—today—at 10:00 a.m. at my house.

Ten on the dot she shows up and we talk for two hours. I sort of open it up, after listening for a time, by saying that the first step has got to be to come to a livable agreement with herself: to help her family, especially individual members of it, as much as she can, but to resign the role of Savior, because realistically, no one can do that. She agrees, says she knows rationally that's not the answer, but feels like she's "abandoning them all to the wolves," "being selfish" (one of her favorite terms). I feel the nitty gritty approaching fast. I mention that one of the false dualisms of our crazed culture is Living for Others vs. Selfishness. She regards me with deep interest in those huge eyes. Now, for ten years this stuff has been all over the talk shows and the best seller list, and Sera has never heard it, never considered that Unselfishness is not equatable with giving yourself away wholesale to anyone who "needs" you, nor that keeping oneself alive and healthy is not equatable with Selfishness, that clearly worst of sins on her list. She tells me that the other night she had a panicky hallucination in which there were pieces of her scattered all around the world, in the possession of various friends and family, and she desperately wanted to get some of them back. She called a male friend here at school, to whom she'd once given a copy (the only copy, of course) of a poem she'd written, and tearfully asked that he bring it over right away. He told her he gave it to his mother, to whom he is currently not speaking. She's virtually hysterical, unable to get this scrap of herself into her own hands. I say firmly that this is a very good sign, that she obviously already knows, in her blood, what I'm telling her.

Then she tells me two stories. In the first, her boyfriend, who's in business school in Chicago, calls her last fall to ask her to get a single in the spring so he can stay on weekends without feeling like he's inconveniencing a roommate. (Yes, they stay together, but chastely.) At first, this is what she wants to do. But the more she thinks about it, the more she doesn't want to be alone this quarter, the more her current roommate, her best friend, is important to her. So she signs up for a double room, not telling the boyfriend until it's an accomplished fact. He finds out and hits the roof. Calls her three times in one day to tell her she's made him very upset and she's being very . . . yep, SELFISH. Say the secret word and win a nervous breakdown. She is horrified, devastated, appalled at herself. And yet . . . she stands her ground, by some miracle, explains to him over and over that she cannot live for weekends and his presence, but must create a life for herself here all the time. And she says to me, tentatively, "And I told him HE was being the selfish one."

The second story is her father blowing up when she confesses to having enrolled in women's studies. "But it's only something I'm doing for MYSELF," she says, plaintively.

Two big points for Sera. By this time I am seeing this thing in very odd metaphors: as if her soul is teetering on the brink. I tell her it's like natural resources: They can't go on giving if they get used up. I tell her life is about reciprocality, renewal, not sacrifice and martyrdom. I tell her the constant givers, the people who are there for everybody, wind up bitter, resentful bargainers: "Dammit, I was there for you; you OWE me!" I tell her there's lots of anger in her life right now—against Mama, Dad, boyfriend, others who've pressured and abandoned her—and that that anger, too, is a sign of a self that needs to be heard and attended to. She says she's always thought that what you do with anger is control it. So I tell her about me and anger—how I learned that "control" lesson as a kid and paid for it and that now, if I could change one thing about myself, it would be to learn to use anger effectively.

Well, Sera's amazed. She's never thought about any of this, she says, never thought about anger positively or acted to affirm herself. I tell her she's wrong: She's been affirming herself all along. Some primal instinct to live, to be, has been saving her. Lots of women would have gotten that single room, I say. Lots of girls would have agreed to forego college or to attend school someplace near home to nurse the sick family and placate the crazed mother. Lots of women wouldn't have called the friend and demanded the poem back. And lots of women wouldn't take women's studies in the face of Daddy's wrath, "just for herself." All your instincts are right, I tell her, including the instinct to care for people, to do what you can for your family, to be the Rock-of-fucking-Gibraltar. None of that is wrong, so long as you also listen to that other voice that says, "I need myself back."

Sera is looking a little dazed. You know that feeling when you discover you've been up to something you didn't realize, been winning all along when you thought you were losing?

She tells me she feels a little out of place in the women's studies seminar. She's always disapproved of the Women's Interest Group (i.e., "feminism")—too radical, too angry, too exclusive and conformist, too confrontative. I ask her to consider specifically what kind of programs WIG does. If it's an anorexia workshop, what's that saying? That a woman who's starving herself needs to feed herself. If it's a program on abused women, what is that about? That a woman is not an object deserving of battering and needs to care for herself. Sera makes the connection somewhere in those eyes of hers. Sera, I say, listen: You aren't out of place in our class. What have we been reading about for three weeks? The Angel in the House? Sera, the class is ABOUT you!

Sera, I say suddenly, what is your full name?

"Serafina," she answers. "It's Italian for 'seraph,' which is a word for . . . " We look straight into each other's eyes. And then we smile. "Perfect, isn't it?" she says wistfully. "I was named after my grandmother, and she IS the Angel in the House."

"Well," I say, "listen to what we've been reading. Listen to what those Victorian women had to say. Haven't we been saying in class all week that caring and healing, shouldn't eradicate the self, that they absolutely require a strong self?"

We're quiet for a moment. Sera looks at me with dry, bright eyes and a real smile and says, "I'm feeling a lot better. Really better."

And then there's a knock on the door, and there stands the Boyfriend. He's truly Mr. MBA, impeccably groomed and polite a la Eddie Haskell. "Good morning, Dr. Griffin, is Sera here?" He comes in, she takes his hand, smiling up at him nervously, and he says, "Jeez, you've been over here a long time." Then, to me, "What is she, a basket case?"

The blood rushes into my eyeballs. I have just spent two hours convincing her she's NOT a basket case but a brave, wise young woman surviving a very difficult time.

"Have you been waiting in the car?" she asks guiltily.

"Yeah, and I got sick of waiting," he responds pleasantly.

I hug her while she tells me over and over how grateful she is. I remind her that she promised to investigate taking a painting course this summer or next year. I had said how important it is to have a form of expression, and that I thought her writing block was a function of her belief in the repression of Self and Feelings. She immediately concurred with that analysis—she's so smart—and she confessed that she's always yearned to learn painting. So she responds, "I will. I really will."

And Boyfriend chimes in, "Yeah, it's when you start learning basket weaving that I'm gonna worry."

And they walk out my back door, hand in hand.

So what's this letter about?

This letter is about the fact that this morning seems to encapsulate my life. I struggle with the devil itself for the soul of somebody like Sera, only to send her happily off into the arms of someone who is fond of defining her as a neurotic child who keeps him waiting in the car while she takes entirely too long trying to save her sanity. Dear God, I was upset. My intestines were just in knots. The fucker should have been on his goddamned KNEES to me if he loves her. Half of me very nearly ran to the door after them and yelled, "Sera! Before the painting course, step one: Get Rid Of HIM!!"

Right now I wonder how I can do this for thirty more years. It's too much—the intensity of working with girlwomen like her, the sense that what I know, what I've learned, is critically important to the Seras fighting for their lives. And at the same time, to have to know that Boyfriend is waiting in the car, that Haggerty and Remington are in the classroom with Sera at their mercy, that most of the people I work with don't know about Sera, don't want to know, wouldn't have a clue as to why she can't finish papers or why she wants to waste her time in women's studies, and won't help me with her, ever. Here's the thing: If I said in a faculty meeting that the college, all colleges, are full of Seras and they are in real peril, I'd get the exasperated looks, the condescension, like when I was a kid and everybody always told me I was exaggerating, being too dramatic. I feel, right now, so tired. Lonely, too. I'm telling you because I need company. And because after Sera left and I sat there wondering if the light in her eyes before Boyfriend arrived could manage to stay shining, I thought to myself, "Shit—Diane does this all the time, for a living!" Sisyphus pushing that damned rock up the hill over and over. Yet what else is there to do? What is more valuable than this, than Sera? I'm looking out my front window and the world seems to be full of Seras, smart and courageous, struggling along, crucified on womanhood, with so little understanding of what's going on, of how good they are. I want to tell them all, right now.

For me, teaching has less and less to do with what I used to think it was about, with the Tradition of the Novel or epic poetry or narrative technique or semicolons. Yet that stuff matters to me and I will always love it, even the semicolons. But it all matters because expression saved my life, my sanity, and can save Sera. Because it saves you two, in words and in paint. Narrative technique matters because there's a reason *Jane Eyre* is told in the first person, a reason Bronte wanted that "I, I, I" voice speaking its story, and the reason has to do with selfhood, authenticity and authority, and thus with Sera, and me, and you. Sometimes this feels so alone. Last week at a department meeting Porter told us not to make the mistake of letting English majors think literature has something to do with life.

Increasingly, it seems, teaching is about using the tools that can reach Sera—women's studies or semicolons or both. Increasingly, teaching is about passing on tools for survival. I know I'm right; it's not that I doubt the life I've chosen. On the contrary: Saturday mornings like this one reconfirm the choice and make me feel that what I went through to get to this day means something. But I watched Sera walk down my walkway with her hand in his, looking up at him, so obviously worried that he's going to be mad for the rest of the day and that she's been Selfish, and I wanted to cry.

Do you know what I mean? Of course you do. Thank Goddess, I sez to meself this morning, there are at least two people in this forsaken world who will understand this.

So coddle your eggs—the two I'm sending and the one inside you—and enjoy the spring on the banks of the Ohio, once the Freedom River. I miss you.

XXOO,

Gail

PS: After Sera, I went out and bought flowers and arranged them in bowls with Lake Michigan colored stones and water, and I taught a couple of them to open up. Not bad for a morning's work, I guess.

Part Two

VOCATION

6

A Good and Worthy Voice

One way or another
you burn for it.

—*Linda Pastan*[1]

The Silent Woman

Driving through Plainwell, Michigan, a small town ten miles north of Kalamazoo, you used to pass a cafe called The Silent Woman. Above the entrance hung a facsimile eighteenth-century inn sign depicting a woman dressed as a serving wench. She had no head.

The first time I saw the sign, I was merely depressed that such an image would be hanging in public in the 1980s. I wondered if any of the locals ever complained. Later, passing it again, I moved on to more philosophical considerations. A quiet act of violence, this decapitation; a quaint morsel of pornography, excising that part of a woman that makes her human and troublesome, leaving only the part that, in male eyes at least, makes her sexual. I turned over in my mind an ironic disparity: the tired stereotype of the babbling female, versus the ringing silence of women historically; the proportional silence of women in mixed groups; the peculiar forms of silence I meet with regularly in women students—for silence has as many hues as speech.

Believing that all stereotypes arise from some distorted truth, I mulled over the possible sources of the Babbling Woman. Perhaps she is the woman among other women, overheard by men—the laughter and overlapping cascades of talk from the kitchen on a holiday; the talk I heard when I came home from school on my mother's bridge days. But even beyond these restricted and thus enabling contexts, I thought, there is indeed something deeply verbal about women. I looked across at us from the male side of the drawing room and saw us as they see us, talking and talking, driving men to distraction with our need to verbalize and our insistence that they do so. "How do you really feel?" "Do you love me?" "I think we need to talk." I thought about the diaries and letters filled with our lives; I thought about how much of female friendship consists in analyzing and comprehending the world by talking it over (a.k.a. "gossip"), experiencing events fully only after constructing and shaping them by retelling them (a.k.a. "inability to keep secrets"), forging human bonds verbally.

But the silence, all the silences—the reticence in classes, the inability to utter anger or dissent, the reluctance to name rape or battering for what it is, the collective silence of our experience, only just now learning its name and history. All the talk of women against all our silence. The Babbling Woman, looking into the mirror, seeing her headless sister not looking back.

✻ঞে✻

> *We women were the ones in the fields in*
> *Africa. . . We were communal even then,*
> *and as we got into bigger fields, we would*
> *call to one another. If you didn't answer*
> *back, we went to see about you.*
>
> —*Nikki Giovanni*[2]

One evening in early spring, I was making my way through a pile of student papers, sitting at my dining room table, regularly looking out my picture window, across the street to the athletic field, which is set in a hollow surrounded by low hills. Beyond are some of the dorms of Western Michigan University, our giant neighbor. The windows were lighting up. Someone was running around our track below. The scoreboard reading "Kalamazoo" and "Visitors" stood blank. Padded metal structures against which the football team rams its shoulders stood in a straight diagonal line. The trees ringing the field were growing black against the sky. The sun was just below the horizon, and the sky had diffused to a gleaming purple-blue, shot with pink, that distinguishes April evenings in Michigan. The evening star, old Venus herself, had risen and was sitting like a diamond chip in deepening blue satin.

The phone rang. "Gail? This is Kitty."

Kitty was a sophomore. Her voice was high with anxiety. "Have you seen Angela?" Angela was her roommate and soul sister. They were one of those inseparable female duos that eighty years ago would have flowered into a Boston Marriage. "No, what's wrong?"

"Well, um, she went out for a walk? And she hasn't come back. Um, and she's been really upset. About Jack. I'm sort of worried."

I assured her that I'd watch for Angela, that she probably needed a good long walk, and that I was sure she'd be back. "OK, thanks," said Kitty sadly. We agreed to phone each other when Angela showed up.

I walked from the study back to the dining room, thinking. Angela had come to Kalamazoo from an urban high school. Her parents were affluent, upright Catholics, much removed from their daughter's reality. She herself looked like a child out of a Julia Cameron photograph, a plump Victorian angel with long, thick hair and a face in which gentle sweetness mingled with sensuality. I knew little of her life before Kalamazoo except that there was a scarifying relationship with someone named Jack. When she had sketched it out for me, in a sort of terse shorthand, I had felt the dissonance I often feel listening to young college women, their faces and voices still full of girl, recounting horrors. Dissonance that often ends in a shudder of fear.

Now, about to sit again at the table and face the white pile, I looked out the big window. There, across the street, inside the hurricane fence around the field, stood Angela, as if she'd appeared there by magic. She was looking away from me across the field toward the pale western light, her body obscured, as usual, by a veil of hair and a long, baggy coat. She stood framed in my window, waiting for me.

I called Kitty quickly and returned to the window. I gave it about thirty seconds, procrastinating, dreading the hard work ahead that would kill my evening, which I had consecrated to the white pile. And then I walked out onto the porch and out the door into the yard, across the street to the fence. When she turned, I knew it would be worse even than I'd thought. I'd expected tears, or maybe that small throwaway smile that says, "Oh, God, here I am again, a mess. Sorry about this." Instead, I was met with a blankness that momentarily set me back. Her big green eyes were pale, flat, and empty. I realized that I was frightened.

I led her back to the house, took off her coat. All my queries received only dumb nods or shakes of the head, or nothing at all. I suggested tea. She nodded slowly. I tried to joke about the array of available flavors—silence, nothing. I selected blackberry, dark and potent, and put on the water. Something warm, steaming, to loosen her throat, something shared to pull her to me out of this silent void. I had left her on the couch, but when I returned with the tea, she had moved to the floor, so I sat there too, close to her. I poured, we drank. I talked sporadically, ridiculously flailing for something that would spring her loose. She would not look at me.

Slowly, in almost whispered fragments, the skeleton of her story emerged. She was sixteen when it started. He was older, had his own place. He told her she was beautiful, sexy, wonderful. She basked in it. Then the violent jealousies began, of other boys and men she knew. One day he was waiting outside after school. He took her arm and propelled her into the subway. As the shriek of the train approached, he pushed her close and closer to the tracks, threatening to push her over, but finally pulling her onto the train. At his apartment, he took her school books and began to rip them apart. (I am madly searching this cryptic, surreal text for significance, I am trying to muster a countertext to give back to her, and I am caught by the power of that metaphor—his terror of her academic life, her mind, her contact with the world through her classes.) He struck her, again and again, and then told her to come back that night. She went home. (I try to imagine dinner with the folks that night in a quiet, tasteful house in a "good" section of the city.) Angela spoke without tears or even visible pain, in a tiny voice just this side of a whisper. After dinner (what pretext do these girls use for getting out to visit deranged lovers?) she went again to Jack's place, bringing with her a music box.

"A music box?" I ask softly, stopped again by a strange, potent image.

"I collected them," she whispered. "I had lots. I took him my favorite one."

"Why?"

She shook her head.

When she arrived, she gave Jack the music box. He took it, walked to the window, opened it, and hurled the music box down into the street. Then he raped her.

Now the looming silence of the room was surrounding me like a malign fog. In my years of teaching I had become proficient, I thought, in responding compassionately, I hoped, helpfully, I hoped, to the confessions of adolescent women—pregnancy and abortion, rape, incest, bulimia, sexual harassment, along with the more mundane realities of uncomprehended anger at boyfriends and teachers and parents, confused struggles with other women and with personal guilt and inadequacy. But now, at this moment, in the gathered dark in my living room, staring at Angela, I was bone dry. There were no words—and not only because none would embrace the enormity of her experience. I had no words because no one was there to hear me. A ghost was narrating Angela's story. She herself was as absent a presence as I had ever known. It was eerie to be in the same room with it. The narrative voice was disembodied, reportorial; the plot factual, unembroidered by physical or emotional detail. Hemingway would have been pleased. In this narrative the central character was without responses. The central consciousness was obliterated. It was a first-person narration as close to third-person as it could get—until the end:

"Finally he let me go. I ran downstairs, out into the street. Then I started screaming. I screamed and screamed."

And she smiled, a brief wisp of a smile.

Physical relief washed over me.

I don't remember what I said then—assertions of her bravery in surviving this, analyses of his psychology, affirmations of the scream in the street—all ineffectual, premature fuel for a fire not yet lit.

But we had only just begun. I could see that there was something more swelling toward utterance. She circled back to the subtext, the heart of it, which the plot had evaded: He told her again and again that she was a slut, a slut, no man would ever want her, she was fat and ugly, a slut. In the voice recounting this there was no inch of ironic distance. She believed every word. Then, after a long silence, she whispered, so softly I could barely hear, "He taped me. Filmed me. Videocamera." Pause. "He has those tapes."

Now I fell over the brink, into fantasy. I would get on a plane, I would go there. I would somehow find and enter his apartment, I would find the tapes. I saw myself ripping out yards of videotape, giving it to death by sun or water, obliterating this record that he had made not as a tool for his own titillation, but as an inspired, ingenious weapon to ensure her humiliation and compliance, her belief in the pornographic image of herself that he needed her to accept.

So, Angela was telling me, he had this knowledge of what I really am, he still has the proof. And now that I know what I really am, I can never forget it. I tried to forget it by leaving home and coming here to school, but it's been a charade. All the people here who think well of me—they've all been conned. You've been conned too. I am a walking lie. Look what I submitted to. Look what I let him do to me.

I gathered my strength like a high jumper and did my damnedest, on and on into the night. I tried closer reading of the text: "Now, why do you think he did that to you?" I tried the wider view, a little depersonalization that might get her to read her own story critically: "Angela, you know the classic response of rape victims is to blame themselves, don't you? Listen: What would you say to a friend—to Kitty, or me—who had gone through this and blamed herself?" I tried personal testimony: "What *I* see is a terrified, victimized girl—*sixteen,* Angela!—who did things out of love and fear and managed to keep herself alive and get out and go on to a healthy life. I call that heroic; listen, I'm not just saying this, I mean it."

My usual adroitness with language seemed facile, my words bodiless, windy. They fell dead on the carpet, and the hopeful, grateful eagerness to believe that usually meets them was absent. She listened, nodded, sometimes smiled weakly, acknowledging my kindness and its futility at once. She cried a little, too little. But the heavy silence never lifted from the room. She was light years away from me, speaking as if far under deep narcotic waters. She could not hear me, because my voice was reaching no voice inside her head. At that moment, a scene from a movie came to me: Anne Bancroft as Annie Sullivan, screaming, "It has a *name!*" to a girl buried in silence and darkness.

Finally I realized I was beaten. I conceded that perhaps all I could give her tonight was protection, so I asked if she wanted to stay with me. She nodded. I had her call Kitty. Then I led her upstairs to the guest room. I held her, and then I looked down into her face, hoping for some glimmer. But a vast blankness stretched far behind her eyes.

Lying in my bed I heard, prowling the house, that third creature that had been in the room with us. The enemy here, I thought, is not Jack. The enemy is this silence.

La Pucelle

friends come

explaining to me that my mind
is the obvious assassin
the terrorist of voices
who has waited
to tell me miraculous lies
all my life. no

I say
friends
the ones who talk to me
their words thin as wire
their chorus fine as crystal
their truth direct as stone
they are present as air.

they are there.
                                        —*Lucille Clifton*[3]

I have just finished Marina Warner's study of Joan of Arc[4] and find myself doing precisely what, the book argues, successive generations have done with the Maid of Orleans: I have responded to her as a symbol defined by my own culture and time. It occurs to me that one significant concept born between Joan's age and mine is the idea of adolescence. Warner reminds us at one point that Joan's sudden and complete immersion at seventeen into the religio-political life of her time was not then extraordinary, when boys her age were accomplished warriors, significant political entities, expensive hostages to the Valois or Anglo-Bergundian parties. When life expectancy was around half what it is now, a decade of adolescence would have been a luxury. But a contemporary reader, especially a feminist, cannot avoid projecting the remarkable events of Joan's short "maturity" against a backdrop of our understanding of adolescence. As time has passed since she was devoured by the flames at Rouen, increasing poignancy and potency have accrued to the fact that she was a girl-warrior, a child-martyr—the age of a senior in high school.

One historical fact, however, tells us that the critical developmental point at which she emerged into French history was not lost upon her or upon her audience. Amid the array of names used then and since to capture her, "the name she always used herself was Jehanne la Pucelle."[5] This is one of those cases where another tongue gives us not merely a word but a concept for which there is no clear English equivalent. "Pucelle" does not translate intact into "girl" or "young woman" or the archaic "maid" or "maiden." It means, Warner tells us, "'virgin,' but in a special way, with distinct shades connoting youth, innocence, and, paradoxically, nubility. . . It denotes a time of passage, not a permanent condition. It is a word that looks forward to a change in state."[6] Etymologically, she continues, it may derive from the Latin "pulcra," or "beautiful"; or, alternately, from "pullicella," or "little animal." The term encapsulates all the ambiguity of female adolescence: vulnerability charged with power, innocence full of the pure sensuality of the beautiful little animal, the moment of quivering balance where a young creature stands on the brink:

> With an instinct for seizing a central image of power, which Joan possessed to an extraordinarily developed degree, she picked a word for virginity that captured with doubled strength the magic of her state in her culture. It expressed not only the incorruption of her body, but also the dangerous border into maturity or full womanhood that she had not crossed and would not cross. In this sense she was a tease. During the whole course of her brief life Joan of Arc placed herself thus, on borders, and then attempted to dissolve them and to heal the

division they delineated. In the very ambiguity of her body, which had to be shown to the crowd to assure them she was a woman, in the name that she chose—which means "virgin" and yet simultaneously captures all the risk of loss—she shows herself to span opposites, to contain irreconcilable oppositions.[7]

Almost all cultures have understood the power of the *pucelle*, enfolding her in elaborate ritual and placing her at the heart of myth and literature. The potent unity of purity and fecundity— paradoxical only where sexuality is regarded as impure, of course—is central to the power of Mary, the Virgin Mother, who was thirteen or so. Juliet was, too, and Romeo was her first encounter with sexuality; hence the pure, furious monomania of her passion. Heloise, the archetypal student in love with her teacher, is the *pucelle* on the verge of "knowledge," as is Eve herself at the moment when the apple sits intact in her hand. One thinks of Henry James' young women, whose innocent—in twentieth-century parlance, "unconscious"—power electrifies their worldly environment.

The *pucelle* as innocent witch turns up in particularly interesting form in Stephen King's *Carrie*. Watching the film, I wondered how much King understood of the mythic sources on which his story draws: The monstrous need and rage of the pubescent girl catalyzes at menarche into terrible supernatural power. Her innate energies explode in flames that devour the hostile outer world and turn in to devour her, like the flames toward which Joan moved inexorably for the six years beginning with the day she first heard her voices.

Much of what is verifiable in Joan's history renders it irresistible as a paradigm for female adolescence: the abusive father, whom she exchanged for another, calling herself "fille de Dieu," her other preferred title; her rebellious escape from home to the big city; her retorts to the assembled Fathers of the Inquisition—insouciant or enigmatic or merely confused and defensive. That Joan did not menstruate, according to testimony at her trial, Warner associates with either stress or anorexia, for Joan was extremely restrictive in the quantity and nature of the food she ingested, vomiting back a particularly rich fish sent her in prison.[8]

And then there are the Voices, which Joan characteristically called her "counsel," and to which she attributed all the actions and habits for which she burned. She first heard them at thirteen. In her trial, she identified them as Saints Michael, Catherine, and Margaret. Though Warner documents a certain degree of confusion surrounding their identification, the bulk of reliable evidence points to this trio. St.

Michael, Warner says, was a natural, as patron saint of France. The two female saints, however, are fascinating choices as mentors for *la pucelle*.[9] They are associated, respectively, with virginity and motherhood, the two mythic poles of female existence, united miraculously in the mother of Christ and perhaps in Joan too, enshrined subsequently as the virgin mother of France. St. Margaret's symbol is the dragon who devoured her and then disgorged her unharmed—hence her association with safe deliveries. St. Catherine's is the wheel on which she was tortured, a machine finally demolished by an avenging angel. Her immediate sin was having spurned the advances of the Emperor Maxentius, pledging herself exclusively to Christ. But Maxentius' proposal apparently came in a rush of infatuation with Catherine's mind after she had confuted fifty learned inquisitors, maintaining her faith in the face of the Emperor's edict ordering the slaughter of Alexandrian Christians. For Catherine was "one of the few women saints to be revered for her brains," often depicted "reading a book, the broken wheel at her feet."[10] She was thus first adored and then tortured and beheaded for refusing to capitulate, mentally or physically, to male dominance. In her the heretical power of the female mind and the mystical power of the virginal female body unite. She is an iconographic episode in the long marriage of two ideas: female intellect and female resistance to male sexual encroachment. Four hundred years later, as women demanded higher education, the concept would be articulated much more simply: Educated women would surely avoid marriage or make incompetent, dangerous childbearers.

Warner explores these saints as reflections of elements in Joan's own life and psychology but she warns us against our ready modern instinct to regard the Voices as internal—medieval correlatives to the subconscious. For Joan lived and died firmly convinced of their empirical reality and reliability. The problem, as Warner outlines it, was that in the context of the trial, faced with an endless parade of inquisitors whose theological and political sophistication was utterly alien to the illiterate pucelle, Joan of Domremy was twisted into speaking a foreign language. Her enemies "were obsessed with determining the extent of Joan's sensual experience of her voices"[11] and insisted that she make concrete, articulate, and rational an experience that could only have been fluid, spiritual, and nonrational. To give voice to her Voices was a contradiction of her experience of them, yet this was her inquisitors' demand. The hook, of course, was that in rendering the Voices solid and apprehensible, she would be damning herself—which was the whole point.

Joan was their plaything, she was lured into a gin she did not even understand to be there, which bit into her deeper and deeper as she struggled to express her truth in a language that she could not fully master and would yet be intelligible to her questioners. As they were adept in branches of learning she hardly knew by name, she took her lead from them, borrowed their images to render explicit the ineffable. The trap into which they prodded her closed inexorably.[12]

In effect, she reenacted the martyrdom of St. Catherine, her mystical "knowledge" ground down on the wheel of academic logic, her experience of light and sound in the gardens and woods of Domremy made hard, fast, and deadly.

Shades of my Ph.D. oral exams. St. Catherine and her protege, St. Joan, should be enshrined in dorm rooms, certainly those occupied by *les pucelles*: Catherine, calmly reading her book as she treads upon that infernal wheel; and Joan, responding in her trial, "I will not tell you everything. . . This voice is good and worthy and I am not bound to answer you."[13] What she is doing here is abjuring one voice to affirm and protect another. Silence becomes the swaddling cloth of speech. The ambiguity of her reference to "this voice" is telling. That she regarded it as external rather than internal becomes wonderfully irrelevant. Joan heard *her* voices.

Daisies

Given that the role of the Mind of Man has long been to discipline untidy and disorderly old Mother Nature, it should not be surprising that the academic year subverts and overturns the natural cycle. Fall is the season of beginnings. Spring is a time of frenzied consummations and conclusions.

Spring quarter at Kalamazoo College is one long nightmare of deadlines. Even the mystical Fiscal Year ends on June 30th. One of the traumatic annual rites of passage is the Departmental Oral Examination. It was also one of my early points of access to the Woman Problem.

In my early years at Kalamazoo, one of the senior English majors was a woman named Robbie—"Roberta," after her father, who persisted and finally got sons but was nonetheless unrelenting in his effort to shove Robbie into an MBA program. In her senior spring she had just shy of a four-point in English, an overall GPA of something like 3.5. The preceding summer she had aced my Victorian Literature course (or, as the students have christened it, "Vicki Lit," a familiarity that would not have amused its namesake) and had discovered Robert

Browning. For her orals, she decided to discuss the monologues. I was one of her two examiners.

Two minutes into the half-hour exam, I was confounded. Robbie fumbled through her initial statement and fell silent. Our gentlest proddings drew more verbal confusion, half-hearted suggestions of answers, always in the interrogative and laced with "ums" and "I guess," and shrivelled with self-deprecation. Both of us threw conspicuous lifelines and pointed out reliable bridges, to no avail. Robbie giggled and effaced herself into oblivion. Efforts to draw her into safe, familiar territory were in vain. My colleague's questions grew odorously patronizing: "Why don't you tell us about some poem you like?" My confusion flared into fury at both of them. Finally, as the usually fleeting thirty minutes dragged themselves to a close, Robbie said, "Um, I know I haven't done very well, I'm really sorry. I guess I just don't do real well in this kind of setting, answering these questions. I guess I sort of read literature with my heart."

When the office door closed behind her, my colleague started to assemble a case for a Low Pass. "Fail her," I snapped. "And before she schedules a retake, let me talk to her."

When she came creeping in, I'm afraid that I gave her hell. "What do you *mean*, you read literature with your heart? You think it's your heart that's gotten you a 3.9 in English?" I pause here to examine my memory closely: Did I excoriate her for saying that she read with her heart, or for denying that she read with her head as well?

She shaped up for the retake, passed, and graduated.

Such performances on oral exams have become common enough to provide some of my more effective exempla in my efforts to heighten departmental awareness of the Woman Problem. They cannot dismiss the Robbies as appealingly daffy girls, though sometimes they try. They know these "girls" and their academic records too well. The dissonance between the two voices of many young women is inescapable: the intelligent, even inspired voice on paper or in class, and the other voice, the one that says, "Don't pay any attention to me, OK? I really don't know anything much. Listen, I'm really sorry, OK?"

It's a time-honored tradition, this female doublespeak. Its manifestations vary. In one case it might be the acute, irreverent, witty, ribald, or angry voice a woman uses among other women, versus the eager, soothing, deferential voice she quickly dons when the gentlemen enter the room. In another case it may be the competent, fluent, cerebral voice in a paper versus the stammering, giggling voice in an oral exam—and neither of these may be authentic, though one at least has some power behind it. The vocal duplicity is complex. The powerless, self-abnegating voice may not be true but may well be honest, conveying the child or idiot or handmaid a woman genuinely sees in herself. Or it may function as a defensive-subversive survival tactic, much as the voices of Jemima and Tom served African Americans. And sometimes it does both.

It did so for Emily Dickinson, I think. This double voice has been at the root of the corruption of Dickinson criticism for decades. When I first read her in high school, I heard—because I was encouraged to hear—only the breathless virgin, the shrill neurotic, the lisping, stammering "Daisy" in the letters to "Master." It was at Kalamazoo that I read her in a different light—a light shed by Adrienne Rich's monumental essay "Vesuvius at Home"[14] and by my immersion in women's studies. I began to listen more carefully to Dickinson, and I heard another voice: clear, urgent, explosive, dead sure of itself and of the hypercharged vision of reality it describes.

Yet another voice exists too. If, as Alicia Ostriker has argued, duplicity is a salient characteristic of the female voice,[15] Emily Dickinson takes the cake: the public silence and recalcitrance of "lawyer Dickinson's half-cracked daughter" versus the private verbosity; the voice of Daisy, tentatively imploring Thomas Wentworth Higginson to tell her, from on high, whether her poems lived, versus the confidence inherent in 1775 poems, tied neatly in groups upstairs in a trunk, a voluminous voice thrown into the future, an extensive letter to the world that never wrote to her. And the duplicity penetrates the poems themselves. In some she cringes before a Master-God; in others she laughs him to oblivion and assumes his throne. In some she is cute, in others acid. In some she quivers, in others she soars. Even formally, the dissonance is central to her work: the rush of each phrase, running up against the silence of each dash; the weight of what is said in such compressed form by each loaded word, against the charged silence of what is unsaid, left unelaborated.

Even the Daisy voice is duplicitous within itself. It contains the cunningly false speech of dramatized, strategic subservience and the all-too-true speech of self-denigration and fear. I submit that most women know all about this duplicity, all these duplicities. Doubleness is second nature to us. And it is because this tension is so familiar to women that Dickinson has benefitted perhaps more than any writer from feminist criticism. Her silences surely were, as Rich and others have maintained, chosen; like Joan, Emily protected her voices, creating space in which they could speak uninterrupted and unadulterated. She judged astutely the prospects for a woman artist in Victorian America, especially one as singular as herself. If you wrote like Emily

Dickinson, transcribing those particular voices, it would be madness not to expect that the world would call you mad, or at least syntactically deficient; that it would ridicule you, ignore you, or just tidy up your punctuation.

The strength of Dickinson's choice is not diminished, however, if we acknowledge that the lisping voice of Daisy is quite real too. That Emily Dickinson may have sustained two polar self-images, one an Amazon, the other a wispy child, only makes her human—and female to the core. Daisy may be a persona, but a mask is always a projection, an emanation, and a dangerous one, too, for it can potentially take over. Like the half-inch of permanent make-up on the face of Elizabeth I when she died, the mask can become inseparable from the skin.

I have known Daisy intimately all my life. I meet her in the classroom regularly. She is the incarnation of our readiness to disbelieve our own good and worthy voices, as well as a tactic for protecting them from a faithless world, which gives us no reason to believe in them in the first place. It is hard sometimes to listen patiently to Daisy, as hard as it is to attend to the tale told by a four-year-old, excruciatingly prolonged by grammatical entanglements, repetitions, inadequate vocabulary, hiati, and encodings. Only the parents listen hungrily—and only sometimes—as the child reports personal discoveries of the world in the form of a small raid on the inarticulate, to borrow T. S. Eliot's wonderful phrase. And it is also hard to distinguish between the false voice that evades and diminishes, and the embryonic true voice stammering toward daylight. When I read Carol Gilligan's *In A Different Voice*[16], I saw for the first time that the equivocation, the inarticulate writhings, the muddiness I was accustomed to hearing from my own mouth and the mouths of young women were not evidence of intellectual inability or cowardice, though they might well represent failures of confidence. They were sometimes salvos in an embattled struggle to express an alternate vision in a foreign language. Thus started my own close examination of the fabric of academic discourse. And I began to see the young women I taught as wrenching the structure of language to let themselves through its bars, much like the woman trapped behind the insidious twisting pattern in Charlotte Perkins Gilman's yellow wallpaper. They love that story—about a woman writing madly for her life, fighting for her voice in the narrowing space between the malevolent discourse of the wallpaper and the silence imposed upon her by her husband and the male medical establishment he represents.

More recently, Gilligan has suggested that the onset of adolescence may take a linguistic toll on girls in a kind of generic laryngitis, a collective loss of voice. That terrible, powerful moment, the shimmering hour at which Joan and Mary heard angelic voices announcing great and frightening destinies, is still one at which awesome signs appear in female lives. But the signs are less glorious than ominous, I fear. Eating disorders erupt, a grotesque and graphic body language. Conceptions occur, but hardly immaculate, clotting lives at the point when aspirations for the future are swelling. Enrollments in "hard subjects" plummet, with dire consequences for subsequent prospects. And, Gilligan suggests, the confident, insouciant voices of eleven-year-old girls dwindle to silence, broken by the "Never mind" and "It's nothing" that confound parents, infuriate teachers, and baffle boy-friends[17]. Gilligan, borrowing Coleridge's priceless phrase, names this another "willing suspension of disbelief"—disbelief, that is, in reality as structured by the dominant culture, in violation of a girl's own experience and authenticity.[18] Its concomitant is the willing suspension of belief in herself. Better, likelier, that we should be wrong than the whole world, for in that case we are lunatics and witches. Safer and healthier to assume its vocabulary than face the awesome work of unnaming and renaming. The non-speech of "It's nothing" is, I think, double-edged, like Joan's "I am not bound to answer you." It is at once a protection of an inner reality, a good and worthy voice that the world's discourse will dissect, smother and deny, and also a capitulation, a concession that the inner voice is probably worthless, sham, only personal.

Joan denied hers, too. Perhaps she was terrified by the fire. Perhaps she humbly accepted the counsel of elders. Perhaps she finally grew so confused and intimidated by the battalion of learned men arrayed against her that the voices simply grew small, so small that even she could no longer hear them. In any case, she recanted, confessed, and put on a dress.

And then something happened—and herein lies the stuff of which legends are made. Perhaps in the silence of her cell the realization that she had saved her life so that it might be lived out in prison struck her as absurd, unbearable. Perhaps it was the prospect of another sort of incarceration, in a prison of inauthenticity, burning in her own silence and burning to hear her betrayed and silenced voices. Or perhaps she simply heard them again, clear as they were at Domremy, and woke smiling, astonished to have wandered so far off course. In any case, she put her warrior clothes back on, the clothes than had transformed her in the public imagination into a mythical androgyne, and she announced to somebody that she wished to recant her recantation. She burned for it.

and you
sister sister
did you not then sigh
my voices my voices of course?

—*Lucille Clifton*[19]

Laughter in the Attic

It was not until my fourth or fifth trip through *Jane Eyre*, preparing to offer it up for the communal feast that traditionally culminates my Literature of Women course, that I suddenly realized that Jane is eighteen. Ten for a few pages, behind the curtain, in the Red Room, at Lowood; and then eighteen for the rest of the book, younger than anyone in my class. I saw that I had been carting Jane along with me in my life since I first read her story at about eighteen. She was surely *me*, my age always. And her self-possession and store of hard experience were so far beyond the callow youths now beginning to read her story. But no, Jane is *une pucelle*. She, of course, would disdain such an un-English appellation. But *pucelle* she is, though her sensuality is so violently repressed that it shows itself only in symbolic, alienated forms. Her narrative is the classic account of female adolescence, that treacherous, dark passage. The novel takes its starting and ending points from tradition: menarche (signified by the Red Room experience) and marriage. But between these poles lies a grim, lonely terrain that no one has charted so memorably as Charlotte Bronte.

Jane Eyre is in many respects a novel about voice and the lack of it. Its climactic moment, the one toward which my own *pucelle* heart pounded, is the point where the hyperconscious, articulate Jane finally comes face to face with the wordless, growling Bertha Mason Rochester, surely the most eloquent silent character in all of fiction. But in fact, a trio of voices joined in a complicated relationship tells the story of *Jane Eyre*. The detailed, precise verbosity of Jane the Narrator mediates between two semi-silences flanking it: the firmly corsetted, tightly reined discourse of Jane the Governess, who guards her tongue and knows better than to give too much away; and the terrible laughter and subhuman snarls of her alter-ego in the attic, whose tale surges under the text of the novel like a subterranean lava river. Or, regarded from another angle, the trio might be seen to realign as follows: At the center is the voice of Jane the Governess—the muted voice of the girl who learned submission and good behavior as well as self-protection and silent defiance. In this constellation, the flanking voices are the buried ones, the authentic ones, those that say what the Governess would say if she could: that of the eloquent Narrator, confessing her passion and vulnerability, exercising her intelligence and acuity; and that of the Madwoman, whose rage is beyond speech.

I wonder if the perennial appeal of *Jane Eyre* for adolescent girls— not to mention the rest of us middle-aged *pucelles*—has not something to do with the novel's sense of tense, barely suppressed voices about to explode in tongues of flame—as in fact they do when Bertha takes her revenge against everything that has rendered her dumb. After all, the mystery at Thornfield is an unexplained *voice*. Bertha's constant threat to the silence of Thornfield is the backdrop for Jane's own difficult relationship with her voice. Or, more accurately, her voices. Four centuries after Rouen, another "Jeanne la Pucelle" hears voices— and stands in danger of burning.

As a child she is very close to these voices, which boil up readily from the unconscious. But Jane always alienates them as external forces possessing her tongue. Barely four pages into the text, the loathsome John Reed, first in the parade of patriarchs presiding over the phases of Jane's pilgrimage, hurls a book at her head, and Jane fires back a comparison of him with murderers, slave-drivers, and Roman emperors. "I had read Goldsmith's 'History of Rome,' and had formed my opinion of Nero, Caligula, &c," she informs us. "Also, I had drawn parallels in silence, which I never thought thus to have declared aloud."[20] Her voice takes her by surprise, that is—as it does Master Reed: "What! What! Did she say that to me?" (9)

Similarly, in chapter IV, when Jane explodes at Mrs. Reed, she tells us that she "cried out suddenly, and without at all deliberating on my words. . ." As punishment, Mrs. Reed demands her silence: She is dared to "utter one syllable, during the remainder of the day."

> "What would uncle Reed say to you, if he were alive?" was my scarcely voluntary demand. I say scarcely voluntary, for it seemed as if my tongue pronounced the words without my will consenting to their utterance: something spoke out of me over which I had no control.

Jane's true voice, which nails John as a mini-Caligula and his mother as a violator of the dead, is so terrible in its audacity that Jane must disown it as "scarcely voluntary," "without my will," "something [that] spoke out of me." Mrs. Reed is likewise terrified of this voice and regards Jane "as if she really did not know whether I was child or fiend." (24)

Mrs. Reed has earlier tried to shut this vocal demon in the Red Room; at this point she decides to immure it at Lowood. After the interview with Brocklehurst (during which Jane's heretically authentic little voice announces that to preserve herself from the fiery pit she must "keep in good health and not die" [27]), Jane lingers in Mrs. Reed's presence, once again overtaken by a compulsion she does not understand: "*Speak* I must; I had been trodden on severely, and *must* turn. . ." (30). And she does, telling Mrs. Reed that she despises her and her family, and pledging one day not to retaliate but to *tell* on them all, to speak their perfidy to the world. The psychic consequence of this outburst is a fascinating two-stage process. First, ecstatic emancipation: "Ere I had finished this reply my soul began to expand, to exult, with the strangest sense of freedom, of triumph, I ever felt. It seemed as if an invisible bond had burst, and that I had struggled out into unhoped-for liberty" (31). This episode becomes paradigmatic: Jane almost always achieves a sense of liberty by exercising her voice against the forces of silence in her life. The second phase, though, is depression, guilt, and remorse. Her image for herself in her passionate voice is "a ridge of lighted heath, alive, glancing, devouring"; afterward she is "the same ridge, black and blasted after the flames are dead" (32). This is not the only instance where Jane's self-imagery adumbrates the imagery surrounding Bertha—the language of fire.

Lowood is a place of profound silence and repression where Jane nonetheless finds a viable, if not finally satisfactory and authentic, self and voice, largely with the help of Helen Burns and Maria Temple. The latter, among other gifts, gives Jane two unprecedented blessings: She allows Jane to tell her story, and she speaks *for* Jane to the community. Thus encouraged, Jane takes from eight years at Lowood a voice to match her "disciplined and subdued character" (72)—the voice of the Governess. The other voice—the one Mrs. Reed recalls on her deathbed as having spoken "like something mad, or like a fiend—no child ever spoke or looked as she did" (203)—got Jane into far too much trouble and was too frightening even to herself, so it disappears. When next she hears it, it is disembodied and completely alienated, emerging from the attic at Thornfield, where Rochester, like Mrs. Reed, has tried to muffle a violent, accusatory voice in an upper room.

The tension in the Jane-Rochester courtship can be attributed largely to the suppression of Jane's voice. Her position—as a woman, a "dependent"—is reactive, for he sets the limits of the game and the tone of the discourse, within which she maneuvers to protect herself.

His secrets and lies, his verbal aggression and withdrawal, his metaphors—notably those of sultans and harems with which the couple
spars so testily, so tellingly, after their engagement—these verbal tools
push Jane into taciturnity, a verbal self-restriction that belies the sympathy and intimacy she asserts between them. This, for me at least, is
the first time that the Narrator seems to be silencing herself as the
Governess does. A lie at the heart of the Jane-Rochester romance is not
being acknowledged, a lie having nothing to do with the existence of
a Mrs. Rochester and everything to do with the man himself. The
Narrator suggests the Governess' discomfort, but that is not enough.
Neither Narrator nor Governess ever admits the rage that is still locked
away. The closest thing to Jane's authentic voice sears through the
verbal game-playing in the climactic "equal—as we are" declaration
in chapter XXIII, where, says the Narrator, she was "roused to something like passion" (225). Not like enough, I say. As eloquent an
assertion of human equality as Jane's pronouncement is, it is primarily
about Jane's humanity, not Rochester's inhumanity. It is desperate,
defensive, too painful to be as angry as it should be. There is laughter
from the attic, where Jane's burning rage accumulates.

     The truest of Jane's voices is growing more insistent. Bertha con-
sistently "speaks for" Jane in her own pure, primal language, at once
expressing what Jane denies and also actively collaborating, trying to
warn Jane and save her from disaster. Her laughter mocks and contra-
dicts Jane's rational conclusions and her passionate delusions; her
language of fire points straight to Rochester's bed as a very dangerous
place; and when she has the chance to slaughter Jane in her bed, she
leaves instead the torn veil, by way of a sign—one denoting cleared
vision as much as disrupted union. And, interestingly, once Jane
knows of Bertha's existence, she returns the favor by speaking on *her*
behalf, in what amounts to her sole reference to Bertha: In the final,
torturous discussion with Rochester before Jane's flight from
Thornfield (which is not much of a discussion, consisting of his long-
winded and self-exculpatory efforts to erode her resistance),
Rochester's contemptuous references to Bertha finally prompt Jane to
interrupt: "Sir, you are inexorable for that unfortunate lady: you speak
of her with hate—with vindictive antipathy. It is cruel— she cannot
help being mad" (265). She who, in Rochester's language, is a hag and
a fiend becomes, in Jane's, "that unfortunate lady"—that is, human.

     But he proceeds with the saga of his life since his marriage, while
distaste for his abuse of women wrestles, in Jane's silence, with pity
for his suffering and loneliness. So overwhelmed is Jane at this point
by the tide of words and emotion that she begins once again to hear

voices. She believes she has not the strength to leave this man, but "a voice within me averred that I could do it" (261). Then, when he finally brings her to the brink of capitulation by reminding her that in staying with him adulterously she, alone in the world, will injure no one, she says that the voices of her "very conscience and reason," now "turned traitor," beg her to think of Rochester's desolation in her absence. "Who in the world cares for you?" they conclude, "or who will be injured by what you do?" And then comes yet another voice, the "still indomitable reply" that says, "I care for myself. The more solitary, the more friendless, the more unsustained I am, the more I will respect myself" (279). Later, in her room, preparing to flee, she turns her eyes to the maternal moon, her guiding spirit, which metamorphoses into a "white human form" that "whispered in my heart—'My daughter, flee temptation!'" (281) And she listens. The preposition here is worth attention: The voice whispers not *into* but *in* her heart, though it comes from a separate human form. The voice is within and beyond her at once, a symbolic celestial mother and a mothering force inside the orphaned girl.

Thus far, Jane's voices are an ambiguous and various lot—subversive spirits speaking through her and out of her, personified elements within herself (conscience and reason), dangerous knowledge and anger that speak through Bertha's growls and laughter at her keyhole, semi-morphous advisers who mediate between inner and outer reality. Once more does Jane hear a voice, and this time it is firmly externalized as Rochester's, calling her name at another critical decision point, when she is once again about to submerge herself in another dominant masculine will expressed in an imperative voice, this time that of St. John Rivers. He, like Rochester, generates more vocal duplicity in *Jane Eyre*. The Narrator and the Governess both regard him with respect, albeit tinged with disapproval of his self-repression, asceticism, and coldness. The novel ends with a paean to him that I have always found dissonant and even dishonest—as if it were guiltily compensating for something.

In their confrontation scene lies what may well be the germ of the narratorial guilt: Jane's furious protest against his unconscionable manipulation of her vulnerable psyche, her religious faith, her susceptibility to guilt. In this respect the encounter is a direct echo of that excruciating conversation preceding her flight from Thornfield. His coercion is stunningly like Rochester's, and perhaps Bronte displaced Jane's rage, which she could not afford to feel at Thornfield, here to Marsh End. She calls St. John a murderer—another interesting echo of her retort to John Reed. This voice is more like that of the heretical, demonic imp of Gateshead than anything we have heard since, but this time she owns up to it, does not attribute it to any outside force. Rivers' response is an adult, socialized version of what she heard from the Reeds: "*I am killing you?* Your words are such as ought not to be used: violent, unfeminine, and untrue" (363)—an interesting ordering of sins indeed. Jane is wounded but stalwart—until a terrible moment slightly later when she wavers, desperate, as at Thornfield, for a guiding voice to disclose divine will. In the silence, however, she hears not God's voice but Rochester's, calling her name three times.

What are we to make of this? Is she still supplanting God with his creature, as she confessed earlier? Is she again alienating her own voice, throwing it like a ventriloquist into the air? Bronte unequivo-cally wishes us to accept the voice as Rochester's, for she takes pains later to confirm that he did indeed speak her name at exactly that moment. Suffice it to say that her own name comes to her, calling her home—and not merely to the "right man" but to the right use of her life as she sees it: self-affirming human love versus self-sacrificing abstract love. For all his duplicity with Jane, dishonesty with himself, and complicity in the ruin of Bertha and several other women, we are asked to see Rochester as a life-source for Jane and his love as a catalyst for her selfhood. That the voice Jane hears at this crucial point is his testifies to Bronte's idea of the great love as that which speaks the beloved's name clearly, reminding her of who she is. Perhaps the best we can do for those we love is to become one of the good and worthy voices they hear.

When Jane hears it, her relief is palpable, something like what Joan must have felt when the voices returned to save her from self-betrayal and spiritual death: "I broke from St. John, who had followed, and would have detained me. It was *my* time to assume ascendancy. *My* powers were in play, and in force" (370). On the strength of those powers, Jane goes home.

There, she finds, Rochester has finally faced the demon in the attic of his life. Quite literally, he has sacrificed an eye and a hand, symbolic of his patriarchal arrogance, attempting to save Bertha's life; and in doing so, he has called her by her name for the first time in the novel. That confrontation has occurred offstage and is not even narrated by Rochester himself. Once again, both Narrator and Governess—and Author, too, I think—are eager to let him off the hook. Yet in a certain sense his confrontation with Bertha is more complete than Jane's. True, her silent glance into the terrible mirror of Bertha took place before our eyes. But does she integrate Bertha, reclaim the alienated voice of the little "fiend" who landed in the Red Room? Finally, I believe that that voice is never really heard or heeded, never affirmed as good or worthy. We hear it in fits and starts in the eighteen-year-old Jane—briefly with Rochester in "equal—as we are"; briefly with Rivers. But it is released only on a short tether and quickly yanked back. It is allowed to remain symbolic, and it dies in the flames with Bertha. It is too much for Jane to own, as Governess or Narrator, and too much for the novel to handle. It threatened disruption for Bronte as it does for her hero. The final page, which should go to Bertha, goes to Rivers, almost as an apology for Jane's fidelity to another voice.

Reader, she marries him, without permitting her rage at him and at what he represents to complicate her love. And the son arrives, and the sight returns. A happy ending. Jane does not burn for it. Someone else has done so in her place.

The Scratching of a Pin

> *. . . the silent women whose voices have been*
> *denied us, the articulate women who have given*
> *us strength to do our work.*
>   *— Adrienne Rich[21]*

In the process of clearing my own throat, finding my own voice, I come repeatedly upon historical and fictional accounts of the moment where the fire within, the burning to speak, meets the fire without, the resistance. It seems a marked moment in women's lives, where the interior voice yearns against a monolithic silence. This silence grows from the injunction of patriarchal culture, the "Hush!" of the Fathers, which may take many forms—legal, social, physical, psychological. But it begets in the Daughter mechanisms by which she gags herself. In doing so she both demeans her voice and spins soft, sound-absorbent layers to protect it. Examples of beleaguered voices coming through—squeaking or bellowing, quavering or clarion-clear—are moving in themselves. But they are even more poignant and heroic projected against all the women's voices that died in silence, those we hear only in their absence, in the echo chamber of imagination.

In Jane's furious retorts to the Reeds I felt, as a young reader, what I think my female students feel today, the ecstacy and terror of possession by the voices of our own visionary rage or insight, so perilous, so "violent, unfeminine, and untrue," that they come over us like demonic forces. In her apprehension of the moon-spirit telling her to flee and the voice calling her home we have women's proclivity to mysticism, our intimacy with visions and saints, vehicles through which we can justify or on which we can blame our rebellions, deviations, glorious and heretical aspirations. Saints Michael, Catherine, and Margaret, after all, enabled Joan to understand her vocation in devout alliance with Church and State. To say that the voices women hear are simply their own, externalized from conditioned psychic necessity, is hardly to diminish those voices, though it may be to patronize those women. Trapped in the twentieth century, we may have no other intellectual choice. Finally such discriminations seem unimportant, and, given the remarkably fluid boundaries of the female ego, "inner" and "outer" may be intrusive concepts anyway. We hear "our" voices. We burn to speak them aloud. And then sometimes, given certain conditions within and around us, we speak.

What precisely are those conditions? This, to me, is an engrossing and central question. The environment in which a woman finds her voice seems sometimes to consist of encouragement and receptivity that produce relaxation and confidence. But just as often the conditions seem to be quite the opposite: resistance and discouragement producing urgency and desperation. The woman who spoke a century-and-a-half ago, like her great-granddaughter in these liberated days, was one whose frightened or merely numb silence was broken when something else took over— not Joan's saints, but something bigger than fear or conviction of her unworthiness. No wonder she often described it as other than herself.

I began to think about the female voice when, in the course of research for a seminar on Victorian women, I started to see that the issue of women's public voice was absolutely central to the Woman Question of the last century. Male writers grumbled in familiar terms about the encroaching battalions of women armed with pens. Suffragists encountered as much contempt and outrage for speaking in public as for what they said in doing so. Speaking publicly, particularly to "promiscuous audiences"—that telling term for groups including both sexes—partook of all that lay within the Victorian use of the word "immodest." The term resonated beyond the sexual connotations surrounding it today, but its suggestion of naked impropriety is useful, explaining not only society's disapproval but the female speaker's own embarrassment and fear. It contains a truth about the vulnerability and audacity of the public voice.

The Victorian male voice met immodesty with immodesty. The *Syracuse Daily Star*, reporting on a women's rights convention, reviled "the mass of corruption, heresies, ridiculous nonsense, and reeking vulgarities which these bad women have vomited forth for the past three days."[22] Interesting final metaphor there, since these women probably were, in fact, on the verge of vomiting as they approached the podium. It is more accurate than its author knew in capturing the sense such women often had of public speech—or any utterance that shattered a safe surface—as an experience of violent upheaval. In Victorian women, speaking was like sexual desire—unnatural, horrible once aroused, best understood and contained by attribution to external forces.

Thus did legions of women writers rationalize their professional commitment to their voices by reference to some external, legitimate, and overriding authority or necessity, often male—a sick husband or father whose medical bills were pressing, a husband or brother who insisted in spite of all modesty's protests that the poor little manuscript go to a publisher, even a larger social evil that outweighed feminine propriety. The *Sonnets from the Portuguese* are in truth an account of a female imagination's struggle with a supportive yet overpowering male. The metaphorical version of this scenario was the woman writer's adoption of a male muse-figure. He is not often merely a trousered brother of her male counterpart's female muse; he is likelier to be an ominous, sometimes violent incubus such as Dickinson describes in "He Fumbles at your Soul."

The most striking poetic treatment of the drama in which the female writer resolves the struggle for her voice by legitimizing it via external male authority is the Prologue to Elizabeth Barrett Browning's "A Curse for a Nation." More interesting than the poem itself and just as long, the Prologue is a dialogue between the female speaker and a male angel. She trots out every conceivable excuse, including her gender, to deflect his injunction that she write against American slavery, and he counters each argument, finally insisting that a curse "from the depths of womanhood," which knows more of suffering than manhood does, "is very salt and bitter and good."

Even in the male and neuter pseudonyms behind which women writers spoke we see the female voice reconstituted acceptably as non-female. In the silence of Haworth Parsonage Charlotte Bronte and her siblings learned to stifle themselves such that when their father wanted genuine speech from them, he had them wear masks. Charlotte and Emily and Anne could not allow themselves to write their remarkable novels until brother Branwell, raised to be the family genius, had succeeded in killing himself. Small wonder that later, discouraged from authorship by Robert Southey—Poet Laureate and thus literary Father Superior—Charlotte resorted to the mask of Currer Bell to protect her powerful voice from illegitimate critical condescension or assault on the basis of gender.

The first American-born woman to speak in public, excluding Native Americans, was Maria W. Stewart, an abolitionist who lectured in Boston in 1832. The astonishing fact—at once wholly unlikely and somehow wholly right—is that she was black, which made her speeches doubly heroic. In her farewell address of 1833 (the brevity of her career speaks volumes), she gave this account of her heretical act:

> I felt that I had a great work to perform, and was in haste to make a profession of my faith in Christ that I might be about my Father's business. Soon after I made this profession the Spirit of God came before me, and I spake before many. When going home, reflecting on what I had said, I felt ashamed and knew not where I should hide myself. And something said within my breast, "press forward, I will be with thee." And my heart made this reply: "Lord, if thou wilt be with me, then will I speak for thee so long as I live." . . .
>
> What if I am a woman; is not the God of ancient times the God of these modern days? Did he not raise up Deborah to be a mother and a judge in Israel? Did not Queen Esther save the lives of the Jews? And Mary Magdalene first declare the resurrection of Christ from the dead? Come, said the woman of Samaria, and see a man that hath told me all the things that I ever did; is this not the Christ? St. Paul declared that it was a shame for a woman to speak in public, yet our High Priest and Advocate did not condemn the woman for a more notorious offense than this; neither will he condemn this worthless worm. . . Did St. Paul but know our wrongs and deprivations, I presume he would make no objection to our pleading in public for our rights. . . [23]

Stewart's genuine terror of what she had done breathes vividly through her prose one hundred fifty years later. For her first public utterance, the buck is passed squarely to the Spirit of God. Her shame is virtually sexual (echoed in her references to Magdalene), the shame of nakedness: "I knew not where I should hide myself." Then comes another voice, that perennial "something" within, and the voice of the heart replies. Next, a litany of Biblical precedents. And finally, transcending St. Paul—going over his head, in effect, to his boss—she lets him off the hook on grounds of ignorance: He could not know the conditions of life for black women in the nineteenth century, conditions that demand public speech, even from a "worthless worm," a phrase in which Stewart makes clear that in her heresy she is but an unworthy vessel of higher powers, larger voices. This last is a classic example of the female "modesty" that permits a woman to endure her own courage. And such were the spiritual, intellectual, and emotional calisthenics necessary to manage the psychic disruption caused by one speech in 1832. But that speech was the maiden voyage of the female voice in the United States.

Another kind of significance belongs to the voices that sputtered through in contexts less historic, less public, but no less dramatic. Many of the small tributaries of the women's movement in the last century had as their primary goal or one of their secondary benefits the education of the female voice. Among these was the Club Movement. Women's clubs, however tame or conservative, brought middle-class women out of their homes, into contact with each other and with issues of the day; and in the process they taught thousands of ordinary women—who would never speak at a podium and might be entirely opposed to women's rights—to speak their minds.

One such was a Scotswoman, Charlotte Carmichael Stopes of Edinburgh:

> [For years I had] heard of discussion Societies of brothers and male friends, of students in that much-hungered-for University, under whose portals no women could enter as undergraduates. When I was ready for it I was, however, taken to a real Literary Society. The Misses Mair had formed one among their class fellows and friends in Abercromby Place, Edinburgh, the house of their mother. . . This was different from other societies of the kind, in having, as the fundamental reason for its existence, the editing of its own Magazine. But it looked forward to include debates, and the very day I joined the members *discussed* a discussion. We were invited to give our opinion if such an exercise would be desirable. I remember replying, "Yes, I think the discussion the most important part of any Society. We can write in any magazine, but we can only learn to speak among ourselves." That was in 1866.
>
> At the next meeting we had a debate on the subject "Ought women to be strong-minded." There was a paper on each side, well written, timidly read, duly supported, but discussion flagged. It was evidently handicapped by some strong things said against "unwomanly strong-minded women." Suddenly I heard my name called, with a mild reproach that I had not seemed very ready to take the opportunity of learning to speak. I had taught myself that when anything unpleasant had to be done, it was better to get it over than to think about it. So I rose at once. . . A tearing traffic seemed to have started through the quiet street, salvos of artillery resounded from the castle, and an earthquake shook the foundations of the rock-built house in which we met. My own sensations matched my surroundings, my ears rang, my head swam, my knees trembled, my back ached, my heart stood still, and then tried to beat down its own bounds, and a lump stuck in my throat larger than ever Adam's apple grew. I spasmodically gasped, "Ought women to be *weak-minded*?" and then my parched tongue absolutely refused to move further, all the ideas that had been coursing through my brain five minutes before had

vanished, and I sat down in shame and confusion. It took half-an-hour before the storm and tremor ceased, and my heart beat normally.[24]

Stopes dwells in comic detail upon her anticipatory terror and subsequent humiliation, when in fact the five words she managed to get out—couched, naturally, in the interrogatory mode beloved of women—say precisely the one thing needful in that debate, which by rights ought to have jerked to a halt then and there.

The deep courage of Maria Stewart, Charlotte Stopes' shining moment, are surrounded by the silence of their sisters. Sojourner Truth, all six feet of her, strode majestically up to take the stage at a white women's suffrage meeting, asserting her unwelcome sisterhood in one interrogatory phrase similar in its simplicity and clarity to that of Stopes: "Ain't I a woman?" But for one of her, one of Stewart, there were thousands of black women whose weapons against imposed silence could consist only of strategic songs, meetings wrapped in secrecy, clever behavioral maneuvers that gauged both the master's power and his ignorance, the ignorance of those whose sensibilities are deadened by the privilege of hearing their own voices too freely, too often. For every Charlotte Stopes, there were thousands of women who could not ask her question, who went home in the silence of small talk, perhaps wondering secretly, later, in their bedchambers, whether Mrs. Stopes' embarrassing question might require an answer.

Sometimes in the records of ordinary women who did not find their voices we hear small chirps, soft whispers, quiet clearings of the throat, and here we have, if not Woolf's "mute, inglorious Jane Austen,"[25] then at least a voice, a genuine female voice, wanting out. Sometimes these are the most eloquent of all. Late in the nineteenth century Ellen Weeton, an Englishwoman, recorded a chapter from her girlhood:

> . . .my mother continually checked any propensity I shewed to writing or composing; representing to me what a useless being I would prove if I were allowed to give up my time to writing or reading, when domestic duties were likely to have so frequent a call upon me. "It is very likely, my dear girl," she would often say, "that you will have to earn your own livelihood, at least in great measure; and a wretched subsistence do they obtain who have it to earn by their literary abilities! Or should you become a wife, think in what a ragged, neglected state your family would be if you gave up much of your time to books." This kind of conversation certainly made a deep impression on me; indeed, it was too frequently repeated to allow a possibility of my forgetting it; and too many living instances were

pointed out to my notice, to permit me to be blind to the injurious consequences of females dedicating their time to the increase of literary knowledge. Yet that impression had little apparent influence; for what I before did openly because my mother seemed pleased with it, I now practised by stealth, till she found it necessary positively to prohibit the use of pen and ink, or slate pencil, except whilst receiving instruction from her or the writing master. My brother was made a spy upon my actions, and by way of deterring me from disobeying my mother, would often threaten to tell her when he had seen me writing upon the wall with a pin, which sometimes I did when I had no other resources. . . As it was almost impossible to be out of either his sight or hers, I had little opportunity of indulging a propensity that was so strong, except during the hour of the writing master's attendance. He was not so watchful, and I could finish more than my expected share of arithmetical or grammatical exercises, and have some time to spare; but alas! I was obliged to rub off my slate, almost as soon as written, what I had transcribed there, lest my mother should come to examine when the writing master was gone. . .[26]

Even from the vantage point of years at which Weeton was writing, we hear her mystification with her small self: Why, given such clearly salient counter-examples and such "negative reinforcement," as a behavioralist would say, should she have persisted in the forbidden act of writing? It is as if it were some compulsion beyond her control, some disease or biological need, like breathing. And so it was. And slowly, inexorably, it was driven underground, to the very edge of silence. The words vanish from the slate, wiped quiet.

What makes for these differences? Sometimes the Babbling Woman never hears the silence beneath her life. Sometimes the Silent Woman never hears her voices. Sometimes, though, she does, and they make their way out, through all the layers of external and internalized resistance, into the listening air. Sometimes she burns for it, sometimes not.

And then again, sometimes, in the silence, we listen and all we can hear is a pin scratching upon a wall.

> *in populated air*
> *our ancestors continue.*
> *i have seen them,*
> *i have heard*
> *their shimmering voices*
> *singing.*
>
> —Lucille Clifton[27]

A Happy Ending

So what you're hearing in our music is nothing
but the sound of a woman calling another woman.

—*Nikki Giovanni*[28]

After the night Angela spent at my house, the tardy spring hurriedly unfolded into summer, as it does in Michigan. Another class
graduated and a week later we rolled into summer quarter. My Lit of
Women class was a beauty—a big, talkative bunch of fifty, with the
usual eight men, ten or so feminists, and thirty other interested parties—some old friends, some unknowns; some ripe to perfection for
the course, others perplexed, resistent, defensive, or simply lacking a
lit credit.

I used Florence Howe and Ellen Bass' anthology *No More Masks!*[29]
that summer, carefully balancing the complex with the crowd-
pleasers. The volume was a big hit. Kitty was in the class and told me,
as others did, how she read the day's assignment to her suitemates
each night, how the poems generated personal testimony and long
discussions. It is a singular and rare gratification to the professorial
ego when a course spreads like that.

Angela was one of her suitemates. The two of them had long been
active in theatre and hatched a brainstorm: a two-woman show, its title
and much of its contents borrowed from our anthology. The theme,
they explained, would be unmasking the woman within, the witch in
the attic, a ubiquitous presence in our course. They dove into compil-
ing, memorizing, and staging poems. They included scenes from *The
Children's Hour* and *Crimes of the Heart*. Officially supervising the
project was a man in the theatre department. I was closet co-director,
advising on selection and interpretation, and dropping in on rehears-
als.

Early on, both Kitty and Angela decided to include monologues of
their own, unmasking hidden selves. After a brief waver, Angela
decided that it was time to write about the episode with Jack. I was
pleased and afraid. Kitty worked closely with me on hers, which
identified a witch-figure lurking under her nice-girl exterior. She
marked the initial appearance of this persona at the time of an anorexic
episode in her early puberty. Angela, meanwhile, kept to herself. She
came by once to discuss dramatic concerns like objective, focus, and
audience, for the director had insisted that a good monologue has a

specific audience. In a moment of inspiration, I said, "Why don't you address it to that younger self—that trapped girl?" She seized on that and rose to leave my office.

"Angela?" She turned. "Be sure to put in the music box."

A month or so later, I pried myself loose from the office one late afternoon and ran across the parking lot to the Fine Arts Building. In the Dungeon, our black-box experimental space, the three of them were at work. I watched for a while, very impressed at the shape it was taking, and it came time for Angela's monologue. I was perplexed to see Kitty bring out a chair, place it in front of the audience seats, facing the performance space, and sit on it, folding her hands in her lap.

A single spot came up and Angela stood there, gathered herself, looked straight at Kitty, and began: "I know what you're thinking. You think you deserve this, don't you?" Quickly she sketched the psychology of her victim-self, just as it had looked to me that April night. But this time she defined it consciously, as one describes another person. Then she began to narrate the story from the beginning, as the story of this other woman represented by the silent Kitty. As she reached the heart of the tale—the shredded textbook, the music box, the rape—her voice built, her eyes blazed, her body tensed. Her arms extended downward, fingers spread. The darkness closed around me; I felt I was in Jack's apartment, watching, barely breathing.

Just before the flight into the street, the scream set free into the night, Angela cried out to her silent image, "He wanted to hurt you—to kill you! You were scared!" And then: "I—I was scared!" For one ecstatic moment, narrator and audience fused. "You" and "I" became one.

Her voice grew quiet again, moving into a gentle, urgent testimony to the beauty and worth of the Other Woman, her loving heart, her integrity, the love of people around her. And finally the voice rose again to a final peak: "Take the risk of loving yourself— and get out!"

In the dark I was crying, knowing that neither Kitty nor the director, nor even Angela herself, could see this avenging angel, thick hair streaming around her in the spotlight, as I did: superimposed upon the dumb animal curled into herself on my living room floor. How had this flaming creature risen from those dead ashes? And what flash of genius had inspired her to place Kitty in that chair, a concrete, incarnate Silent Woman? With that stroke, Angela became Demeter, reclaiming her Persephone, her lost younger self. The monologue became an exhortation to an actual symbolic Other, to every woman sitting numb and voiceless. The Angela standing and speaking embodied a voice, the one for which I had listened so desperately that night.

The moment when "She" became "I" was not merely Angela's acceptance and transformation of her own nightmare, but a merger of herself with every other woman beaten physically or psychically into nonbeing. It was a stunning act of love. In positing an Other who needed to hear her voice, Angela had found it.

I sat for a while afterward, the passionate, furious voice winging around the rafters of the little theatre like a wild bird. A good and worthy voice, verily. I still hear it.

7

Man Hating: Voices in the Dark

The ringing yanks me from sleep. I realize that it is the phone, not the alarm, and that the clock radio reads 1:36 a.m. My heart is thudding as it does when I am suddenly awakened. I have always been frightened by phones in the night. I have tried many times to locate the root of the fear in my past, but I can't. I reach across the bed to pull the receiver to my ear. "Hello?"

Foggy as I am, I recognize immediately the background sounds of a dorm room. Clatter, male voices. A pause, and then a young male voice, heavily accented, says, "Men hate to bitch."

"What?"

"Men hate to bitch."

I replace the receiver, turn over, think a minute about the odd words, relieved that the call wasn't obscene. I never receive obscene calls. I am the only woman in North America who does not receive regular obscene calls. Men hate to bitch. Odd. Do they? Not that I've noticed. Well, good for them. I slide quickly back into sleep.

I am up for an hour or so the next morning before the call floats up to the surface. I turn the strange message over and over in my mind, like one of those prophetic 8-balls we consulted in my childhood. Suddenly, on one turn, it comes up different. "Men hate you, bitch." That was what he said.

There is no dismissing it as a random crank call. It was for me, and it was from one of ours, in a dorm minutes from my house. Then, in a flash, I make the connection: I have recently written an editorial for the campus newspaper on nonsexist language. Oh, the power of the press, and of the word, which is what my editorial was about. This guy understands that power all too well.

The immediate weight of shock and then sadness gives way to the old sense of nakedness, the vulnerability of women violated in the night by phones and other weapons. And then the paranoia slithers in. Was he not simply one of ours but one of mine? A foreign student: I file through the male foreign students in my classes over the past couple quarters. The accent, through my sleepiness, suggested Hispanic or Middle Eastern rather than Asian or African or Northern European. Paul? Hakim? Carlos? When I bring their faces before me, they are smiling, joking, shaking their heads in frustration at English prepositions, handing me a paper, asking me a question after class. Was that voice, that hateful voice at 1:36 in the morning, embedded between the lines of that paper about the contrasts between high schools in Argentina and the U.S.? Was the razor edge of that anger waiting behind the friendly brown eyes?

A shadow falls across the rest of the day.

✵╲(⚇)╱✵

> *It is ironic, to say the least, that the first verbal attack slung at*
> *the woman who demonstrates a primary loyalty to herself and other*
> *women is man-hater. The fear of appearing or being named as a*
> *man-hater still causes many women to deny the reality of gynepho-*
> *bia, the concrete evidences of woman-hating embedded in our cul-*
> *ture, in language, image, and act.*
>
> —*Adrienne Rich*[1]

I remember the first time I heard that voice—or rather, heard it coming. It was early fall, early in my career at Kalamazoo, and I was comparing notes on the new crop with a colleague. He chuckled and told me that one of his new advisees had consulted with him about which Expository Prose teacher to try for at registration. He had recommended me, and the student had hesitated, then asked, in a low voice, man to man, "whether, you know, a guy could get a fair break from her." My friend had assured him that there was every chance. Now he laughed, and, since he is wont to mock my tendency to take everything seriously, I tried to laugh with him. As we went on with our quiet drink, I pondered the fact that the new students had been on campus for four days and already the grapevine in the male wing of a dorm had nailed me with the dirty F-word.

Afterward, I tried to analyze my reaction. Which bothers me more: the simplistic cliche about feminism, or the slur on my professional ethics? Interestingly, I decided that it was a tie.

So it had begun with "You hate men," evolving in the intervening years into "Men hate you." Cause and effect? Crime and punishment? Or were those statements identical after all? Different constructions of the same phenomenon, faces of a Janus who has presided over my life more than I like to admit. A sentence looking at itself in the mirror, subject and object transposed, like the first and third shell in the game, whipped around the table, making me dizzy as I try to follow with my eyes, pursuing some elusive pea of truth.

After that message leaked by a friend, I stumbled over it regularly, this gnarled outcropping in the generally green and pleasant land of Kalamazoo College. As before, the message usually came to me via friendly intermediaries. Sometimes it was a male student—often one whose outlines are softer than the others', whose presence partakes of what I could never tell him can only be called sweetness—who sat in my office, moving quickly through the presenting problem (his test, his paper topic) to the real agenda. I can now smell it coming, sentences away: "You know, before I took your course I was kind of scared, because, well, you know what they say . . ." He falters, wondering if I do know, wondering if he's over his head here. "That, you know, you don't like guys, or guys can't get a grade from you or something." I assure him we are on solid ground. "But it's not true, you know?" he says, obviously genuinely disturbed by an injustice. I thank him for telling me and I lodge him in a mental file, a resource against future need.

Such as arose during my tenure review. This most mythic of academic rites used to be prolonged for nearly a year at Kalamazoo. You got a massive file together in the fall, documenting your every waking moment for the past six years and attesting to your brilliance (pedagogical, creative, scholarly), your community spirit, your promise for the future, your worthiness of what the provost repeatedly reminded me amounts to a million-dollar investment. You secured an advocate, preferably a senior colleague in a different academic division. During the winter and spring the faculty personnel committee deliberated. Their recommendation went to the provost and then to the president in the summer, and the president conveyed his recommendation to the Board of Trustees at their October meeting.

As my advocate I had secured the help of a senior woman. Not above a little dramatic symbolism myself, I had asked her because she would be the first woman ever to act as a tenure advocate, but also because she understood women's studies. If there's a problem with me, I told her, it will be women's studies—or rather, the question of disciplinary depth and seriousness within which the question of women's studies is tangled. So she went into action, did her extensive homework, read the file from start to finish—scholarship, teaching evaluations, poetry, letters of support—and met with the committee to advocate me for adoption as a permanent member of the family.

One morning in June, she and I began to discuss her most recent appearance before the committee. Everything went fine, she said, but a cloud passed over her eyes and she added in a low voice that while the general discourse was overwhelmingly positive, the committee had raised the issue of male students. "Male students?" I repeated, sinking fast. "You know," she said (rather sadly, I thought), "whether you're fair to men and all that. What male students say about you."

Unburdening myself to female colleagues that day and that week, I was met with reassurance and sometimes with a little impatience. "Good grief, they feel that they have to raise some problem or other; it's part of their job to check every nook and cranny." "Oh, they're finding something so they can say they've done a thorough job." "Listen, *they* don't believe that; it's just something that's said, so they have to address it. What do you want, anyway?" But they have my evaluations for six years. If I were routinely unfair to Generic Men, wouldn't it show up there?

I worried the thing to the bone, wholly out of proportion to its role in the review process—which is the whole point, as I recognized even then. The power of a whisper of male disapproval to unbalance me— that recognition in itself disturbed me. It frightened me that I had heard two distinct issues in what my advocate had said: whether I were fair to men, and what the male students say about me. Would the committee know the difference? And where would they seek an authoritative answer? And what *did* men say about me anyway? Maybe I was living in sweet ignorance. And what men? Sporadic men? Scores of men? Those clammy scales of paranoia around my neck.

I had expected that the glitch would be women's studies. I was ready for the clear public voice of male scholarly tradition saying, "Explain yourself." But instead I heard a secret voice, an anonymous, disembodied voice, mumbling what is, to the female ear, the grossest of obscenities: "Men don't like you."

And then I did something that even at the time carried a whiff of humiliation I did not stop to examine. I went to a male student— one who had taken several courses with me, a strong student, a friend— and I asked him to write a letter for my file. And I told him why, as archly as I could. "It seems they need some evidence that I'm fair to male students." Translation: "Please tell them you like me." Subtext: "You do like me, don't you?"

ᵃᵍ⚭ᵍᵉ

Now, at the end of my first decade in academe, I like to think that I've stopped worrying about it. I tell myself that I haven't energy to devote to defending myself against amorphous public perceptions; that the problem is rooted not in me or my behavior but in a knee-jerk free association with the F-word that I am powerless to combat, other than by being myself and doing my work. Sometimes I wonder why the Man-hater should be such a cherished stereotype, what advantage it holds for twenty-year-olds (or their fathers).

But I have not stopped worrying. Sometimes I sit alone with the question, taking it seriously, asking myself, "Well, OK, *do* you like men?" Usually it seems meaningless, a ludicrous wrestle with an abstraction. Once in a while I am defenseless enough actually to tally up in my head the men I love, have loved, men who have loved me—students, friends, family, lovers—as if each name were a talisman against that unnatural monster, the woman who does not like men and is righteously condemned to not being liked by them in return.

Sometimes, mid-sentence, mid-act, I am suddenly aware that I am tailoring myself to counter that anonymous, ubiquitous accuser on the telephone. I see myself snap into super-friendly, hyper-nurturant gear around male students, especially the jocks or the seemingly hostile or diffident. I suspect that at times I have given such as these the benefit of the doubt in that awful moment when the hand hangs above the page before inscribing a grade. After a faculty meeting I have stood across the room and cringed to watch myself going into overdrive for the benefit of a male colleague who might be suspicious of me.

This is My Secret Life. Many who've worked with me for years would not believe it. I am one of those women who has achieved symbolic status in her particular milieu: I am Woman, hear me roar. I am a feminist and therefore I eat men like air. I have always suspected that Sylvia Plath loaded that line with irony, that in fact the whole poem is self-parody, a cartoon portrait of the Scary Woman as hallucinated by men frightened of being eaten. In my daily life, the ludicrous stereotype has its occasional advantages. But most of the time they are outweighed by the heft of the lie. Most of the time I know the obeisance I do to the Fathers—even in the form of the Sons, even now when I am approaching the age where they could well be my sons.

My Secret Life is also the secret life of every woman who ever strode—or more likely stumbled—into that wilderness beyond the hedged garden of male approval. Watching myself scurry back inside or deform myself in trying to keep one foot in and the other out is uncomfortable. But it is also salutary, a bitter tonic, for it keeps me in touch with the deep fear that grips women students skirting the edges of feminist insight. There be dragons, indeed. And my impatience with their timidity or willed obtuseness subsides in the face of my own daily compromises and contortions.

For a teacher, I think, the struggle may be further complicated. Teachers want and need their students. The students' general trust and acceptance form part of the subtle, powerful contract implicit in education. If liking, affection, and admiration are there too, then the wonderful things can happen. That one's ego also hungers for these tributes is a secondary point. The Olympian professor who couldn't care less what they think is no one I can or want to be; and anyway, he is a rare species at a little college where distillations of the "purely pedagogical" from the personal are virtually impossible and at odds with the atmosphere. Above all, teaching is relationship—with a text, with individual students, with a collective being called a class. The quality of the relationship merits a teacher's concern.

And if I am a feminist as well as a teacher, and if that makes me that other thing, a feminist teacher, then I cannot simply say, "I am what I am; screw the bastards." I am obligated to convey what I am—which is a product, after all, of what I know and what I know they need—in a way that tries to be as congenial as it is challenging and disturbing. With feminism, as with semicolons and Shakespeare, that task demands concessions to their unreadiness, accommodations to their ignorance, empathy for their resistance, and thus modulations of myself designed to disarm their fear and hostility. But I go on wondering how much of the modulation is a terrible acknowledgement of the entrenched power of the Father/Son bond, and how much is a viable teaching tactic by which I mediate my equally terrible demand that the Sons begin to see that power, examine it, question it, maybe eventually understand it, even possibly disown it.

※❦❦❦※

I have spent much thought on power and powerlessness in the voices of my women students. Only after the phone call in the night did I begin to think about the various voices of my male students across the years. The sociology of speech, especially in the classroom, generally describes female silence and male speech. But I am surprised to realize how often the male student's voice has made itself heard in my life by its resounding silence. Boys' silence is, of course, quite different from girls'. Generally speaking, it is not polite, deferential, or timid. It is palpable, weighty, intrusive. It imitates not the demure damsel but the strong, silent cowboy or the sullen, rebellious James Dean. It is the silence of a voice that need not speak because the entire culture speaks for it, not the silence of a voice that doesn't know itself, has no language, and hears no echo in the world (including the curriculum) around it. It is the silence of resistance, refusal, disengagement. In my classroom it is likely to be the withdrawal of young men, in fear or antipathy or mere confusion, from the female voice at the front of the room or in the text.

The peculiar silence of men in women's studies courses rings a slight change on this theme. At Kalamazoo, a women's studies course is an entirely voluntary experience. The only such course I teach in which there is a regular critical mass of men is Literature of Women. A big course by Kalamazoo standards, it generally enrolls forty to fifty, perhaps eight to ten of them male. I am subtly encouraged to keep tabs on male enrollment during the first week of the quarter, when the perennial collegial question, "How many have you got?", is followed closely by another, "How many men?", as if the course's legitimacy depended upon it.

The classroom dynamics tend to be depressingly predictable: The eight-to-ten, with perhaps two exceptions, are always silent; the thirty to forty women are seriously bothered by this and blame the course severely for it. The blame floats free; it will not light on the men themselves; it lights first on me or on the other women or on the subject matter. It is truly as if male silence indicted what we are doing. In midterm and final course evaluations and in informal feedback, the silence of the men speaks loud and clear in the voices of the women. In true female style they castigate themselves for the men's refusal to speak, for some deficiency on their part in something that would make the men "feel more comfortable."

If eight women were silent in a course with forty men, I doubt they would even be noticed, much less thrust to the center of collective concern. I know this, yet the issue the women press must concern me, because it concerns them and because the comfort to speak is fundamental to the classroom I strive to create. But then, women's studies, by its nature and its function, ought to produce at least a little discomfort in everybody and certainly in a man. Such a context *ought* to render him hesitant to speak—at least in his customary voice. He is the Outsider, for once, and this role is profoundly educative.

And if his silence is in some ways desirable—though one wishes he might speak more often in the form of questions—it is also eminently understandable. It is often the shy or troubled or openly vulnerable young man who gravitates to women's studies (though just as often it is the guy with something to prove to me or his mother or his girlfriend, or the guy with a bone to pick, which is unspeakably tiresome). And a man may be understandably disconcerted or intimidated by this anomaly in his academic life, an overwhelmingly female context, guided by female "authority" in the form of not only the teacher but the majority of his fellow students and the material itself. Female experience *is* the authority in a women's studies classroom, and that is unprecedented in his life. And in the women's lives too; hence their discomfort and guilt. They are not used to being at the center, though they are usually not aware that they have existed at the margins. If a womanly landscape is, for them, a brave new world, whether delightful or suspect or both, then for a man it is likely to be a chaotic wilderness where the laws of nature are suspended and carnivores snarl behind every tree. The commonplace that men are "threatened" in a women's studies class is quite true, and necessarily so. Any education worth its salt ought to be deeply threatening, and the education of a man about women even more so. The women in the class, and sometimes the men, personalize the threat: They are threatening him, or I am threatening him. In fact, no one may be actively, personally threatening him, and yet he is still threatened—by two forces. One is those growls from behind the trees, which he names "man-haters," "male-bashers," "ball-busters." As usual, he is only simplistic, not wrong. There is something hungry and angry back there, a creature that above all others terrifies him and the woman sitting beside him: female anger. The great art of teaching women's studies is to lead everybody to confront and comprehend the anger without letting it eat anybody. But the other threatening presence is the very strangeness of the place. If only, I have thought, hearing his silence, if only he would once begin asking his way, watching the trees for signposts, crying for help, anything but hacking through the underbrush or sitting down in the middle of the woods and refusing to move.

Or if he would begin telling his way, telling it truly. I think of Muriel Rukeyser's line about what would happen if one woman told the truth about her life. The classroom, if not the world, would surely split gloriously open if one man told the truth about his life— the costs, the glories, the terrors and deformations of manhood. In women's studies we talk constantly of manhood, and still he does not speak. For he is used to the comfort of hearing his experience disguised as "human," and to hear it defined specifically as male makes him feel naked; it seems to diminish, not enhance, his masculinity because it circumscribes and isolates it. In this context, he, like his sisters, does not know the language. The difference is that he does not often want to speak it. Sometimes he comes to me privately and speaks, as he goes privately to his girlfriend or his mother and speaks. But mostly he is like the brawny athlete described by my colleague Karen, who had the unenviable task of teaching him French: he grunts and mumbles through the uncomfortably feminine syllables and relapses into a silence that may be deferential, fearful, confused, or angry. Often I can't tell which. His truth may finally blurt itself into the telephone at 1:36 a.m., in the only language he knows.

✥✥✥

Or it may announce itself publicly, as blithely unself-conscious as the Emperor in his New Clothes. One day in my first years at Kalamazoo, an Expository Prose class was winding down and the class was filing out. Still struggling with names at the beginning of the quarter, I called to one student, naming him "Frank." "It's Fred," he said, and I apologized. "Who's Frank?" he asked. "Your boyfriend?"

In the long instant that followed, and in the hour afterward back in my office, Fred's wholly benign question stood aside at the door it had opened while a small swarm of troublesome recognitions rushed in upon me. I checked out my own reaction first: Was it simply discomfort at a green freshman's inappropriately personal remark? And was such discomfort evidence of my hypocrisy, my inability to live with the informality I cultivate in class? But no, I decided, that was not the kind of question I would ask a student, in or out of class. I tried next to imagine a female student asking a male professor, "Who's Linda? Your girlfriend?" Never. Could I imagine this very Fred asking one of my male colleagues the same thing? Impossible. Why? Primarily because, even if he wondered about Dr. X's personal life (as they all do, of course, wonder about our personal lives; I haven't been out of school long enough to forget that particular fascination), his solidly ingrained sense of the professor-student relation would render him mute. Not that I especially favor the kind of professor-student relation that renders the latter mute. I was bothered by what Fred saw in me that opened the way for the question: to wit, femaleness.

The fact was that for Fred, I was not Professor but Woman Teacher, a creature whose romantic life was at the forefront of her consciousness even in a class on writing introductory paragraphs. And for Fred, Woman Teacher was someone who saw him primarily as Sexual Man, in the same category as the apocryphal Frank the Boyfriend. After all these insights had settled in, another, larger one continued to trouble me. It was above all Fred's innocence that angered me, his absolute unawareness that he might have said, or assumed, anything inappropriate. Just like the Emperor, Fred was blinded by unexamined assumptions, insulated by the thick swaddling of privilege of which he was completely ignorant. I began to consider how such a precondition affected my ability to teach him to write a paper and his ability to learn, but I quickly decided I'd had enough for one day. That way madness lies.

I heard his voice again several years later, in considerably more and also less sophisticated form. It came in a letter from Winston, who was working off-campus in his Career Development internship, which made him a sophomore at the time. Age nineteen or twenty. It was a genial, newsy letter, which suddenly announced, in a final paragraph about his plans for returning to campus, "I thought about having an affair with you this summer."

Now, Winston had always been a conundrum to those of us on the faculty who knew him. He was bright, friendly, cooperative, if a little bit of a con artist, and always somehow slightly askew, so that it was easy to regard the end of the letter (and I did, in part) as an unfortunate outcropping of that weird, troubled streak. But given that troubled streaks in students are hardly exceptional and that they manifest themselves in myriad ways, this is only a partial explanation. It may also have been purely a joke—but in this case the joke could not be quite pure. Once more, the issue was not his lust for a faculty member, another ubiquitous phenomenon of student life, but rather his blitheness in voicing the proposition. I am still in sporadic contact with Winston, now several years out of school. For what reason, I muse, have I never drawn his attention to this letter, which sits between us unacknowledged despite and because of its ponderousness? What nasty things would fly out in our faces were I to open the closed envelope and say, "Hey, remember this?"

What I heard in Winston's naive proposition was what I heard in the voice in the night—though Winston, who adopted the relative safety and distance of a letter instead of the anonymity of a telephone, would be horrified to see himself in such company. After all, he was my friend and fan, and the two messages were entirely distinct, even opposite. Weren't they? But they both, and Fred's question too, came from the same power source that assumes its right to remind me that I am female, that it is not, and that certain privileges appertain to its maleness, privileges so ancient that they could thus, in all three instances, reverse the customary formidable power dynamics of the teacher-student relation. Winston's affable voice and the growl on the phone were flip sides of the same coin, the coin of the realm.

Therein lies the dissonance of the female academic. She walks through the corridors of her world as an authority until, once in a while, she comes upon disturbing graffiti to remind her of the hard truths of the street.

It was, in fact, graffiti in the case of my colleague Susan. It appeared in the tiny and excruciatingly slow elevator in our main classroom building. A chalkboard is pragmatically provided on one of its walls to afford an outlet for the universal student impulse to anonymous self-expression. It is characteristic of Kalamazoo that such expression ranges from quotations from Whitehead to German salutations to simple, reliable, four-letter Anglo-Saxon derivatives. One day, years ago, the elevator announced that "Sue_____ gives good head." It will be hard for those accustomed to large universities to comprehend how public an announcement in one three-by-four elevator can be. At a very small college, excrescences of the eccentric, neurotic, ugly, or possibly dangerous are thrown into high relief. They are conspicuous, observed, reported, discussed. For about a week, as the message was regularly erased and reinscribed, Sue was embarrassed, humiliated—and frightened. Facing her classes each day meant wondering which of the benign faces before her was that of the author. Magnify that incident about five hundred times and you have the case of my friend at another college who opened the student newspaper to discover that the entire issue was about her—a "joke" issue concerning her body and her sex life as well as her classes and her personality.

A college provides yet another medium for anonymous messages: the course evaluation form. By now it is redundant to suggest that these forms often mitigate against female professors. Male and female students tend to disclose a tidy array of biases and double standards rooted in their gendered expectations of faculty behavior. Our forms now carry a space for an optional signature, but even when they didn't, it was often easy to discern the identity of the author. Sometimes it's easier when you know who it is; sometimes not. In general, where women faculty are concerned, the students consider more of our territory as fair ground when they write their judgments of us. Martha, who is elegant, professional, and nervous, gets "bitch" regularly. Elaine, who wears pants a lot, gets excoriated for that offense. I seem to suffer relatively few personal insults; I get resentment of authority and intellectual quarrels, from students of both genders. But occasionally that peculiarly male voice is so clear on that piece of paper that it shocks me, like that voice in the dark.

The form was signed, not surprisingly. Some Evaluation Terrorists cultivate anonymity, but some in fact make it a point of pride that they are not afraid to reveal themselves. The signature was that of one of the eight-or-ten in Lit of Women. Early in the course, after I had stressed in class the value I placed on student discussion and collective responsibility for the class, he had arrived in my office to tell me that he didn't speak in classes. Like many non-speakers, he told me contemptuously that he considered most classroom discussion to consist of cheap attempts to impress authority or to outdo other students. (Ah, I thought: James Dean. The rebel without a voice.) These rationales were firmly in place, clearly part of an identity of which silence was an essential part, a shield against his own potential failure and his fear of finding himself to be either one of the herd or one apart from it. So I quickly abandoned my attempt to persuade him of the value of participation in the collective discourse. In the office that day he was diffident, obscure, opening and then shutting tight, a classic example of sullenness and shyness, arrogance and vulnerability flooding each other's boundaries. Yet he came in to see me and he stayed a while. As he walked out, I thought, "It's a toss-up. He wants something from me, from the course, and he wants me to know who he is. There's a chance we'll be friends before the next nine weeks are out. But I can't call it."

He kept to his word, or lack thereof, all quarter. He did extremely good written work, thoughtful, articulate, provocative, original, sophisticated. And he said not one word in class and never came to the office again. But his evaluation was a thing to see. It was written in closely pencilled scrawl inscribed *diagonally* across the page, bottom to top, obscuring the typed instructions, the individual questions, in gigantically unsubtle defiance of the strictures of official forms and requirements. A verbose, articulate, graffiti-evaluation. It was also, of course, designed to make my reading as difficult as possible. The "essay" itself was a lucid, beautifully written, wholly condescending assault on the course—its premises, my methods, the other students, specific questions I'd asked and remarks I'd made six weeks ago in class. The gist was that the course was not serious enough for him—a charge which he couldn't have improved upon had he deliberated for months as to the quickest way to my jugular, for the charge of insufficient intellectual seriousness is the recurring nightmare of women's studies teachers. The use of personal experience; the concern for the female sides of life—the emotional, sexual, familial, maternal, mundane; even the primary concern with gender itself—all these make us sitting ducks in an academy constructed upon some fairly rigid and exclusive notions of seriousness. I was impressed by the accuracy of Edwin's aim.

For this very reason I rubbed my nose in his pencil marks, forcing myself to think about each criticism, trying to separate it from the form in which it was conveyed. Trying to be fair, objective, unemotional. That long afternoon in the office, I reexamined the course itself, its premises and my teaching. But after I'd done this duty and swallowed what he threw at me, what stayed in my mouth was the taste of his anger, his need to best me, to have the last word, which amounted to his first word as well and therefore kept him safe in the odd purity he craved. His torrent—an educated, eloquent torrent it was, one that promised him a good shot at a place among my academic brethren— washed over me at the end of a long quarter and left me flat on the beach, heartless, winded, lonely. Well, I thought—slipping his evalua- tion in with the others, marking the packet to be shipped over to the provost's office, imagining male eyes reading it— at least he didn't say I was unfair to men. But this is one man who sure enough doesn't like me.

I could peel through the layers of Edwin's prose to the simple reality beneath, as Virginia Woolf peered through Professor von X's erudite misogyny in the British Museum and asked archly, "What is this man angry about?" Edwin's was simply a more ornate variation on the theme—which description might serve fairly well for the rela- tion of academic inquiry to life's realities. These voices all wind to- gether in a sort of dissonant fugue: Fred's insouciant oboe, Winston's cheerful, brash flute, Edwin's baroque, sophisticated cello, all un- dergirded by the relentless simplicity of the bass on the telephone line.

❋⟨⟨✦⟩⟩❋

I hear one other voice in the male chorus, this one something like a clarinet, high, sad, whining. It is perhaps the least anonymous, for it speaks directly and in public at virtually every open gathering whose subject matter is women or feminism. At some point during the dis- cussion session after the main program, he will stand to speak—usu- ally but not always a young man, often sitting with female friends. The approach varies, but the landing is always the same. First come his credentials: He is in sympathy with what is happening here and with the Women's Movement. He believes in equal rights, or has many women friends, or has taken a women's studies course, or even, "I consider myself a feminist." But this casting of men as the enemy disturbs him. It is often the case, mind you, that men have not even been mentioned in the program (which may, in fact, be exactly what rankles: whether 'tis more dangerous to mention them or not to mention them is a question I've yet to resolve). His speech has nothing to do with the specific subject at hand—film or talk or panel or whatever. But his agenda is urgent. He must address his relation to what is going on in the room—that is to say, the Women's Movement, which by definition assumes an Other, men, who must be the enemy. Sometimes he couches his discomfort as sympathetic advice: "This won't get you anywhere. It alienates us." The advice can grow patronizing: "You women really ought to . . ." Then there may come an account of discouraging experience with a woman, or a group of women, or "feminists": a meeting that excluded him, a car door opened and not gratefully acknowledged, a friend who got mad. He is standing proof that the political is personal, and he is full of authentic confusion and hurt: *He* hasn't oppressed women; he's tried hard in his relationships with women to be aware of things, to treat women with respect. He resents being lumped with the oppressors. "It doesn't help, you know," he concludes, plaintively and admonishingly, meaning perhaps that it doesn't help the women's cause but more probably that it doesn't help him. And at this moment, it doesn't. He is authentically bewildered, frustrated, pained.

In a college audience, the response to this small guerrilla warrior is unvarying: Young women leap to their feet to assume the burden of his feelings, assuaging his hurt or explaining to him or assuring him that he's *not* the oppressor, that what it's really all about is Humanism. The waters then close over the leviathan he has raised, leaving a smooth surface on which we can all float away and drift homeward.

And so I start walking home, always thinking more about him than about the program, a fact in itself annoying to me. The feminist in me is exasperated, wondering how it is possible for a twenty-year-old to speak in 1987 as if the Women's Movement were some startling, outrageous new phenomenon just yesterday sprung upon the public consciousness. The teacher in me calms her down, reminding her that to be twenty *is* to discover the ragged old universe for the first time. She recites the Perry Stages of Development (based, after all, on the study of boys), which locate this young man firmly at the point where the old dualistic, individualistic cosmos is having its last hurrah before collapsing in the face of the relativistic, complex new vision.

The Teacher then remembers herself back to 1969. She is nineteen, white, upper-middle class, very bright, pathetically sincere in her dutiful liberal commitment to a naive idea of equality. Seasoned by the racial tensions of a big high school, she is readier than some for the explosive dialogue in black and white on a college campus in those days. She yearns to keep her mental and spiritual energies safe within the realms of academics and private interpersonal dramas, but she can't do it. She can't let herself do it. Maybe it's the times, but maybe it's something in her—some guilt, some training, and maybe some determination to understand, to live an examined life—that keeps her studying the sociopolitical curriculum outside the classroom as diligently as she studies Henry James, also distasteful but necessary. She listens to the black women in her dorm. She goes to demonstrations and listens to black anger. She frets and writhes. But she thinks a lot, reads some. And above all, she grows accustomed to the angry black voice. She normalizes it. And gradually it becomes less an unjust personal accusation than a potent medium for knowing the world and her own uncomfortable place in it.

And now, the Teacher wants very much to roll back tonight's tape, just to the point where he said, "It doesn't help, you know."

"Doesn't it?" she asks him. "Oh, but it might. It might just be extremely salutary, this uncomprehended female anger, if you could face it rather than run from it or deny it. This Medusa head might turn you to flesh, not stone. It might galvanize you, propel you through doors you wouldn't otherwise open. You might come through with the ability to live consciously and well as a man among women. Believe me, it might help. 'In the destructive element immerse'—E. M. Forster."

The Feminist, meanwhile, is standing aside, nodding across the walkway with a jaundiced eye. "All true," she says, "so maybe you'd better find some way to work that moving speech into a class sometime. In the interim, you do realize what happened to that room when he stood himself up to speak, don't you? You did notice that the focus shot from the speaker and the subject right across the room to his suffering maleness? You did feel the energy change, in the blink of a sympathetic female eye, into mother-love, with all those Little Women falling over themselves to make him feel better?"

The Teacher nods slowly. She is awed by the power of his voice, even more by his unconscious understanding of its power. In all his confusion, he had a confidence deeper than he can see, deeper than any specific lack of confidence he may have felt in rising to speak. However alone he may have felt at that moment, he was in old and powerful company. He stood and spoke from the innocent assumption that his concerns, his struggles, and his voice were legitimate enough to divert the meeting from its purpose, and that his personal discomfort was inherently unjust and unwarranted. Two assumptions that few women in that room would share and on which even fewer would act.

His voice was not anonymous. But it was archetypal. His text was, "You women are on the wrong track." Translation: "Why don't you women love me?" Subtext: "If you don't love me, pretty soon I won't love you anymore." From which it is a sad, short downhill route to "Men hate you, bitch."

As I walk slowly home, I pass alongside one of the dorms and look up at the lighted windows. Music, laughter, a shriek, the sound of a typewriter. What's going on up there?

≈ᴥⅭℰᴥᵏ

A few nights ago, far from Kalamazoo in another college town, the phone rang after midnight. Expecting a call from a friend who often calls late, I picked up the receiver without qualm. "Hello?"

Silence. A bad sign.

"Who is this?" said a male voice, a young male voice.

I don't bite. "Well, who is *this*?"

"Tom."

Will it be? This one? The obscene call with my name on it?

"Whom did you want to speak to?" Why don't I ask, "Tom who?"

"Um . . . could I talk to you for a while?" The voice is small and sad.

I don't hang up. I don't know why. But I don't respond to the question, either. Instead, I go into some kind of weird overdrive, plowing over the top of it. "What?" I ask, having heard him distinctly.

"Uh, could I talk to you for a while?"

"I'm afraid you have the wrong number," I say in the voice of a pleasant machine, and hang up.

I try to go back to work and can't. His voice was a kid's. I am suddenly very homesick for my students, for the young men who speak in those voices. I am sure it was a college kid. I have easily deflected the intrusion of his voice, simply by breaking the mechanical connection. And that is what I am left with, the feeling of broken connection. I sit, half-expecting the phone to ring again, wondering what I will do if it does. Nothing in Tom's voice threatened obscenity. To my amazement, I feel in my stomach the growing germ of guilt. I think about the dorms within blocks of me, stretching away for miles across this sprawling multiversity, so unlike my little college. Yet dorms are universals and I know them here as well as at Kalamazoo.

I think of the ones I lived in. I can hear the music, the voices down the hall, the typewriters, the phones ringing. I can feel the claustrophobia, the bleakness of late night or early morning, the loneliness in a crowd. I imagine Tom physically and construct a life for him, culminating in some crisis to account for his random calling out into the night—a broken romance, a drug problem, a divorce or death at home, a failed exam, the coming-out terror, the waves of inadequacy and doubt and fear, all the crises woven deeply into the fabric of my Kalamazoo life. I realize I am regretting having hung up. And I am ashamed. I should have talked to him. Maybe it was serious, maybe I could have helped, maybe . . .

It was an unknown male voice on the phone late at night. I hung up. It was by-the-book, unexceptionable female behavior.

Then I realize that I am sad not for Tom but for me.

8

Teacher's Pet

The Professor and the Coed

The sexuality infusing the powerful drama of The Professor and the Coed has been openly acknowledged and usually celebrated through centuries of cultural lore, from Abelard and Heloise to Clark Gable and Doris Day. There is about this relation a special kind of charisma and romance that feminists engaged with the problem of sexual harassment do ill to ignore, deny, or minimize. Most of us, if we are honest with ourselves, remember it all too clearly.

Well into our own century the potential for "romance" between male professor and female student was acknowledged without embarrassment or alarm. If a professor singled out a student to pursue, that was charming. The classroom was as delightful a target area for Cupid's arrow as any other site. In fact, Lucinda Stone, my Kalamazoo College archangel, found her husband in her Greek professor at the Hinesburg Academy in Vermont in the 1830s. Today, when committees on the status of women bring the awkward issue of classroom sexuality out of the closet, they are likely to meet with some older professors, married to former students for years, who are genuinely bewildered. The lines we have come to see so clearly are very blurry to those who have not stood on the other side of them or studied them very closely.

Harassment of women students certainly has existed as long as men have taught women. But I believe a shift has taken place in the socio-sexual environment surrounding the issue. The Sexual Revolution has robbed the professor-student liaison of an innocence and good faith it often had one hundred years ago, or even fifty. The rigidity of Victorian heterosexual romance amongst the middle and upper classes—structured as courtship, with firm rules and a singular end in mind—was, if debilitating and deforming in many ways, protective of women in others. That a woman's sexuality was not her own but instead hogtied to family and other social connections, trammelled in formalities as her body was trammelled in underclothing, horrifies us.

But as we have come to understand, the sexually "free" woman is in many respects hardly freer than her great-grandmother. More often than not she is "free" only in the economic sense—she costs nothing. After the revolution as before, her sexuality is commodified. Once the old layer of convention and ritual was stripped away, predatory heterosexuality lay exposed, red in tooth and claw. The "free" woman may be an effective agent in her own sexual life in many ways, but she is also more often than her great-grandmother sexual prey—on the street, on the job, after the prom, in a bar, in a clinic, and in the classroom. At twenty she is likely to see this as but the price of her "freedom." And while academe, like corporations and legal firms and convenience stores and factories, is full of men taking full advantage of that odd notion of freedom, it still harbors men who remember Honorable Intentions and thus are confused by our insistence that active sexuality has no place in the faculty-student relationship. I believe that there is honest confusion among the younger male professoriat too. I would wager that the men I work with would agree unanimously that "a lay for an A" is wrong, as is forcing "sexual attention," as it is called, upon an unwilling female student. But these extreme forms of sexual harassment are but the tip of the iceberg. The kind of harassment women in academe deal with most often, as student victims or as faculty counselors and confidantes, is more subtle, often less physical or not physical at all. While sexual blackmail and rape inflict hideous scars, this "lower level" harassment carries its own particular venom. For it is this kind of harassment that the victim herself may be unable to define, to name, and thus to confront. And then there are the so-called "consensual" faculty-student sexual relations, which preclude "victims" by definition.

It is this behavior that both male professor and female student have such difficulty seeing for what we keep saying it is. No wonder: it usually consists of what is called Normal Behavior on the part of men to women. At this end of the spectrum of professor-student sexuality, the feminist work of naming and renaming is most critical, as well as most difficult.

Confessions

Colleges and universities began instituting sexual harassment policies in the late 1970s. Kalamazoo's came into being in 1982. The initiative emerged from the office of the Dean of Students, which was politically convenient since it could not be seen as a women's studies plot, though the Dean's concern was at least as much to cover the

College's ass as it was to protect its students. In presenting the proposed policy to the faculty, the Dean consulted with me and we decided to request that one of the sporadic Friday-afternoon faculty advisors' workshops be given over to him and to the Women's Studies Committee to explain the policy, review the literature on sexual harassment, and try to establish a context for discussion of the problem as it exists on our little campus. To do the latter, we made the unprecedented move of inviting students to a faculty workshop. The three women students on the Women's Studies Committee were charged to bring anecdotal data—an explosive charge, we knew, but crucial in bringing the issue home from the realm of abstraction, giving it a human face.

The turnout was healthy, though we always gripe that these workshops tend to draw the already converted. The colleagues you want to address are precisely those who avoid gatherings where the interpersonal aspects of pedagogy are discussed.

The Dean presented the policy. The reference librarian, a member of the Women's Studies Committee, reviewed the literature and available resources. Another member offered established definitions of sexual harassment from federal law and the policies of other institutions. And then it was my turn. I proposed to offer a little autobiographical testimony by way of pulling this discussion down from the abstract.

⁂

I was a born student. An eager, impassioned student. Even when I griped about soporific classes, tyrannical rules, abhorrent subjects, monstrous or ridiculous teachers, I was loving school. Like most good female students, I was devoted to school for two reasons: I took the subject matter personally, and I wanted to please, to shine, to be thought good.

From the day I hit college, and perhaps even before that, I was falling in love with male teachers, of which there were proportionally more in college than in high school, even in English. (It is, in fact, in college that English stops being a "girl's subject" and the female English major begins to feel a little alien in her chosen field.) The increase in numbers of men at the front of the classroom meant an increase in the glamor, prestige, and, well, *sexiness* of classes and study. The passion of reading literature, dreaming and thinking and talking about it, writing about it, existed in and of itself, but it often mingled happily with passion for the eminence in corduroy at the front of the

room. The intellectual element of the passion was often indistinguish-
able from the rest. The passion usually dissipated quickly after exams,
to make way for a new one the next quarter. By the time I was a senior,
considering graduate school, crushes had given way to full-blown
fantasies of liaisons with professors. There was nothing, nothing more
romantic in the world, more illicit, more thrilling. This development
was facilitated by a senior seminar taught by a wonderful young
assistant professor with shining brown eyes, thick, wavy, dark hair,
and a bountiful moustache. He also had a beloved wife, but I merely
factored her out of the fantasy. Put that combination together with the
orgasmic lyricism of Keats and Shelley for fifteen weeks, and you have
quite an elixir.

   He was the finest of a species that fascinated me and dominated
my life. Professors—I loved their hairiness, their corduroys and pipes
(he had both). I loved their witty, literate humor and their passion. I
loved them in contrast to their crude, dense, graceless brethren, my
peers. As men go, they seemed to have more of the woman about
them—especially, of course, in literature. I loved their potency, their
ability to inseminate my head. I positively hungered for their praise.
The papers I "submitted" to them—always too long, always on time—
were my surrogates in the affair. In person I felt ugly, awkward, dull,
and went home from their offices in despair and disgust with myself.

   Looking back, I see what was really going on: What I loved was
the professoriat, and what I wanted was to join it. I wanted to *be* that
vital, inspiring, charismatic young man. I think this is often the case
with the bright young women who worship their professors. Like the
horses they adore at eleven, the professors they adore at nineteen
embody the power they have in themselves but have learned to submerge and alienate. The longing to identify with the professor trans-
mutes into a longing for sexual connection, which is, of course, the
traditional female relation to power. It is true that power is an aphrodisiac, but only because women's usual access to power has been
through the bedroom. As students we respond to collective memory.
Boys emulate them; we fantasize about them, seduce them, or allow
ourselves to be seduced.

⁂

   Before the students spoke at that faculty meeting, we laid groundwork by stressing that all evidence defines sexual harassment as a
problem perpetuated on most campuses by a small number of repeat
offenders, usually renowned among the student body. (At this point I

could see the wheels spinning in the audience.) We also emphasized that on our campus we deal almost exclusively with "lower level" forms of harassment—the comments, invitations, insinuations, and gestures that suddenly charge a classroom or an office with sexuality in a way that is anything but titillating, flattering, or humorous to the woman involved.

Then the students took over with their reports. Interestingly, several of the anecdotes came from foreign language classrooms—as if, somehow, an alien tongue removed some kind of restraint, releasing that other self linguists speak of discovering in a second language. There was the guy whose habit it was, in the course of dialogues designed to increase fluency, to ask female students if they would go out with him or sleep with him. Another incident involved a woman who had gradually stopped attending a language course because the instructor focussed on the physical and romantic attributes of the women by way of enlarging vocabulary. Sometimes he asked whether a particular student was a slut.

I had been very worried about this part of the workshop. Would the students' testimony be resented? Disregarded as grapevine gossip? Would we be blamed for bringing them and their distasteful scraps of reality into our midst? But the faculty listened attentively. They asked questions; occasionally they challenged one of the students, but respectfully, without professorial condescension or rancor. One man asked if "we" weren't encouraging students to perceive and report harassment where it might not exist. How odd, I thought, that they think we enjoy this, that they can imagine that making, hearing, or forwarding reports of sexual harassment is in any way gratifying. I thought of the sick dread in my stomach when a woman closed my office door and began a story whose ending I already knew. I thought of how encumbered the student always was with fear, confusion, and worst of all, that monstrous guilt about harming the perpetrator. So strange, I mused, that these men honestly see themselves as the vulnerable ones, potential martyrs in crucifixion-without-trial in our tight, cautious little academic village. In response, I tried differentiating between *encouraging* and *enabling*, but I'm not sure I succeeded. And in my own English teacher's mind, I considered the word *encouraging* and decided that I should simply have confessed: Yes, it's true. We are about the subversive task of giving them courage—that is, heart (Latin: *cor*).

Near the close of the meeting, a senior professor rose to thank us all, especially the students, and to say that the anecdotes especially would help him to be more conscious of his own verbal and physical behavior. What is the difference, I mused, between him and the other man, who was sure that he was going to be falsely incriminated? Is the one sure of his innocence while the other is uneasy about his possible guilt? Is the one listening while the other is playing with abstractions like the "rights of the accused"? Is the one the father of daughters, while the other is not?

The meeting dissolved and people collected around the table bearing wine and cheese—the small bribes that encourage attendance. A young colleague strode up to me. "Some of what they said was good to hear, valuable," he said. "But some of this— I really wonder if we're getting into individual style, placing much too much weight on personal idiosyncracies."

Like what?

"Well, the story about the language teacher calling somebody beautiful and asking if somebody was a slut, or whatever. I know that's Lloyd, it was obvious. He's probably upset about it. But look, isn't that just Lloyd? He's an older man, he's from another generation, he's got that debonair, sort of flirtatious style—that's just him. Can't we accept that? Does that have to be a big deal?"

Peripherally I could see Lloyd with a couple other men, smiling gently, shaking his head. Probably his advocate here was right. Probably Lloyd was at least surprised to hear himself classed among the bad guys, perhaps hurt. The intimacy of the group that day, reflecting that of the College itself, embarrassed me for Lloyd, who would never think of imposing sexually upon a student beyond using her for his private fantasies. Doubtless Lloyd had never had cause to ruminate upon the word "slut," its history, its lack of a masculine counterpart, its effect upon the woman who hears it. Doubtless Lloyd had never heard himself evaluated physically in class by a professor; or, in the remote event that he had, he might have found it a little embarrassing, but that's all. That experience would not have been replicated everywhere around him in his culture. That experience would not have reinforced an objectification he felt everywhere else in his life.

Yes, I said, I think it has to be a fairly big deal.

Tall Grass and Deep Water

Academe was never built to deal with sex. Academe was constructed as a temple for the cranium, and the rest of the vile body was to be kept securely outside the gates. That's one reason women were physically shut out for centuries and are intellectually excluded today.

Once you decide to confront and understand sex in academe, you're into the tall grass. It's very murky there. Men with whom you deal daily and easily suddenly become more complicated. If they are men you love, then you really find yourself in the deep water. A heterosexual friendship is, to me, like any intercultural relationship. However loving and authentic, it carries an explosive subtext. There is that gulf called History, and you watch yourself twist into strange contortions, trying to swim across.

A close friend invited me to guest-lecture in his class. In the ensuing discussion, my friend launched into a Freudian analysis of evil: Our normal manners are part of the veneer of civilization and keep the beast in check, he said, masking our "natural" urges and responses. "For instance," he continued, "if Liz spoke in class, I might say, 'That's an interesting point, Liz, and I think blah blah blah.' But outside class I might be talking to Dave here and I'd say, 'Wow, Liz is gorgeous. I'd just love to get her alone.' You see what I mean?"

I was next to him at the front of the room. As he spoke, my smile froze, my eyes fell to the desktop on which we sat. A ripple of nervous laughter. I could feel the students' eyes turn to Liz's chair. From the rear of the room I was sure I also felt the attention of a handful of feminist women shift to me. Perhaps I imagined it, a tension spreading across the room: What will she do? Will she laugh? Will she blow up? I sat silent.

All afternoon and evening it ate at me: I must confront him. I owe it to that class, to those women. To him, too, a friend I love. But there was something lying heavy on me, like a tarp. The old terror of "breaking the roundness," as the Chinese say, of disturbing the sunny, normal surface of our friendship to acknowledge the deep water below it.

Yet I know how easily the calm of concord can easily turn to the mendacity of denial. I should have spoken up immediately, for the sake of those women. No, that would have been to embarrass him in front of his own class. No, I should have spoken up immediately after class. But there we were, walking away, he telling me I was great, thanking me for coming, saying what a great class it was.

I'm a fraud. A hopeless humbug like the Wizard of Oz, hiding behind my curtain, cranking out a big feminist voice. There is no escaping the sorry truth and there is no excuse for me. I have just confirmed for the women in that class the eternal natural law that when one man appears on the scene, sisterhood flies out the window. When the going gets tough, the tough get timid. I sat miserably, awaiting the arrival of the Sisters to strip me publicly of my credentials.

The next day my friend collared me to tell me that he'd received a four-page handwritten letter from one of the group at the back of the room—a brilliant student whom we both knew well and respected highly. It was a carefully argued explanation of the effect of his remark. "Four pages!" he said, looking at me in genuine wonder. "Did you know about this? Did you react this way to what I said?"

"Well, yes, I did, and I was going to . . ."

"But I didn't mean I really wanted to screw Liz! Could anybody believe I'd say that in a class if I really meant it?"

"But that's not the point." And I told him what the point was. He listened, brow furrowed.

"But what *should* I have said, then?"

As I answered, I was thinking, "He really doesn't know this. He really doesn't."

"OK. OK. I see. All right. I'll say something tomorrow." Good. This is good. "But. . . four pages! Do you believe this?" He saw my point, he accepted her point. But he still couldn't fathom why this molehill should merit a mountainous four pages.

I suggested that he take it as a compliment: His brightest student took the time to write at such length, trusting him and caring enough about him to communicate honestly and directly, instead of just resenting him and badmouthing him outside of class.

"Yeah. I guess so," he said, thoughtful.

The next day, the letter-writer dropped by to tell me that he had opened class with a full apology.

On the whole, I thought, this one turned out OK. I'd give him a 5, me a zero, and the woman in the back of the room a 15.

❧

Shortly after the passage of our sexual harassment policy, the campus paper did a special feature article. One of the staff told me they were going to do some informal interviewing amongst their peers. OK, I said, but be careful—be very careful—of accusations in print. You could undermine the whole article.

A few nights later, the phone rang after 11:00. It was a student I knew quite well, clearly upset. In her talks with women who spoke of faculty whose behavior had made them uneasy, a few names kept cropping up again and again. Well, that's perfectly typical, I said.

"Yes, I know. But one of them's . . . One of them's Paul." Paul was a man dear to both of our hearts. "Sharon's one of the people who named him. She's never talked about it to anybody, but it's really upsetting her, because she thinks of him as a friend."

I knew exactly how Sharon felt.

"She's considering writing about it for the article."

Writing what?

"Writing an account of it—how he acts, what he says, how she feels."

"Wait," I said. Wait. Wait. "How can she do that without making it obvious who she's talking about?"

"I don't know. I guess she can't."

Wait. Wait. "Listen, would Sharon talk to me? Ask her if she'll come see me tomorrow."

"OK."

"Look, this could really be trouble. You can't indict somebody in the pages of the newspaper without any . . . without. . . I mean, she's never talked to him about it, right?"

Just whom, a voice whispered, are you trying to convince?

Sharon was very bright, extremely nervous, hyperarticulate and eager, a perfectionist, probably anorexic by the look of her. Exactly the kind who is crippled by something like this. As I sat for a few minutes after replacing the receiver, I remembered that just two days ago Paul had asked if I thought Sharon was attractive.

I met Sharon for coffee the next afternoon. The problem had come up in a class two quarters before. A wonderful class, she said, small and friendly, full of vitality. But periodically Paul would use her as an example, a case in point, citing her attractiveness, referring to her sexuality, to hypothetical sexual encounters between them. As she described her feelings, I could feel it too: some alien substance dropped into clear water. I could feel her ambivalence—the unmitigated respect for his teaching and appreciation for the class, but the anger, the embarrassment, the mistrust. The star pupil suddenly finds herself out on a limb, naked, exposed. And betrayed.

Immediately I saw that what she needed was to talk about it, and not in the pages of the newspaper, the only venue she'd been offered. It was also obvious that she wanted very much to preserve her friendship with Paul. I easily convinced her to make an appointment with him. She was very frightened, tense and brittle, but she did it immediately. I coached her through the hard day-long waiting period, stressing his respect for her, his probable ignorance of the pain he'd inflicted. To myself I wondered for the hundredth time how it was possible, this ignorance.

Later the next day she arrived at my office, smiling, visibly relieved. He had listened carefully and then apologized sincerely. She
had said her say, and they were still friends.

I waited for him to mention it. He didn't, not then, not since. Why,
I wondered. We tell each other things like this, unusual encounters
with students. Was it unimportant to him, or so important he was
afraid to tell me?

I was pleased with my negotiation here. I had worked with concern for her, above all, but also for him, a man learning the power of
his words, a man I cared about. Sharon was strengthened by the
knowledge of having named and validated her experience, having
acted, having precipitated an intimidating confrontation with a friend
who was nonetheless an authority figure, a man, a professor. Good, all
good. Their friendship was intact, maybe deeper. And he, my friend,
was doubtless wiser, sensitized, more aware.

But a corner of my mind would not clear up. In it sat a cobwebbed
thing that kept asking why I had so quickly headed off Sharon's
interest in writing her story for the paper. Would you have worked so
hard, so anxiously, I queried myself, to avoid exposing Morton, whose
sleaziness is legendary but who happens not to lodge near your heart?

The Sex Meeting

1983. The Faculty Council, the chief faculty governance organ at
Kalamazoo College, traditionally met at 4:00 on Wednesday after-
noons in a grim, airless faculty lounge with plastic furniture. I was
tearing up the hill at 4:15, waylaid by a long conference with a student.
I slipped into the lounge with an apologetic smile and took my seat.
The other eleven members looked up when I entered, but then kept
watching me, cryptically, expectantly, I thought. The provost, who
attended occasionally, grinned and said, "Guess what *we* just did."

I confessed that I couldn't. The Council chair then read a short
resolution. It announced very simply that sexual relations between
faculty and students would hereafter be considered potential grounds
for dismissal of the faculty member.

I looked around the circle of men smiling like little boys who've
done something daring behind Mom's back. I started to laugh.

Sexual harassment policies were multiplying like flies around the
country's colleges and universities. But "consensual" relationships—
that was a hot potato that no institution, to my knowledge, had
touched.

The new president, apparently, had received his second report of predatory faculty sexuality and had, in his direct way, sent the Provost to the Council to propose this resolution. It had just passed unanimously.

I pulled myself together as quickly as I could and asked for a revision in the wording, which at present omitted any rationale. I quickly devised one, saying that the faculty-student relation was always inequitable in its balance of power and that a sexual relationship held too much potential for abuse of power and distortion of the learning environment.

That was written in without objection. Then a small discussion opened. The resolution had obviously been passed so quickly that some members were still spinning from their immediate capitulation to Presidential will. The chair of the Council at that time was a man imbued by a wholehearted, profound, constitutional moderation, intellectual, political, and personal. And his brow was profoundly furrowed.

For a fleeting moment I felt what this must be like for him. In the academe he had entered three decades ago, faculty committees didn't talk about sex.

Thoughtfully, slowly, he was saying that he understood why sex would compromise the relationship of a faculty member and a student over whom he had direct power—a student in his class, a student worker in his office, an advisee. But in all cases was there necessarily a power differential?

I tried to articulate the potential for psychic damage to the student in the wake of the professor's omnipresent, abstract power and influence, regardless of his particular role in the student's campus life. But the brow remained furrowed.

I shifted gears and went for the specific: "Well, think about this: On this campus, how often do we find ourselves in positions of power over students we may never have taught or advised—students we maybe haven't even met: scholarship committees, Phi Beta Kappa selection, Judicial Council, prizes and honors? There are even a couple of senior athletic awards we vote on in full faculty meeting, right?"

Sold.

He nodded. "You're right. OK. That's right."

Funny, I thought, walking down the hill at 5:30. They don't seem to see their power unless it is being consciously exercised. That's dangerous, when power is so pervasive it's invisible, like air. Like radiation.

The faculty meeting where the resolution was passed was convened by that same Council chair, who also had an important budget item to propose. He called us to order and opened the meeting thus: "Well, today we have two issues I think you'll agree are pretty significant—sex and money."

The laughter was welcome. Everyone had received advance copies of the resolution.

The civil libertarians were vocal. Individual rights all around. Invasions of privacy. Moral watchdogging. Examples were delicately cited of faculty who had married students shortly after their graduation. The provost himself finally settled the issue by explaining that the resolution defined grounds for termination but did not stipulate termination and thus could be interpreted case by case. This seemed to assure all but the most adamant, and in the ensuing vote, the resolution passed by a heavy majority.

In the wine-and-cheese aftermath I had to swear up and down and across the room that the resolution had not originated with me.

That meeting quickly entered College lore as "The Sex Meeting."

No Harm Done

If power is often invisible to the dominant, it is likewise invisible to the subordinate.

The widespread student reaction to the Sex Policy was negative. A long letter appeared in the campus paper protesting the Policy's paternalism. Its author was male, but many of the women I spoke to had similar objections to what they saw as the policy's assumption that they were helpless, immature children. At 21, I realized, I would have agreed with them.

✳➷⟲➶✳

I was talking with my friend who directed the media center, chatting about the strengths and weaknesses of the policy, the faculty reaction. Her student worker, Sally, was listening in. At one point she began reminiscing about a class during her sophomore year, two years earlier. She'd become the object of classroom professorial flirtation, in the form of constant jokes about dating her and having a crush on her, hands on her shoulders as he wandered around the room, and on tests, story problems starring Sally. As she told the story, she was neither pained nor angry, but instead sarcastic, dismissive. She laughed a lot. It wasn't a big deal. "That jerk."

How did the other students react? we asked. Slowly, her face darkened. She had a lot of male friends in the class. "Some of those guys were *good friends*, you know? And it was just never the same with us. They kept telling me I couldn't go wrong with him. I had it made. It was a really tough class and we were all dying in there. When I made a B on the final and a B- in the course, man, I was ecstatic. I mean, I really busted my ass in there, and I was *so* happy at first. But after what they said . . . I mean, I wasn't sure anymore, whether I really earned the B, you know?"

❈❨♡❩❈

I was chatting over coffee in the Snack Bar with a woman student about the policy. "What if a woman comes on to a prof, though?" she asked. "I mean, I know some who've done it."

"So do I," I replied. I thought a minute. "Let me ask you this: What should the prof's role be there? Is he helpless? Is he no longer a prof? What's his *job* there, do you think?"

She looked at me as if those questions had never before entered her mind.

"What would be good for the student in that case?" I continued. "What would help her take herself seriously? Who's the grownup? Who's the professional? Who's in charge here, really?"

"Yeah," she said, nodding slowly. "Yeah."

I walked back to the office shaking my head. How ready she was to let Dr. X off the hook. How absolutely ready and willing.

❈❨♡❩❈

There was a young man at the College on a short-term contract. A brilliant teacher by all accounts, and he rapidly developed a devoted student following. His social life, in fact, was predominantly student-oriented, and how they love that—going with him to bars, having him over to the dorm or the apartment for dinner, being invited to his house. Only a rare murmur reached me from a disenchanted handful of women who resented his sexualizing of the classroom, his constant personal references, his double entendres. When his contract ran out, then, he was easily able to engineer a large student outcry on his behalf, which ultimately failed to get him a tenure-track slot but succeeded in generating some support for keeping his file active in case of future openings in his department.

Just before he left, I learned that among his groupies was a first-year advisee of mine. I found this out when her family enlisted me to try to find her after she disappeared from her dorm for several days. Jeannette was brilliant, scores off the charts, a gifted musician, and a born rebel, a classic Bad Girl. A history emerged—drugs, legal and emotional problems. Now this disappearance. Her roommate came to see me and told me about the liaison with our faculty rock star. The relationship, she said, had been extremely important to Jeannette. They had talked of meeting in another time, another place, maybe California. My God, all this and California too? In the middle of a Michigan winter, that's no small inducement.

We found Jeannette unharmed, staying with friends. She duly came to see me, to say she was fine and was leaving "this place." She agreed with Him—this place was nowhere. She had to get out. After all, the place was driving Him away, so it was no place for her.

I wrote a letter to the Provost saying that in the event of a serious initiative to rehire him, I would go the President with what I knew about Jeannette. The Provost wrote back, thanking me, telling me my letter would be in the guy's file. I was first gratified. Then suddenly I felt embarrassed, then frightened. What had I done? What kind of informer was I turning into here? *Who elected you the Sex Police?*

Jeannette wrote me later from California to say she was fine, to say that leaving school had been the right thing. She also said that His interest in her, His understanding of her situation, His friendship had gotten her through. He was "the one good thing about this place" for her.

Maybe she was right. Maybe he was.

~(T)~

In July a just-graduated woman came back to campus for a few days and wandered up to see me. In the course of an hour's conversation, she mentioned that a married faculty member had propositioned her the preceding summer.

Did she feel she'd been pressured?

"Oh, no. Nothing like that at all. I mean, he was a friend, we were pretty close. I told him no, but I wasn't angry or frightened or anything. I don't see that as harassment."

"No, me neither, but we do have a policy against that."

"Yeah, and it's always bothered me a bit. I mean, if you've got two consenting people, I don't think there's anything wrong with it."

"I see your point. But I'm concerned about the faculty-student relationship, about the power there. I think a lot of damage can be done if it gets sexual. I think it can really distort things, you know? I mean, maybe somebody like you can handle it without a lot of damage, but not all college women can."

"That's true," she said. "That's true. And it did piss me off." She paused, I waited. "I don't know. Last summer was pretty shitty anyway. Part of it was that it just seemed like every single relationship I had with a man had to get sexual, you know? I mean, sooner or later, even with some of my best friends, guys I'd known for years, the pressure would come: Will you or won't you? I was beginning to think it was impossible for a man and a woman to be friends, just friends. And so when that happened with *him*, I thought, 'Shit, did you have to do this to me too?' I thought we were friends. You know?"

I know.

"I felt kind of betrayed."

But no harm was done. No harm.

Family Secrets

And if, in that languid spring of 1972, Professor Wonderful had made the same suggestion to me, what would I have done? He didn't, and I headed off to his graduate school, wanting to become just like him.

Now that I *am* him, I find I am not. For the magic, the charisma, is only partially in the role; the rest of it is gender. I sensed very quickly in my first year on the job that the power I wielded over my students, both male and female, was qualitatively different from that exuded by my male counterparts. I have compared notes on this often with women friends on the faculty: We may be admired, even revered; we may be loved and cherished; we may even be feared at times. But in the students' reactions to the men we work with there is that other ingredient, that quiver of the animal who smells where the real power lies.

Never were we so careful about our pronouns as in those discussions about the sexual harassment policy and the "Sex Policy." Grammatical pretzels emerged: "If student feels that he or she has been harassed, he or she should be encouraged to confront the faculty member about his or her behavior." There was a sort of unspoken warning that if we gave in to male pronouns in referring to harassers, lightning would strike. Gender was the sleeping giant we were loath to awaken. Strange, I thought. Passing strange that *role* is a legitimate category of analysis, but *gender* is not. *Gender* is political, dangerous, explosive. The eighty percent of our faculty that was male was quite willing to talk about their power as faculty members, but not about their power as men. So, for the sake of peace in the family, we pretended that if the roles are reversed—female professor, male student— nothing changes. Of course, the third model— professor and student of the same gender—lay at the very bottom of the ocean.

The woman professor's sense of her authority is a complicated phenomenon. Her power lies in her role, her job contract, and not in her. It does not mesh with the mystique, the prestige, the tradition that the male professor has behind him. It is not reinforced by the power structures of the extra-academic world, except to the extent that Mom is seen as a power, and her power is likewise ambivalent and complex. It is often this dissonance between the authority vested in one by the college and one's marginality as a woman that renders the woman professor insecure and touchy. If she has any doubt about her illegitimacy as an authority figure, it disappears when she exerts that authority in a negative form—bad grades, harsh criticism, distant or formal demeanor. Then she feels what an imposter she is. In sundry oblique and direct ways, she is made aware of expectations that she will be "nicer" than her male counterpart and of surprise, resentment, and double-standard judgment when she is not. She receives the hostility and condescension accorded to Mom, to the librarian, to the high-school English teacher, though she may also receive the affection they get. She is likely to find herself unwittingly and unwillingly worrying too often about her authority, striving too often to prove it. And then, of course, her students and male colleagues alike wonder why professional women are so neurotic.

A male student may bring into her office considerable deference toward authority and eagerness to please Mom, but it may be interestingly cut with the eighteen-year-old boy's ongoing struggle to disengage from the female world, to ditch Mom and fly into the transcendent, invincible maleness the world has promised him. Into her office he carries the invisible baggage of immutable natural laws he has breathed since birth, though we may all tacitly agree here in the rarified air of academe that these laws are temporarily suspended, or at least that we will politely ignore them. He is most unlikely to see her as someone he wishes to be, to perceive her power as something to emulate, because it comes in female form, and emulation of the female is wholly beyond his imagination. He may develop a crush on her, but the aphrodisiac will probably not be power.

And she is unlikely to put sexual pressure on him; for her, unlike her academic brethren, that would be an aberration from, not an extension of, normal behavior in the "real world." The real world reinforces male sexual advantage, part of which is the model of the older man and younger woman, whereas it still marginalizes and ridicules the model of the older woman and younger man. The silver-haired man with a twenty-year-old woman on his arm is congratulated; his stock rises. This image is fundamentally incestuous. And the academic family has its dirty little secrets like any other.

I tend to be physically affectionate with students, moreso with women, I think, because of a tacit assumption that men are less easy with physical displays of affection. Yet I wonder if a young man has ever wondered uncomfortably about my hand on his shoulder, a quick hug. I also wonder if academic men think we are immune to the attractions of twenty-year-old men within that peculiar intimacy that develops between teacher and student.

It happens. Generally the young men are younger than the young women, and I think it is less likely that a heterosexual woman in her thirties or forties or fifties will find them seriously sexually alluring. And when she does, the script reads slightly differently. But it happens.

❦

One tropical summer there was Tim, who used to amble—late—into Literature of Women in very short cut-offs and tank tops or T-shirts bearing interesting messages. I used to falter when he cut in front of me to reach his seat, watching his compact, muscular body, wholly at ease with itself. My mouth would go dry. He was an office regular, too, and I juggled other needy souls most unprofessionally in order to clear whole half hours for Tim with his wide smile and his green eyes. He was a psychology major with broad, diverse interests who read a lot and thought a lot. He asked wonderful questions. His mother had just remarried and he and she were at odds; he was taking the course out of frustrated curiosity about women. "Especially anger," he announced in my office in June. "I want to understand why she's so angry, why women are so angry." So I told him, all summer long.

One gentle spring Brad showed up in a course of mine, shaggy auburn hair shot with gold, eyelashes so lush I could barely listen while he spoke to me. Long and thin, he reminded me of a beautiful yearling colt with the look of a champion. After the course ended, we remained friends. I was often the consultant about his love life. Once he confessed a fear that he was going to turn out to be a "shit to women. I don't want to be that," he said. He asked me how to avoid it. So I told him, long into the night.

And I used to muse, when Tim or Brad was imminent or had just left; I used to wonder and fantasize and ask myself, "How could I possibly do them any harm?"

Lenore

It is five in the afternoon, at the ragged end of a long grey line of anxious, inarticulate people from Expository Prose. I am looking around my desk again and again, trying to formulate a plan of attack to deal with the memos, book order forms, requests for information, articles to be filed, department business, women's studies account reports from the Business office, reminders, more memos correcting previous memos, student papers. I think back to my first quarter at Kalamazoo with the distinct memory of having used the late afternoon hours to grade papers at my clean, neat desk.

Lenore appears in the doorway and asks very softly if I have some time. Bidden in, she closes the door behind her, always a bad sign. No, I think. Not today. Please. I breathe deeply and muster what resources I have left.

Lenore is a junior who has taken one course from me, in which I rapidly learned to save her papers for the bottom of the bottom pile to read last, when my patience is tearing at the seams and I waver on the edge of despair. Lenore moved in language like an Olympic swimmer. Assigned the usual eight-to-ten-page paper, Lenore submitted twenty gleaming pages of careful, serious, detailed thinking in rich, sophisticated prose. She is double majoring in social science and humanities, and she has graduate school written all over her. She is warm and friendly, but with a stillness, a darkness about her.

As she sits down in the chair beside my desk, I think how lovely she is, with ivory skin, fine bones, and long, shiny dark hair. She has never come to see me before.

She is trembling, and then she begins to cry. I reach into the bottom left-hand drawer for the large box of Kleenex I keep there. "Just take your time. Take your time and then tell me."

It is a course in one of her majors. Before class, after class, during the break the prof has something to say about her clothes, her legs, her hair, always in front of a group of other students. Such public harassment carries its own particular burden, embarrassing a student before her peers and damaging her relations with them. I remember Sally. But

Lenore will never have to bust her ass for a B-. She knows how good she is. In her many of us already see Fulbright or even Rhodes. In her, however, one of us sees Legs.

She has tried avoiding him, leaving class quickly, arriving just in time, fleeing to the bathroom at breaks. But he follows her, calls her back, corners her. By this time, as her story emerges in short, tight bursts, she is shaking, her eyes shut, the musculature of her face tightly clenched. Hurt, tension, and something more, I thought: rage. Inarticulate rage.

Like most victims on first appearance in my office, she does not divulge his name. Since I know her two majors, it isn't hard to guess. I wonder if he's still in his office. I wonder what would happen if I took her arm and dragged her to his door and thrust her into his sight and said, *"Look at this. Look at this."* Brilliant, promising Lenore, a scholar, quaking in this chair, her beautiful face shiny with tears.

I am suddenly very tired, a different sort of tired from what I felt before Lenore arrived. I feel exactly as if I were standing at the foot of a mountain, looking up. There is so much to do, because of Lenore. There is himself, sitting in his office, ignorant of what he's done. Yes he is, ignorant. And that is the worst of it. If he were twirling his moustache, chortling about the destruction he's caused, that would be simpler. His ignorance makes everything more difficult. There are the rest of them out there, in their offices or committee meetings or heading home, ignorant too. They don't know about Lenore, and at this moment I want them all to know about Lenore. At this moment Lenore is the most significant issue facing us. Lenore is a crisis in Liberal Education. Lenore takes precedence over whatever else they're working on or worrying about.

There is also the question of what Lenore will wish to do after this hour is over, and what role I will play in her decision as to what to do. What will be the best thing to advise her to do? Is it legitimate to advise her to do anything? *Who made you the Sex Police?* Should she decide to do something, there is the college mechanism for dealing with sexual harassment—inadequate, sanctionless, abstract. There is the probability that she will wish to do nothing, nothing at all. There is the probability that she wants only to verbalize this to me. That is, she wants to give it to me to rid herself of some of its weight. I see myself going home that night, laden with it. I have papers to grade. I have a novel to finish in order to lecture on it tomorrow, and the lecture to write. . .

But first, there is the simple, enormous fact of Lenore, sitting here, shaking, tears not so much falling as squeezed out of the corners of her eyes. First and foremost, there is Lenore, here, now. So I begin.

9

Orphans of the Storm

The F-Word and the Post-Feminist Generation

The Crest of a Wave

During office hours, there comes a soft, tentative knock on the doorframe. Shelley's face appears, timorous. "Are you busy?"

I summon her in. She was in a class of mine the year before; she is now a sophomore. After having done her Career Development Internship last quarter at the local Domestic Assault Program, she has become involved this quarter with the campus women's group. She is thin and delicate, with ivory skin and wavy brown hair.

She moves noiselessly to the chair beside my desk and lights on the edge of it, her hands clasped in her lap, her shoulders drawn in, her eyes darting around the floor. I am prepared for a terrible confession—probably, I guess, the crime of being sexually harassed.

"Um. . . " A gathering of breath. "I wanted to ask you something." Her voice is whisper soft.

"OK."

"Um. . . I wanted to ask you . . . whether you think . . . that. . . um . . . being a feminist makes you . . . you know, narrow." Her eyes shoot up to mine.

I rein in a smile. She might be asking me whether Tampax destroyed one's virginity.

"Well. . . ," I begin.

I know, as they say, exactly where Shelley is coming from. It is a prominent feature of this student body, the philosophy that commitment to a belief system defines you, thus narrows you. They want all options open, no bridges burned; they also want no labels to hamper their social lives, to make them feel exposed, known, and categorized. I remember this. I remember myself at exactly this age, seeking a kind of freedom and also a kind of shelter in fuzziness. In indefinition I could be anything, and thus didn't have to be anything in particular.

I do my best to explain to Shelley my thinking as it has evolved on this very central developmental issue. I conclude by saying that my own feminism has, I believe, broadened me.

She nods shortly. "OK. Thanks." And she's gone, like a sprite, ten minutes after she arrived. I expected a fairly extensive conversation here, so I'm surprised. But apparently all Shelley wanted was a brief answer. Perhaps she didn't want the conversation to turn toward her. Perhaps she didn't want to have to confess that the virulent, narrowing disease was metastasizing in her very own sophomore self.

A few days after this, a deeply antifeminist colleague was telling me that he knew his stand did not make him popular. "You, on the other hand, have it easy," he said. My eyes must have widened. "Oh, yes, you certainly do. You're riding the crest of a wave."

Taking refuge behind my office door, I sank into my chair. My eyes sought the trees outside the window. With that wonderful imaginative flexibility bred in the female of the species, I moved to his vantage point quite as easily as I had to Shelley's. I saw magazine racks laden with *Ms.* and *Self* and *Working Woman*. I saw Donahue and Oprah devoting afternoon upon afternoon to women who love too much, women who love the men who hate them, Cinderella women, Wendy women. I saw advertisements celebrating women who had come a long way, baby, bringing home the bacon, frying it up in a pan, and never letting him forget he's a man (though I have to wonder about the kind of man who could forget a thing like that). I saw Geraldine Ferraro and Sally Ride. That is, I saw the Women's Movement, broadly defined, everywhere, changing the face, if not the body or heart, of the culture. And I said to myself, He's right; I'm riding the crest of a wave.

So why is it that I feel I'm always about to wipe out?

And, more to the point, why is it that Shelley sat in this chair here, quaking with embarrassment, asking me whether feminism was narrowing in exactly the same tone in which her mother, thirty years before, would have asked a female mentor—assuming she could have found one—whether you could get pregnant the first time?

Goddess, if being a feminist is easy, preserve me from a really hard life.

An old familiar dissonance danced between my temples, an atonal fugue heralding a wicked headache.

Reinventing the Wheel

Around the same time I perused Ann Beattie's *New York Times* piece on the opening of the National Museum of Women in the Arts in Washington. An article by a woman artist in the pages of the notoriously "liberal" *Times*, positively redolent, absolutely squeamish with discomfort about the whole enterprise. The nervousness was wonderfully reflected in the headline on the jump-page where the article continued: A MUSEUM OF WOMEN'S ART? Ah, the power of punctuation. That potent little question mark, turning fact to questionable proposition. Such a headline atop such an article would hardly have been surprising in 1970. Since then there have been countless shows of women's art, so identified or not; there has been *The Dinner Party*, outraging the Fathers of Art History and trekking around the country seeking gallery space big enough—physically, intellectually—to shelter it; there have been articles, journals, texts defining and exploring the female tradition in visual art. And it all comes down to a question mark—tentative, or disdainful?—in the *New York Times*.

I sometimes think the peculiar exhaustion I see in myself and other feminist educators, within and beyond academe, comes from the inordinate proportion of our energy that goes to reinventing the wheel. The trip back to Square One every time takes a lot out of us.

And the primary objections to the NMWA raised in the *Times* boiled down to the two questions every women's studies teacher I know has come up against so many times that she could recite them and her responses to them in her sleep:

1. This is separatist; it excludes men.
2. This is (insert current year); we're beyond this now.

That is: this is both exclusive and regressive. That is: this is narrow. Adrienne Rich has written:

> The entire history of women's struggle for self- determination has been muffled in silence over and over. One serious cultural obstacle encountered by any feminist writer is that each feminist work has tended to be received as if it emerged from nowhere; as if each of us had lived, thought, and worked without any historical past or contextual present. This is one of the ways in which women's work and thinking has been made to seem sporadic, errant, orphaned of any tradition of its own. . . So also is each contemporary feminist theorist

attacked or dismissed ad feminam, as if her politics were simply an outburst of personal bitterness or rage.[1]

That is, feminists and feminism are made to seem narrow. And so Shelley, instead of feeling the opening-out that comes with entering an honorable tradition of thought and work, feels that she is becoming neurotic, obsessive, myopic, deformed, cramped—and isolated. Where she might feel her mind expanding, she feels her personality contracting. A complex historical and cultural phenomenon has become a personality disorder.

One craves a reprieve; one wishes to stop explaining. The hell with it, one thinks. But then there is Shelley, who must know. And if one is Shelley's teacher, one has not the liberty to say the hell with it. This is one's job: to educate Shelley. To give Shelley what belongs to her. A mind is a terrible thing to waste. Climb back on that board and head on down the pipeline.

Generation Gap

The relationship of college students to their parent culture is always ambivalent—as ambivalent as their relationship to their parents. The particular tension of adolescence, after all, is born of a classic conflict of desires: Every adolescent wants more than anything to fit in as a group member and more than anything to break loose as a distinctive individual. Hence the tired old parental joke about teenagers wanting to prove they're different by looking like everybody else. Conformist nonconformity is the nature of the beast. It signals not confusion but the onset of the continuing human struggle, very pronounced in the West, to find some accommodation between self and other, individuality and communality.

Thus most college students admire a limited, safe nonconformity. The majority of them are likely to approve forms of "individual" self-expression that distinguish the individual without really challenging or undermining the dominant paradigm. Thus they often adore the hip, iconoclastic teacher but resist or resent the one who offers a profound critique of their society, their values, their lives. I recall loving the teachers who wore jeans, drank and smoked dope with us, bucked formal authority, and taught literature in a radical, liberating way; but I also recall disapproving mightily of the hairy, intense young man who explained to us why he felt he must cancel classes in the wake of the strike of May 1970. Rather than making me feel included, approved, an insider, he unnerved me by trying to make me think about the project and priorities of my education and of his profession.

The students of the eighties have come in for their share of denigration, especially from the students of the sixties. Some of the former have come to me concerned about their generational public image, in fact, wanting to know if they're as self-centered, oblivious, boring, and materialistic as the media tells them they are. It's sort of sad.

Yet these sons and daughters are precise mirrors of their culture, and one of the prime benefits—or detriments, depending on what kind of day you're having—of teaching them is that one sees so clearly what's going on out there. If they are predominantly the children of the white middle class, what they show you is the mainstream culture, which merits surveillance. This perennial contact with our collective children is said to keep teachers young. I have found the opposite to be true. They age me.

I think we can all agree that students today are on the whole less willing to ask or to hear large, troubling questions, less open to radical (in whatever direction) points of view, more concerned with finding the quickest way to a comfy, lucrative niche in society as presently constituted, than their parents were. Their adolescent rebelliousness tends to remain social and personal, not evolving into the moral and political, or not nearly so quickly. Theirs is the resistance to authority of the thirteen-year-old rather than the informed, thoughtful dissidence of the young adult. To be sure, the obvious descendants of the sixties are around, but fewer in number, ill informed, and they tell me they feel very isolated and out of place.

Even the more conservative among us teachers find the studious moderation of our students a source of annoyance, for it makes teaching less dynamic. My overriding emotion toward them is less annoyance than an obscure sadness. I find myself feeling sorry for them, for what they're missing. I cannot make college for them what it was for me: a harrowing, in which everything well fastened shook loose, everything carefully constructed trembled and collapsed, and anything might be imagined to replace it. In short, an education.

To teach young adults these days is to be particularly intimate with the collective loss of memory that seems to have settled over the country in the Reagan eighties—that benign, terrifying blankness where, in the course of watching TV or checking out at the supermarket or listening to a political candidate, one thinks of "Invasion of the Body Snatchers." Part of that cultural amnesia has been a reversion to a simplistic, dualistic world-view much like that which, according to the developmental stages defined by Perry, marks adolescence. That is, the country has retreated from adulthood—from complexity, multiplicity, and relativity—to an endless summer of cowboy movies where we are all fourteen and it is 1955 and we're out to vanquish the Evil Empire. The fact is that as I write this against a backdrop of a couple of terrifying epidemics, a complete breakdown in health care, a crisis in education, and a national shame in the shape of millions of homeless people, we have endured a presidential campaign one of whose central issues was the Pledge of Allegiance.

There seems to be a general will not-to-know, a general amnesia. And to be a teacher in this lotus-land is a study in frustration, if not an outright contradiction in terms. For education is about memory.

They say that what the kids lack most of all is a sense of history. This is quite true. Of history traditionally defined they are woefully ignorant. Of the other histories, the hidden histories, they are still being robbed. This is the genuine, bona fide closing of the American mind. And their understanding of what was going on while they were growing up—the painful, tumultuous chapter in the evolution of the American soul which resulted in the frightened, protective regression that has nurtured them—this is sketchy and cartoonish at best. The class of 1989, seniors as I write, was born in 1967. We who were coming of age at that time are marked indelibly, conclusively. And we bring to the classroom certain assumptions that we find ourselves having to check again and again as they meet the resistance, the silence, or the simple ignorance of our charges. To put it simply, they are culturally deprived, all of these privileged kids whom I teach.

Case in point: the Civil Rights Movement. Now, they're not idiots; they all know that there was such a thing, they know who Martin Luther King was (his birthday now being a day off from high school). But that's about all they know. A few years back I did a unit on black women in American in my all-white senior women's studies seminar. I asked a black colleague to come in to talk from her research on the black family after emancipation. But as the hour moved along, she wandered up to the more recent past. She talked about growing up on the black side of a southern Ohio town, about making the transition from segregated to integrated schools, including a most interesting assessment of what was lost in the transition. Sensing as I did the class' ignorance and interest, she broadened her scope to sketch the general outlines of Jim Crow America. The group was galvanized, full of wonder and outrage—a splendid sight to see, believe me. One woman, daughter of two professionals, worldly and astute, articulate and well read, shook her head after class and said, "I had no idea those things were going on in this country right up into the sixties."

But if their understanding of Civil Rights is patchy or superficial, their concept of the Women's Movement is enough to induce PMS. And its chronicle runs something like this:

> From the dawn of time until 1960, women were housewives and mothers and weren't allowed to do anything. They were very suppressed (or "repressed"). They were passive and quiet and stayed home all the time. They didn't do any work because men wouldn't let them. Somewhere about 100 years ago men gave them the vote. Then in the sixties some of them got mad, had protest marches, and burned their bras in public. Some of them began to be lesbians. A lot of them hated men, though some didn't and just wanted equality. They carried signs. Some of them founded a radical group called "NOW" and a radical magazine called *Ms*. They fought for their rights, which was good, but some of the radical ones and the lesbians went too far. They said everything was men's fault and men were the enemy, or else they wanted to be men. Then around 1975 everything changed, and women could become lawyers and doctors and astronauts and vice-presidential candidates. Some people say women only make sixty cents for every dollar men make, but that's changing now. Everything's changing now. Now women can be anything they want. They can have careers and families. They can be CEOs of big corporations. Now no woman is discriminated against unless she lets herself be, and people are judged more as individuals. Most women have realized they don't want to be men and that they can have equality and still be feminine. Women will continue to become equal as long as radical lesbians don't ruin it by turning women and men more against each other. Now we've gone beyond feminism to humanism, where everyone is equal and neither men or women are discriminated against.

World without end, amen. These kids are not stupid, mind you. Far from it. They are extremely retentive. They recite this story pretty accurately as they have learned it, from their parents, from the media, and from the respectable publications they read at school and at home.

And the rest of the story? The rest, as they say, is History.

And it is history that Shelley and her sisters lack. They are the daughters "orphaned of any tradition of [their] own," to borrow Rich's words. They have no context for themselves.

So one of them, at nineteen, finds herself working with battered women. It is a simple, ready point of entry: She sees woman after woman beaten and terrified out of her home, and she wonders why. Upon her return to campus, she finds herself gravitating toward the campus women's group. On her way out of the dorm one night to go to one of the meetings, she hears another resident—maybe male, maybe female—say, "There goes Shelley, off to another bra-burning session with the dykes. Or is it male-bashing tonight?" She thinks, "Omigod, am I one of Them?" Her roommate is less hostile; she says, "I'm for equal rights and everything, Shelley, but those feminists are always seeing everything as Male Versus Female. It just makes them so narrow." Her boyfriend says, "Look, I'm trying to understand what you're going through, but it seems like lately all you can talk about is this feminist stuff. You're getting so narrow I'm afraid to talk to you." And so, one afternoon when she finds a little time, she finds herself creeping up to the office of an Avowed Feminist who seems to have made it past thirty with her sanity and eye make-up intact, to whisper a small question.

That's where she finds herself. And it's scary there.

Against the Grain

Shelley's little private drama is microcosmic. It tells a crucial story. For every Shelley there are those voices, multiplied exponentially, warning her away from self-knowledge, from her history. If she persists in her madness, she will encounter the identical resistance, writ large, in what she calls the "real world." She is not a typical late adolescent, nor are her peers a typical group of students in the late eighties; as I have said, they are an elite. But it is precisely their elite that is empowered to create, preserve, or alter the dominant culture. So their resistance to feminism (which can be quite distinct from anti-feminism, as Shelley herself demonstrates) is significant to me. It saddens me that the immediate response of nineteen-year-old Americans should not be naively sympathetic to a liberation movement, but I remind myself that adolescence is as rigid, judgmental, and intolerant as it is passionate, rebellious, and imaginative.

Which is to return to my initial analysis of American adolescence as a struggle between conformism and rebellious individualism. Those two forces, which interplay to construct Shelley's reality, also happen to be powerful forces in the American cultural tradition and character. And both collaborate against feminism in interesting ways.

Individualism, vaguely conceived, is for most of my students an inherent Good. Thus they are extremely resistant to class analysis of any kind—unless it involves a class to which they do not belong (people of any color other than white, other nationalities, homosexuals, about all of whom they are quite ready to generalize). That is, they are good Americans, firm believers in the efficacy of individual effort in overcoming circumstances, so that institutional oppression is both unreal to them and suspect, intellectually, as a convenient "excuse" for individual failure. They quite understandably do not want their burgeoning selfhoods subsumed and swallowed by some group to which they belong by accident of birth. They do not want to believe that their individual gifts and efforts might be of limited effectiveness in altering their lives. And they surely don't want to think of their privileges as undeserved. They want—and who can blame them?—to be and to think of themselves as self-reliant, self-determining, and unique. When feminism talks to them in 1960s terms about equality and opportunity, they are with it all the way. Stereotypes violate individuality, they agree. Overt job discrimination violates individual rights, they concur. In this respect, oddly, they are true children of the sixties.

But something has happened to feminist thought since then, something as problematic for seasoned feminist theorists as for a nineteen-year-old from Farmington Hills, Michigan. Put simplistically, it is this: The focus moved from equality to difference. Women's studies was born of the premise of some degree of integrity and continuity in women's experience, its *difference* from male experience, constructed in academe as normative. "Equality" and "difference" are just not easy for the western mind—especially at nineteen—to reconcile. A legal system grounded in notions of individual equality is having a bloody time dealing with reproductive rights, child care, and pregnant workers. The emphasis on distinctive female experience leads inevitably to assumptions or speculations about distinctive female qualities and capacities, and this thinking troubles the most committed feminist. It smacks of the essentialism against which feminism has often fought, and it threatens a vicious circle straight back to the Separate Sphere of the last century, in which the Delicate and Mysterious Female Organism was incarcerated. It is a short route from Difference to Exclusion. My students sense this and wonder how continued accentuation of difference can lead either to enhanced female freedom or to harmony between the sexes.

If this feminist "separatism" violates their individualism by underscoring collective identity, it also, paradoxically, threatens their need to conform. My students naturally wish to be healthy, functional swimmers in the mainstream, and feminism represents—and promises—resistance and alienation. For the young men, of course, the alienation in embracing feminism is double: It expels them from the mainstream and it exiles them from the Brotherhood, where all power lies. The women's fear of feminist alienation is of particular interest to me, because once upon a time it was my own deepest reservation about the feminist I was inexorably becoming. From where they stand—that is, historically ignorant and educationally deprived—to be a feminist means not to join an historical life-force, but to cut oneself off from one—that is, the continuity of regular, normal female life and behavior, particularly as it involves relations with men, family, children. And normal female life and behavior have been defined by just those relations. Make no mistake: These daughters are in no way interested in a return to the fifties. They want, all of them, to be strong, self-sufficient women. The college woman who does not plan on a career is a complete anomaly in my life these days. But they also want to be sexy, loved, loving, belonging deeply to that web of relationships that has—they're dead right about this—constituted female reality for centuries. They see feminism as removing them from that web, leaving them isolated, odd, exiled, peculiar, humorless.

And angry. Above all, angry. Their fear of being angry is a wonder. I have seen them, in and out of class, in matters intellectual and personal, go to exhausting lengths and into astonishing contortions to avoid angry conclusions. When I lose patience with them, I remind myself of the mucky detours I took twenty, fifteen, ten years ago to dodge the anger to which my experience wanted to lead me. As adolescent conformists, and as female web-spinners, they see the Angry Woman as a death's head, an awful warning. They see her as apart from the race, alone, unloved, unloving. As American individualists, they see her as someone with a Problem, the result of her own psyche and experiences, and one that is hers to solve, not to blame on Men. The wider historical analysis that can stabilize and clarify that anger, without robbing the sacred Individual of her sacred duty to "deal with it," as they say—that waits down the road for most of them. It involves pretty sophisticated thinking, and more living.

Of course they are, especially the heterosexuals, particularly wary of anger against men—with whom, I must concur, it is very dangerous indeed to be at odds. They want, if they are heterosexual, attention from and intimacy with men here, now, during their college years. They treasure their male friends and lovers and teachers, so they are troubled when asked to explore some deep historic gulf between them and these brothers, these fathers. They also want very much to believe that men are not the enemy, as they put it; that men are changing, are capable of change. I often think they want to believe this more than the men do. To explain to these women the difference between "men" and "patriarchy" is, in the words of T. S. Eliot, an occupation for the saint. It also leads into class analysis and thus to further trouble.

The fear of alienation from men and from heterosexual tradition both nourishes and is fed by homophobia. That is, it is at once ingredient in and product of their nervousness about The Lesbian Thing.

That they will be perceived as gay or suspected of gayness is terrifying. Even the most stalwart are concerned about the cost to their romantic/sexual lives of alignment with feminism—and, again, with good reason. The men who involve themselves fear most of all the price they will pay among their brothers, the sundering of the male bond, the allegation if not of "fag" then of "wimp" (a term of such wide currency among them that it has trickled up into our political discourse, so that Wimpiness, also, becomes a major issue in a presidential campaign). "Wimp" is at once a watered-down version of "fag" and a more deadly label, since it is a sort of extension of "fag" that subsumes a greater variety of people and qualities. But the men will not suffer in the dating game; if anything, their sympathy for feminism makes them more attractive. The women will be not wimps (a female wimp exists but is a quite different phenomenon) but ball-busters, dykes, man-haters. And so the heterosexual woman risks a decimated social life; the closeted lesbian risks a confrontation with herself and the surrounding campus culture for which she may not yet be ready; and the "out" lesbian risks the double-barrelled abuse of homophobia and gynephobia conjoined.

Working with a student women's group means an endless, vicious circle around this issue. I have seen several generations of women's groups come and go, enter and graduate; and without fail, sooner or later, one of the leaders will come to me and announce that The Problem With the Group has finally been discovered and named: They are perceived as a bunch of lesbians. It gets you nowhere to assure them—or their detractors among the rest of the student body, the faculty, and the administration—that this perception is perennial and permanent, has accompanied every one of the group's incarnations, and is in fact endemic to women's groups everywhere. For the students wishing to make the group successful in serving the diversity of the women and men in the campus community, the problem is brand new and devastating. It is a hard lesson for them: that a group of women whose purpose is anything other than cuisine, cosmetics, or child care will sooner or later be labelled Lesbian. It is the free-floating catch-all that collects the general unexamined suspicion and fear accruing to women in groups—rightly suspect, of course, and rightly feared. The saddest byproduct of this kind of verbal harassment is that it serves the end of dividing and conquering, easily alarming heterosexual feminists into homophobic self-defense by asking them to separate themselves conclusively from lesbianism. As for the non-feminist students, they rarely come to the conclusion that homophobia is the problem. Homosexuality is the problem. If only the dirty F-word could dissociate itself from the even dirtier L-word, maybe it could make itself more appealing to such as they. How can I blame them for this thinking, when I have heard their mothers say the same thing?

And so, when the F-word raises its ugly head, I am likely to hear from them the very same thing I heard from the *New York Times*: "That's separatist. We're beyond that now." Both of which statements merit some analysis.

"We're beyond that now" says that feminist protest was a temporary, corrective deviance of a decade ago, targeting isolated, blatant pockets of discrimination. Feminism was a detour leading us all back onto the improved freeway. "We're beyond that now" also implies, as a corollary, that equity is now a matter of individual effort and behavior. "Nowadays, no woman has to be treated that way if she doesn't want to be." These daughters and sons are startlingly willing to blame the victim of sexism for her predicament—or, if given to sympathy for her, to sympathize strictly in terms of what she might do personally to correct her situation.

"That's separatist" says that Difference and Equity are at odds, that Distinctness and Concord are enemies. Feminism thus becomes what they love to call "reverse sexism." Its "separatism" is scary because they do not wish to be separate. They fight for the middle ground, the main stream—which is implicitly male, though they deny it; to them it is comprised of collective individuals doing their own thing. To introduce the gender factor is, for them, to define people as members of groups, which is, they remind me, at the root of sexism and racism. It also threatens them personally. To speak of "women" in class is not merely a matter of selective emphasis—as would be, for instance, to speak of "Americans" or of "physicians." When the men hear "women," they are being left out, excluded, "discriminated against." When the women hear "women," their responses are, I think, more diverse, more convoluted. They feel their individuality is violated; they are being stereotyped. Or they fear the vague, insidious Lesbianism of it. Or, conversely, they resist being identified with a group they see as weak, trivial, limited. They are a transitional generation, these daughters; half of them still see "women" as a source of weakness, the other half see "women" as a source of strength—but dangerous strength that will get them into trouble. More accurately, I suspect lots of them see both at once and are deeply confused.

To teach truly requires that you gird up your loins and enter the minds of your students, so that you see where they are in order that you can find them. It isn't pretty. When I consider the terrible F-word as it resonates in those heads bobbing in front of me every day, Shelley's fear of the growth swelling inside her seems hardly remarkable at all.

Coming to We

The project of feminist education, as I have come to see it, reinforces the general project of education: to help people move from the simplistic, dualistic universe to the complex universe of multiplicity and relativity in which "I" and "We" are no longer experienced as conflicting alternatives or adversaries but as complements, mutualities. A core premise of contemporary feminism has always been that the depletion of female individuality corresponds to the fragmentation of female collectivity—and, conversely, that a healthy, coherent sense of female collectivity strengthens the female "I." This re-formed I/We relation is fundamental to human development. It is a feminist issue because patriarchy systematically decimates female collectivity and individuality, and because within patriarchy these must be assiduously, concertedly reconstructed and preserved, against the odds.

For a young woman today to say "we" is an educationally healthy sign. It gives her the collective memory that brings her a regenerated "I." For her brother to hear her say "we" is also salutary, in that he sees more clearly the perimeters of his own being and learns some valuable truths about limitation and otherness which he is less than likely to learn in an academic system which teaches him that He is All, and that We is Him.

I am often struck by the willingness of white, middle-class students to hear black Americans say "we." This collective self-identification does not seem to bother them much. The truth is that the Civil Rights Movement, however limited and superficial their understanding of it, succeeded in leaving an important mark on them: They know that there is a black experience, and mostly they respect it. They may integrate this consciousness of Otherness into an Us-versus-Them mentality hardly distinct from the outright racism of their grandparents. They may use it as an excuse for ignorance: "They're different from Us." They may struggle innocently against it toward a simplistic ideal of equality: "But we're all human and all individuals are different and we should get beyond that now." They may still speak of "people" versus "black people." But at the very least, they entertain the concepts of black experience and historical institutional white racism. The feminist movement as yet has failed to get the same point about women broadly accepted.

I was startled to realize this discrepancy in the wake of the Howard Beach violence in late 1986. Watching a day full of news reports, I was struck by the ubiquity of the phrase "racial violence." It bespoke a general consensus amongst the media that violence between members of different races belongs to a special category, that it is a more significant, serious kind of violence than your run-of-the-mill street fight between white boys or black boys. If the attack in Howard Beach had been either, the rest of the country would never have heard of it. Instead, it was deemed symbolic of a larger problem. What would happen, I wondered as I watched, if the term "sexual violence" or "gender violence" were as current, as acceptable, as readily understood? What if the TV specials on "hate crimes" included rape and assault against women?

Lo and behold, shortly thereafter, the leader of the New York-based National Youth Movement, in a radio interview, pulled the issue into sharp focus for me. "If you kill someone because of his race or religion," he said, "that's a crime against society, more than if you get in an argument with your girlfriend and kill her—that's a crime against an individual."[2]

But what if that victimized Individual is perceived as part of a We?

If Shelley, who has worked for ten weeks with battered women, is ever beaten by a boyfriend or a husband, will she see the crime against her as private, domestic, individually motivated? Or will she see herself as part of the We whose acquaintance she made during her Career Development Internship?

How strange, I mused, that the consciousness of one's relation to history and to a larger whole should be perceived as narrow, more narrow than the tiny cell of Individuality.

Candidates

Though they don't know it, they come to college seeking ways out of that cell, extensions beyond themselves into the realm of human experience in which they are at once very tiny and much larger than they thought. For Shelley, that route took her to the Domestic Assault Program, to Wednesday-night meetings of the Women's Interest Group, and up the stairs to the second storey of Humphrey House. By the standards of my own life, she's a prodigy, actually. It took me much longer.

Each fall, I look out over the new crop and wonder which of them will, by the end of this academic year or early in the next, appear at my door with a question, a need like Shelley's. She is probably not the most obvious candidate.

The most obvious candidate, the one *Time* magazine would use in a cover story on Young Feminism, is pre-law or pre-business. She owns several suits when she arrives at college and acquires a couple more on a Career Development internship at General Motors or in the Attorney General's office. She is very well groomed, uses make-up carefully and conservatively, looks you straight in the eye, and speaks articulately. Her grades are excellent, as she has superior verbal and quantitative skills at once. She is much better informed about current events than her peers, and she knows about "women's issues" too. She can tell you discrimination stories. She knows what percentage of Fortune 500 executives are female, and she did her final poli sci paper on the Congressional Women's Caucus.

How can she not be a feminist? She's feminism's showroom model. She's clearly come a long way, baby. Without feminism, she'd be an impossibility. And she will do us proud: She will step off the platform at Commencement and into a junior-executive position at the World Bank, or into Harvard Law. She will publish or lecture or move up quickly, sending glowing reports to the alumni magazine. We will brag about her, maybe invite her back to receive an award. I will brag about her with the rest.

Yet if you watch her closely, listen attentively, you will notice something. Most of her friends are male. The professors of whom she is fondest are male. She has a wonderful relationship with her father. She speaks contemptuously of traditional female things. She does not often speak fondly of women; in fact, she announces in class that men have always treated her more fairly than women. In fact, she does not like women much, as a species. Women's Liberation means, to her, liberation from women, from woman-ness. She is a large, sturdy branch that shot off the trunk around 1970 and thrived. She is a stunning byproduct of the marriage of popular feminism with American individualism. Her feminism, if she uses that word (she is likely to call herself a humanist), means her right to compete in the same arena as her boyfriend, who is also primed for a stellar career.

As a senior with one remaining elective, she takes women's studies, thinking it might be worth her while to do some thinking about women, since she's moving into a male-dominated world. From Day One, she is miserable. She walks into class wearing clean blue jeans and an impeccable sweater. She sits, with her hands folded in front of her, as far as possible from the Women's Interest Group types, who arrive in overalls and "Take Back the Night" T-shirts, harem pants brought back from Foreign Study in Africa, or long cotton skirts, walking in braless with their arms around each other.

As the weeks go by, I feel sorry for her and bend over backwards to integrate her into the group, to make sure she is heard, all the time wondering if these disparate cousins on the feminist family tree can even recognize each other. In her journal she confides that she particularly despises Margo, who is into feminist spirituality and did her Senior Project on witchcraft. She tells me that Margo and her friends make her feel like a leper. Likewise, Margo despises her and in her journal calls her a travesty of feminism.

If we're extremely lucky, a moment will come—outside of class surely, late at night, while I'm home reading their attacks on each other in their journals—when they wind up in the snack bar at the same moment. One of them asks the other a nervous question about an assignment. They find themselves at a booth together. An hour later they go to the dorm room of one or the other and talk until 2 a.m. The next week their journals are full of astonishment at how similar their families are and how they hate the same guy in calculus and how they're maybe going to live together next year in Boston, when one is at Harvard Law and the other is working at the Women's Health Collective.

Usually we're not so lucky. Usually the result is a class where Jerry Falwell's arrival would be a relief.

In either case, I take refuge in a vision: Two letters arrive in my mailbox ten years hence. One tells me about coordinating services for battered women in the Boston area as the result of new federal money. The other, from Washington, tells me about co-sponsoring the bill that released the money.

Margo is a different case, but an equally obvious candidate. She, three years ago, was the obvious sixties legacy. She wore OshKoshes to freshman orientation, with a bandanna around her neck and a button reading "Keep Your Hands Off My Body!" She annoyed her freshman seminar by knowing something about Nicaragua. She was in my office by the second week of fall quarter discovering that she couldn't major in women's studies. She chose anthropology instead, with a slight, late deviation into theology in the wake of her discovery of goddess worship through a paper on witches. Margo and Shelley are friends. When Shelley agonizes with Margo about whether feminism makes you narrow, Margo sometimes talks passionately with her until two in the morning. On other days she throws a cucumber slice across the dinner table at her and says, "Oh, Shelley, get over it!"

But there is another one, harder to describe except to say that in some obscure, clear way she is not like the others. She catches my attention the first day of class. Perhaps she dresses differently or has unusual hair. Perhaps she is more articulate than the others or, if not, has more to say but can't say it. She may be the bright, troubled one. She has been assaulted, maybe, by a boyfriend or stepfather. She is bulimic, perchance. She is a gifted painter, poet, actress, deeply unsure of herself. Both Margo and the Showroom Model scare her to death.

In her case, it is struggle, not success, that leads her to feminism. Her life has not been a liberated one; on the contrary, her life has probably been one of difficult female experience. It has generated pain. This first year at college the pain will bloom into anger, and into thought.

Once, after I had confessed to a male colleague that I have a terrible time standing up to authority figures, he said, in genuine incredulity, "But you're the arch-feminist around here! I thought you were a tough cookie!" Sorry, Charlie. Tough cookies have little need to hear what feminism has to say. Tough cookies are the ones who believe that if the rest of us wimpy women would toughen up and be more like them, we wouldn't need this Women's Movement stuff. I myself am a gingerbread woman. And I can spot another one when I see her. She is that soulful girl off in the corner. Friends are very important to her. And she is likely to be utterly apolitical.

She is not seeking refuge from her problems. She is not looking for excuses. Neither is she looking for a cause or a group, though when she finds the group, this network of other women will become inseparable from feminism in her mind. What she is looking for is strength, her own strength. She is deeply womanly and she wants, though she cannot frame this want, to plumb that womanliness for its vein of vital force. She wants to locate the underground springs in herself. What will take her there may be any number of things—a teacher, a friend, a novel, a course. Her quest is deeply personal. She is the orphan daughter seeking her origins, her source.

Outstanding Debts

It is a perilous journey. We who play significant roles in it— the witches proffering apples, explaining the uses of red shoes to get home—must be acutely conscious of the danger in what we do, the potential for abuse and manipulation. She will put frightening trust in us. She will empower us beyond our wildest dreams. We owe her our most conscientious attention, for we have entered into a blood-bond with her, one that carries obligations for us.

First of all, we who translate the legacy of her foremothers owe her a feminism that is neither too easy nor too hard. It cannot be so comfy that she can use it to rationalize or escape anything, nor so congenial that it does not push her, as it constantly pushes us, beyond herself. But neither can it be so hard—rigid, single-minded, pure—that she cannot admit it into her life as her life is now. It should inform her life, not pass judgments upon it. If her goal, for instance, is to work for a pharmaceutical company whose contraceptive products have damaged women, we cannot face her with a feminism that demands that she work for a women's health collective instead, though that is what our feminism tells us. The most we can do is to give her the information that lets her know, inescapably, that such issues exist and that hers must be an examined life in its interconnection with the life and lives around it.

We owe her a sympathetic awareness of the prices she is paying along her way, having paid a few of our own. We must consider her new conflicts with her boyfriend of equal importance with her senior thesis on black women writers. We must remind ourselves daily that the difficulty of our own feminist lives is magnified manyfold in her life, that the intellectual and psychological humps we surmounted long since are looming real and large for her.

And we owe her joy. We who insist on giving her a legacy of suffering owe her the whole truth, which includes triumph and heroism of the first order. We must remind ourselves that part of her original resistance to feminism was her fear of anger and negativity. If all she gets from the troubling world we open to her is rage and depression, we have abandoned her to the wilderness. I remember a student coming to me, talking about some research on women that was yielding horrifying information, and asking, with genuine weariness, "How do you do it? How do you live with it all for years and years? How do you do this for the rest of your life?" The "you" was collective, not singular, but I had to take it as a personal question. In fact, I took it so personally—it was so pertinent to me—that for a few minutes I was speechless. I answered, finally, that one made regular, intentional celebration a part of the plan, that one found victories and paragons to honor and en-joy.

For me, occasions for celebration are probably more frequent than for a lot of working feminists, because, as Christa MacAuliffe put it, "I touch the future. I teach." Every June I get to watch them walk across the platform towards a diploma, and I remember where they began, and then I believe, if only for a half hour, in Progress, in the Future, in the Goddess, in things to which I haven't lent credence in years. They are smarter, stronger, wiser than I ever dreamed of being at twenty-one. They are going on to lead remarkable lives, valuable lives, intelligent lives, ethical lives, examined, responsible lives. And they will do so from a consciousness of themselves as women, from a We that makes them doubly wise, doubly strong, doubly beautiful. They are women to the core. They are as old as the earth, and as revolutionary.

10

Vocation

*"In an ultimate sense, I don't know
what I do in this place."*

—Dr. Martin Dysart, Equus

Vocabulary

"Job"—a piece of work.

"occupation"—from Latin, *occupare*, to seize. That which seizes or takes over one's time.

"profession"—that which one professes to the world. A job for which extensive formal academic training is required. Formerly, one "made a profession"—of faith in something.

"career"—from Latin, *carraria*, a road, which became, in French, *carriere*, a racecourse. A rapid course or swift progression; a charge at full tilt.

"vocation"—from "vox," a voice. A voicing; a calling.

Job description

profess: 1. to affirm openly; declare or claim.
2. to make a pretense of.
3. to claim skill or knowledge in.
4. to affirm belief in.
5. to receive into a religious order.
(from the Latin: to declare publicly. *pro*, forth, in public; + *fateri*, to acknowledge, confess.)

professor: a teacher of the highest rank in an institution of higher learning.

teach: 1. to impart knowledge or skill to; to give instruction to.

           2. to provide knowledge of; to instruct in.

           3. to cause to learn by example or experience.

           4. to advocate; preach. (from Middle English: *techen*, tahte.)

teacher: one who teaches; especially, a person hired by a school to teach.

Affirm, declare, claim, make a pretense of. Versus impart, provide, cause, example, experience. Austere old Latin versus grubby old Anglo-Saxon. Two verbs, the one taking an intellectual object (to profess some*thing*), the other, primarily, a human one (to teach some*one*). A friend of mine, a middle-school teacher, when asked what she teaches, responds, "I teach kids."

Poor Professor, standing up there in the highest rank in an institution of higher learning, affirming and declaring and claiming and making a pretense, before the entire world, or, for all we know, the empty air. One somehow feels he has something to defend.

Teacher, on the other hand, is very much of this earth, "hired by a school." To profess is to speak; to teach is to speak to and with someone. To profess is an act; to teach, a relationship.

Once I tried an experiment with a freshman composition class. Under the guise of a "comparison/contrast" assignment, I asked them to make two lists of connotative qualities they associated with the terms "professor" and "teacher." There was remarkable homogeneity in the lists. The images corresponded pretty closely to those offered by Webster, though the students described them slightly differently. The teacher, they told me, was someone who worked really hard, long hours and wasn't paid very well. Also, the teacher was likely to be female.

Job Qualifications

In 1986 I attended the annual convention of the Modern Language Association. The first time I had been part of that massive post-Christmas cattle auction was exactly ten years earlier, when I had been the heifer on the block. This time I was one of the buyers. We were interviewing thirteen bright particular stars to determine which of them would actually abandon the academic fast lane ("career") for the westward trek to an absurdly named college that calls itself a Teaching Institution. That is to say that while we are interested in the permanent impact the candidates might have upon literary criticism as we know it, we are still more interested in what they are going to do to their students.

We asked one brilliant young man what he considered to be the foremost attribute of a good teacher. Without a beat he replied, "An open mouth." A small silence passed and then, pressed for detail, he elaborated: A professor should not be afraid to talk. He should cure himself of guilt about the dearth of discussion or student participation in his classroom. He is there because of his expertise; the students want and need what he knows. He should let 'em have it.

I felt rather sorry for this guy; clearly, he had had a bad year as a graduate instructor of composition or a T.A. in World Lit.

Another of our baker's dozen was a brilliant young woman to whom we posed the same question. She thought a bit and then said, in the gentle, tentative voice that passes for insecurity among those who don't really attend to women's speech, that she thought a teacher ought to be "a sort of midwife of ideas?" The question mark at the end was too perfect.

I was struck by her metaphor. Only a month earlier I had been reading what was then a brand-new study of female epistemology, *Women's Ways of Knowing*, in which female learners are classified according to degrees of "voice." At one point the authors discuss Paolo Freire's concept of the "banker-teacher," who sees his role as filling the students up with his store of knowledge. Their research indicates that this pedagogical style is uncongenial and even destructive to women's learning process. This interested me, because I had always been uncomfortable conceptualizing what I do in this way, yet I constantly heard colleagues describing their work as essentially that of intellectual depositors.

> Many women expressed—some firmly, some shakily—that they possessed latent knowledge. The kind of teacher they praised and the kind for which they yearned was the one who would help them articulate and expand their latent knowledge—a midwife-teacher Midwife-teachers are the opposite of banker-teachers. While the bankers deposit something in the learner's head, the midwives draw it out.[1] To put something in, rather like insemination. To draw something out, for which a synonym is "to educe"—to educate. "One who would help them articulate"—that is, one who provides a voice; one who speaks for them and with them in order that they might speak for themselves, learn what they know, bring forth what is in them, achieve a voice[1]

Midwives should not be sentimentalized. Midwives neither were nor are romantic. They were and are skilled, trained professionals.

They facilitate a great change, enormous movement. The midwife-teacher is no security blanket—usually quite the contrary. She is an authority. She too has an open mouth. But she gives information as food, to be digested as fuel. And she speaks with a mind to the dynamics of voice.

A thought struck me and I asked our candidate, "Is it a matter of 'teacher' versus 'professor'?"

She thought again, smiled, and said, "Yes. I think it is."

The Wilderness, Answering

We are *in loco parentis*. We try to talk our way out of this; we say we are teaching the students to be our colleagues; we say we are fellow learners; we say we are partners in education; we say we are mentors, intellectual models, friends. It may be true, all of it. But we are also inescapably Mom and Dad. We who are Mom—and we who are uncomfortable as Dad—feel it most. Especially when we speak the mother tongue, here in this shrine of the father tongue.

"The essential gesture of the father tongue," writes Ursula Le Guin,

> is not reasoning but distancing—making a gap, a space, between the subject or self and the object or other. Enormous energy is generated by that rending, that forcing of a gap between Man and the World.... The father tongue is spoken from above. It goes one way. No answer is expected, or heard.[2]

It is, in short, professorial. It is the language that, in the west, has created knowledge as we understand it, has defined the enterprise of education, and has drawn the outlines of academe. It is the language that commands attention in faculty meetings.

It is dualistic, not only in its essential project of distancing, but in its dependence upon another tongue, a mother tongue, for its survival. It initially defined itself and continues to define itself against its opposite, its enemy, the dark yin to its clear white yang:

> The mother tongue, spoken or written, expects an answer. It is conversation, a word the root of which means "turning together." The mother tongue is language not as mere communication but as relation, relationship. It connects. . . Its power is not in dividing but in binding, not in distancing but in uniting.[3]

It is "a language always on the verge of silence and often on the verge of song."[4] But always on the verge. It is a renegade, outlaw language in academe. It is obscenity. It defies basic academic principles. It subverts the very nature of knowing as knowing is understood. It gets you nowhere in faculty meetings.

It is, Le Guin reminds us, the first language we heard, the language of our infancy, male or female. It is our natural tongue. Therefore, it is the language we are supposed to outgrow. We learn the father tongue to prove we have outgrown the mother tongue. We who are mothers rather than fathers work extra hard to learn it, for we have to prove we are not what we are. And our students, even at eighteen, know all about it. They may not yet be proficients in the father tongue, but they know it as the language they are here to learn. When Teacher speaks Mother Tongue instead, they are as likely as their Fathers to recoil, to suspect, to sneer, to think "not serious, not important."

Even as I write this, and often as I speak Mother Tongue in class, I hear the father tongue, so deeply embedded in me that I often think it is my own. It cavils, it analyzes, it takes exception, it accuses. "All the time I wrote the book," says Susan Griffin of *Woman and Nature*, "the patriarchal voice was in me, whispering to me . . . that I had no proof for any of my writing, that I was wildly in error, that the vision I had . . . was absurd."[5] To speak on, listening intently to your own voice despite the persistent drone of that other voice is truly to cry out of the wilderness—and to cry from and for the wilderness. To attend to your vocation.

This first, primal language is Wilderness. The father tongue is Pioneer, naming, taming, measuring, controlling, conquering Wilderness. What, in fact, is happening when Mother Tongue is spoken in academe?

"What is happening here," says Le Guin, "is that the wilderness is answering."[6]

Called Out of Your Name

At Kalamazoo, they use "Doctor." Coming from institutions where "Professor" or "Mr./Miss/Mrs./Ms." is the norm, you are repeatedly jolted when you hear yourself called "Doctor." Maybe it's a delightful shock: You've made it. Maybe it's a disconcerting or downright uncomfortable shock: Who do they think you are? If you're female, it's probably the latter.

You haven't thought much about what you will be called by your students, but this suddenly becomes a real and pressing issue. Perhaps you think "Doctor" hopelessly pretentious. Will you go to Professor? But that's not the coin of the realm here, and it feels itchy. What did you call Them when you were student? You called most of Them "Mr." until, as a senior major, you crossed that wonderful threshold where one of the junior faculty said, "Hey, call me Tom."

You notice that some of them are making the decision for themselves and calling you "Miss" or "Mrs." These commonalities suddenly sound strange, even absurd to you. The sheer irrelevance of your marital status strikes you as worth making a small deal about. But you notice that when they ask if it's one or the other and you respond, "It's Ms.," they either are embarrassed or start drawing conclusions about you, looking scared, or hostile, or mocking. "Oh, *Ms. Excuse* me." You see bras burning wildly behind their eyes.

You also notice that they do not make this distinction with your colleague Dennis, who is unfailingly "Dr. Vaughan." You and he are introduced by a student to her father one Parents' Weekend as follows: "Dad, this is Dr. Vaughan. And this is Gail." This really pisses you off. And then you realize with a jolt that you're getting awfully concerned with superficialities, aren't you, and you've never known yourself to fret so about hierarchies and authority and titles. What's happening to you?

Toughen up, you tell yourself. Insist on Doctor. Yet when you say the word to yourself, you see a clear image: beard, jacket with elbow patches, pipe, rumpled shirt, wool tie. No way in your wildest dreams are you ever going to wake up looking like Him.

After a while you give up and go back to basics: "Please call me Gail." Some of the kids love it, instantly loosen and warm up. Others are nervous for a while. Some few, still enjoying the high school mindset whereby the object of the game is to shore up whatever power you can against the Teacher, take it as license. Regardless, you decide you will have to draw your authority from something other than your title.

The Voice of Authority

If their voices surprise and confuse you, no less does your own.

Half the time, in those first months, you feel like a foreigner, you do not speak the language. You become intensely aware of vocal blunders—the moments when your voice sounds terribly high amongst a chorus of baritones and tenors; when you have laughed too loudly, too freely; when you have sounded suddenly shrill, emotional in a committee meeting; when you mentally replay a meeting with the provost and it sounds like a little girl talking to her father; when you have confessed your classroom anxieties to the department chair and subsequently realize how patronizing he sounded as you left, how delighted to learn that you were struggling.

You find yourself listening intently as an immigrant does to learn the lingua franca: High Father Tongue. Your gift for mimicry deepens in those first years, and you learn which voice goes with which setting. In particular, you learn to do Blase, Disinterested Intellectual, Cynical Questioner, and Rational Proponent to perfection. Rational Adversary you still struggle with; when you're fighting, your vocal cords tend still to tighten, so that you sound, god help you, Emotional.

You become vocally nimble beyond your wildest dreams: You can switch instantly from the Classroom Voice to the Office Voice to the Committee Voice to the Faculty Meeting Voice; from the Motherly to the Sisterly to the Collegial—that is, the Brotherly. You speak to the smart-ass from the comp class in one tone, to the sweetheart from the novel class in entirely another. And you're surprised by your own relief when you are in a roomful of female voices.

Some voices you decide not to master. You walk into a department office and hear a colleague speaking to the secretary as if she were a favorite dog. You recall that just yesterday, when you called this number and identified yourself, her voice took on shades of deference and eagerness to please that made you squirm in your chair. In such conversations, you sometimes call upon the old female modes of speech—the interrogatory endings, the apologies, the underscoring of your own ignorance and ineptness—in order to demote yourself, to assure her that you're female too.

One of the first shocks of the new is the power of the professorial voice, including even your own. Suddenly, in the space of a month or two, you seem to have come to own the voice toward which you have been striving for seventeen years. It is yours. When you speak in class, forty heads dip, forty hands go for the pen, especially if you have uttered the word "exam" or "assignment." One negative word turns out to have haunted a young soul for weeks. One positive word redeems that same soul, at least for a few days. One word from you and a student's proposed Senior Project is certified Legitimate and funded. A letter from you is at least one significant factor in whether he will attend law school or not. One sentence of support and her Senior Project is granted Honors and she thus has Honors in English at graduation. One private word to the registrar and he is admitted to an overbooked course. On your word she is exempt from the writing requirement.

It is not nearly as much fun as you assumed it was as a student, this vocal power. In fact, it is somewhat frightening. No, it is very frightening. You begin to see what havoc you could wreak. Remember Mr. Margolis, who wrote at the end of one of your papers that your writing was "clear as a bell"? Remember how you heard that very bell in your head for months afterward? What if he had said you really ought to consider another major?

The campus paper comes out one Thursday and you are chagrined to see the women's basketball team termed the "Lady Hornets." You consider a letter to the editor and decide against it; faculty letters of complaint send the whole beleaguered staff into nervous collapse. So you write a private letter to the editor, who is a friend of yours, and you make sure the tone is gentle and jesting. She rushes in to assure you that it was a mistake on the part of a new sports editor rather than policy. You laugh about it together. Next edition: an editorial by someone on the staff, attacking faculty censorship of the paper. It appears that the sports editor has sworn to abandon journalism for good as a result of a letter of complaint from an unnamed "feminist in the English Department." You find out who this person is whose career you have just torpedoed, and you realize you have never laid eyes on him.

You become highly attuned to the power of voices. A woman student comes to see you, distraught. Dr. X has said her idea for a Senior Project is "not really very serious." You, in fact, find her idea rather intriguing, and you spend half an hour convincing her that it is, and another half suggesting how she might go about exploring it further. When she leaves, smiling, full of thanks, you know that you have exerted considerable power. You are amazed that you can do it. You are disturbed that you have had to do it.

Another woman creeps in and closes the door. Dr. Y has said she might have problems in her chosen field because she "exudes a sexuality" that will be troublesome for male co-workers. Is it true? Should she think about other options?

Does your voice stand a chance against those of X and Y?

The phone rings at eleven one night, and it is a student who graduated two years earlier. "Remember me?" she asks, tentatively. She is about to start applying to graduate schools in philosophy. You talk with her aimlessly about this for fifteen minutes or so, in a fog as to why she has called you. Finally she unwraps the real problem: She finds herself unaccountably interested in finding out which programs have women's studies emphases, and how many woman there are on the faculty. She cannot even articulate why this is suddenly important to her; she knows only that it is important. Her boyfriend thinks she's nuts. Clearly, part of her is in agreement. Forty-five minutes later, she signs off: "Oh, thanks so much. I'm really sorry to have bothered you with this, but I just didn't know who else to call. I just wanted to hear you say that. I just needed to hear it from somebody, I guess."

You are surprised to discover how often this is the case, how often all they need and want from you is to hear you say it. What that means is that something in them is saying it, and they need the close harmony of another, external, more authoritative voice.

You are even more surprised to discover that it is yours, that voice that they need. You, who have never felt like you had much authority or even the right to much, hear yourself speaking in that voice, firmly and easily. Because they need it, you have it.

And finally, you are amazed to hear yourself saying, with perfect confidence, things you yourself have needed to believe all your life.

When one true voice calls and another responds, that is a vocation.

Name Calling

Often I have begun my Literature of Women class with a one-page gem of a story by Ursula Le Guin called "She Unnames Them." Eve, significantly unnamed throughout, recounts her process of releasing the earth's creatures from the names Adam imposed on them. She watches them fly, swim, crawl, run away to freedom, discussing their future identities. Finally, she tells her preoccupied mate that she is on her way out too, leaving behind the keys to the garden and her own name.

It's a formidable fable of the work of the female writer, this story. But it is only In the Beginning. The problem of clearing the slate is a real one. The problem of inscribing it with our own hands is another. Creation cannot go nameless.

An eighteen-year-old comes to college equipped with a whole store of names, expecting it to be richly augmented. A professor is first and foremost a giver of names. As noblemen used to have certain offices "in their gift," so the professoriat has in its gift the names by which academe constructs knowledge, divides it into compartments, determines how knowledge is obtained and what knowledge is obtainable and what knowledge is important enough to obtain.

The feminist teacher is primarily an unnamer and a renamer. This puts her or him in steady conflict with the lingua franca, and often with the student body, who do not like to be told that the names by which they know reality are false.

Several years back the campus paper reviewed the Theatre Department production of Pinter's *The Birthday Party*. The reviewer commented on one performance as follows: "Jane Schaeffer was most convincing in her portrayal of the slut."

I was at my typewriter within hours. The reviewer, whom I knew, wrote me a long personal reply, protesting that he had meant no insult. *He* was not asserting that she was a slut; that was merely the role she had played—and played extremely well.

In other words, for him, the verbal category "slut" had intrinsic validity. It was objectively real. I went to the typewriter again, addressing this interesting philosophical point. But he continued to believe that the issue was the feelings of the actress involved. We were at such cross purposes that significant communication was impossible. How was I to deconstruct his entire culture, especially when the local newspaper joined forces against me by using exactly the same word in assessing—again in glowing terms—Jane's performance? Such a simple little four-letter Anglo-Saxon word, and I couldn't strip it away and send it flying into the linguistic dumpster.

As it happened, the feelings of the actress provided another dimension of this, to me, critical educational moment. After both reviews were out, she came to see me, looking defeated. "No matter what I do onstage, I'm a slut. Everybody's been telling me I'm supposed to be really excited about two positive reviews. Then why do I feel like shit?"

We talked for a long time, and as she walked out, I thought to myself, This is what it means, Teaching English. This is what I do. My vocation.

Hearing Voices

When we say that someone "has a voice" in some body or proceeding, we mean not that this person speaks, but that this person is heard. The individual voice is thus a function of a collectivity, empowered by its context. True, its inherent strength—the intelligence and artistry of its owner—can influence its reception. But without the audience's willingness to legitimize it, all the intelligence and artistry in the world can dissipate in the deaf air.

The outcry against the public female voice in the last century was the reaction of an audience that had not empowered such a voice. The female voice was heretical in its arrogance, in the truest sense: That is, it arrogated significance, inspiration, the right to be.

One of the most interesting lessons in the history of the voice is how often the voiceless describe their experience of voice as collective or collaborative, rather than discretely individual. This is difficult to understand for those of us nourished on the white, western, male notion of "originality." Yet those who come to voice against the weight of this tradition, or from other traditions, frequently understand voice as *something speaking through them* or as *speaking on behalf of someone else.* Whether this conception is the cause or the product of the powerful experience of voice is moot.

Today, women of color often speak of their art and their role as "creators" by means of the metaphor of the medium through which other forces speak—the voice of a divine power, the lost voices of the silenced ancestors. Alice Walker's essay "Writing *The Color Purple*"[7] is the best example I know. As Walker recounts her long, frustrating effort to enable her characters to speak through her, one comes to understand why she signs herself, at the close of the novel, "A. W., author and medium," and why she thanks "everybody for coming."[8] Of the tales comprising her stunning first novel, *The Joy Luck Club*, Amy Tan says, "It was like people would tell me the stories, and I would write them down as fast as I could."[9]

In such a tradition, writing—the voice on paper—is an act of service and collaboration, rather than a solipsistic, masturbatory assertion. Among people to whom voice was forcibly denied, among whom active, steady, careful collaboration was necessary in order to enable communication to take place, this conception should not be surprising. Nor should it be surprising that to women activists and preachers, voice should have come literally as *inspiration*: something breathing into them, through them, out of them to others.

One does not merely open one's mouth and speak. It is not so simple. First, there is convergence. Forces without meet forces within. Past voices meet the present for the sake of the future. Past and present silences demand utterance. The individual voice arches to meet the willingness of others to hear it—not necessarily to hear it happily, or to agree with it, but to hear it. Collective power informs individual power.

Whenever a voice speaks or sings, many voices are at work. One hears voices, like other witches, saints, crazies. One also hears the silences of those past or present for whom one must speak. One hears the implied voice of the audience, saying yes. And one speaks.

When you teach, and especially when you teach language, literature, writing, it is largely a matter of voice. When you teach consciously as a woman, the matter is urgent—a vocation.

Teaching Language

"I think of myself," says Adrienne Rich, "as a teacher of language:"

> that is, someone for whom language has implied freedom, who is
> trying to aid others to free themselves through the written (and
> spoken) word, and above all through learning to write (and speak) it
> for themselves. I cannot know for them what it is they need to free,
> or what words they need to write (or speak); I can only try with them
> to get an approximation of the story they have to tell.[10]

The problem is that so many of them think they have no story to
tell.

I have frequently taught courses in autobiography, and when
asked to write their lives, they not only say that nothing has happened
to them, but cannot conceive any shape in their stories. I have taught
composition more often than any other course, and their invariable
response, when asked their biggest writing problem, is "thinking up
things to say," as if eighteen years of living left them blank, vacant.

In literature courses "the story they have to tell" is a little more
complex, for it is a story told through and with another story, the
author's story. The vocal interplay in a literature course is very convoluted, very hard to orchestrate successfully. Who is the authority in a
Shakespeare course? There is first the voice of the author, preeminent,
predominant. It is difficult to achieve the kind of deference to the
author's voice—the willing suspension of self—that will allow entry
into the author's world and thus yield genuine understanding without
seeming to ask an unhealthy suppression of the authentic individual
voice—the very kind of self-obliteration that creates the Generic
Reader I was in 1972. It is also difficult to establish a Teacher Voice that
at once serves and critiques both the Author Voice and the Student
Voice(s). And for the average student, it is difficult not to fall back on
a position of silence, to let those two mighty authoritative voices speak
through you, like the voice of the ventriloquist filtered through the
dummy's moving jaw.

And in a women's studies course, whatever the "subject matter,"
the problem of voice is central. When I go to conferences where
feminism is spoken, I am often frustrated by the discourse surrounding
feminist pedagogy. It usually paints a picture of a blissful academic
Herland whose inhabitants are magically freed from silence, literal and
figurative. On the contrary. I submit that a women's studies classroom
is infiltrated by weirder silences than any other. I submit that the

potential for chaos and cacophony is greater than in your basic Introduction to the Novel. To speak *as a woman* is, for most young women (and perhaps for most not-so-young women), unnatural, frightening, or just confusing, every bit as much as it may also be liberating, exciting, and fun.

I look forward to my annual spring interdisciplinary women's studies seminar rather as a runner must anticipate the Boston Marathon: It's what I do and I love it, but it's going to hurt like hell, and round about Mile 16 I am going to hit The Wall and wonder what madness possessed me when I signed on for this. One year the class sort of tacitly decided that to speak as women meant to chat about anything that crossed their minds, and only after three days or so of assigning Wollstonecraft and Daly and hearing about boyfriends and moms did I throw feminist principles to the wind, adopt my authoritative voice, and suggest that we get serious. Another year the extracurricular sociosexual relationships of a large and incestuous portion of the class became such a throbbing subtext that I was weeping in the office afterward. Still another year, having realized the fruitlessness of conducting a discussion with people who considered the reading assignments optional, I failed to show up for class one day, leaving instead a xeroxed letter for each member of the class, instructing them, in short, to get their shit together and then to let me know what the course was going to be about.

And then there was the year we began with Gerda Lerner's essay "The Challenges of Women's History." I quickly discerned the outlines of a classic pedagogical problem: the one where you suddenly realize you've been operating on some fairly basic assumptions not shared by the students. In the first place, according to my class, history was history; how could one rewrite it without falsifying it? This took me aback, but only briefly. I came back like a pro: What about the untold experience of women? If we add that into the pot, doesn't the nature of the stew change? And then they hit me with the biggie: We can't add it to the pot, because we can't talk about women as a group.

We can't?

Then what in the name of Simone de Beauvoir are we doing here?

And what were you thinking when you enrolled in something called "Women's Studies 600"?

So I came to class the next day and announced, "We have a problem." If you are correct that we can't talk about women as a group, I said, then we have no course. So what shall we do for the next nine and a half weeks? And, believe it or not, we proceeded from there.

It was a conceptual problem, of course, and one that every feminist educator has addressed many times. It was a more than legitimate issue, too; they were questioning the premises of the course and the uniformity of women's experience, a very healthy sign. But it was more than a conceptual problem; it was a critical issue of identity for each of them. It was just as personal and every bit as political as it could be. The fact, and it was patently clear to me, was that they enrolled in the course because they were dying to talk about women as women, but they were also frightened, confused, and even guilty when they attempted to do so, for to do so was to undermine the entire substructure of fifteen or more years of education.

In moments such as these, when the voices of the classroom—Teacher, Student, Students, Author—are at such odds, one struggles for vocation. One strains to hear clear voices clearly. The Devil sits on one's shoulder, reminding one that this noise will stop if one just exerts one's professorial voice. It is bloody hard to resist this temptation, to opt instead to talk together through the dissonance.

At moments such as these, one does well to call up other moments. For instance, remember the day thirteen white women filed in, having read fifty pages of nineteenth-century black women's reminiscences—of rape and lynching, hiding in trees to listen to the white folks tell news of the War, seeing children sold away, selling pies to found colleges, scrubbing floors to clothe children? Remember the looks on their faces? The sorrow and respect and amazement in their voices? Remember how you sat back, quiet, knowing that they had heard with pristine clarity some voices they had never heard before, and hearing them speak so beautifully in response?

But even here there is a disturbing silence to your right. One woman is totally silent for the full hour, and the day after, and the day after that. Finally you ask her to come see you. She tells you that she has never experienced anything like this before, but these readings feel like lead in her soul. She cannot make herself talk about such suffering. Its enormity clogs her throat, renders her silent. Is this an eloquent silence, the silence of humility and respect? No. This is the dead silence of despair and futility.

You, as a teacher, have likewise never experienced anything like this before. You ask her to think about the triumph, the beauty, the power in these testimonies, as well as the horror. You remind her that these women survived to voice their lives, and that we give them voice by speaking about them in class. You ask her to think about her class journal as a means to give voice to her own silence. And as she walks out, you think: The truth does not immediately set you free after all. It sometimes leaves you speechless. Education can be unspeakable.

The Unspeakable

Once upon a summer, we were finishing up *The Color Purple* in Lit of Women. We had one half-hour left. We had already extended our discussion of the book by a couple days, and we really had to move on. I asked the class at large—and it was large—if they were satisfied by the ending of the novel. Several people immediately spoke up to say that they saw Celie's rebirth as incomplete. In a really full recovery from the initial nightmare of her life, they said, she would accept Albert's proposal of remarriage. But Celie declines rather firmly, avowing that she "still don't like frogs."[11] This bothered them. This seemed hostile to them. It indicated, they said, that Celie had not really "gotten over" her antipathy to men, and thus her flowering was not complete.

Terrific discussion erupted. Some students argued that such a romantic resolution would be unrealistic in so gritty a book. Celie, they said, has been through too much at Albert's hands to kiss and make up with him, however transformed he may be. Others said that Celie ought to stay single, within the bosom of her rediscovered family; that was the thrust of the novel, to them. Still others believed that the non-sexual amity between Celie and Albert was accomplishment enough, an achievement that would be adulterated by sexuality or romance.

As this wonderful interchange progressed, I felt an obscure uneasiness. Then I realized that one name was not being voiced at all: Shug Avery's. And I also heard a silence, down to my left, where four lesbian women were sitting.

Now, *The Color Purple* is a most subversive novel. It makes a homosexual relationship so inescapably, irrefutably superior to any heterosexual choice, so absolutely healthy, vital, and liberating, that only the most rigid of homophobes can possibly resist it. Although genitals appear specifically and prominently in its pages, it is so little about genital sexuality that the issue is virtually moot. For this reason, however, the novel can be dangerous. You can, in fact, get away with teaching *The Color Purple* without ever mentioning the L-word. I had, I realized, just done so. Acceptance had slid into avoidance.

I was actually a little frightened to raise the issue, as I had initially been to teach the book the first time. This was the eighties. Who knew who sat out there in my classroom—what fundamentalist, what agent for Accuracy in Academe, what child of a trustee? Yet there was Shug, standing apart in all her glory, leaning against the wall, smiling sardonically. And there sat Annie, Liz, Tricia, and Sean, silent, watching me.

The hour was nearing its close when I let my voice arc out over the others. "I think we might be ignoring something important." The class went still. "The fact is that Celie cares for Albert but is in love with Shug. She has chosen another woman to love. If we make her victory contingent upon her choosing a man, I think we're missing the point." Silence. And the class ended.

Down to the front flew a woman sitting up in back, her eyes wide. Patty was extremely intelligent and articulate, an avid class participant. "Thank you!" she said. "I *never* thought of that, what you said! I really didn't. That she *chose* another woman. Wow!"

The room cleared slowly, as I dealt with questions, requests for appointments, problems. I noticed the four on my left, still seated, waiting. When we were alone, Annie came up. "We just want to say thanks," she smiled. "We were sitting there listening and wondering if anybody was going to say it or would we have to do it, and I was trying to get up the nerve, and you saved us." We both laughed.

Walking back down the hill to the office, I contemplated once more the mysteries of voice. What I had just said was, for me, relatively easy. I hadn't said it earlier because, again, I had assumed until those final moments that it was understood. But clearly not— not by Patty, one of the brightest in the bunch. It had never occurred to her that a woman might choose another woman. Perhaps on the part of other students it was understood on some level. But perhaps that isn't enough, if they weren't willing to say it. It needed voice, the way people need voice, to give it presence, weight. It cost me nothing to say it, at most perhaps a small ripple along the student grapevine. Yet for that quartet on my left who waited patiently until the room cleared even to speak to me about it, the statement I had made would have entailed considerable risk on our small campus. Annie was a rising senior English major, an A student, a woman with many and diverse friends and campus involvements, and a woman who was pretty completely out as a lesbian. Yet—or because of that, because of the focus she would take— even she was hesitant to make a simple statement of truth about a novel. For that moment, she had been without voice.

When I spoke, I saw myself as speaking for—that is, on behalf of—Shug and Celie and Alice (just as Alice saw herself as speaking for them). I also saw myself as speaking for—that is, for the benefit of—those in the class who were oblivious to the truth I spoke, willfully or not. For Patty, with her incomplete $10,000-per-year education. I had not realized that I was speaking for Annie, for Liz and Tricia and Sean. Annie had made it her business to tell me so.

I have felt most easy with the terrible power of the Professorial Voice at moments like these, when students tell me I have given voice to them—to something they wished to say, didn't know how to say, or just didn't know.

Teachers have always been voices for culture, passing on accumulated knowledge. Academe thus amounts to oral history. If in thinking of oneself as a voice a teacher has in mind a sort of funnel through which culture transmits itself into the waiting student-shaped bottle—or, conversely, as a megaphone through which culture spreads to the little pitchers with big ears—then one's task is relatively simple. If, however, one sees oneself as inescapably changing the story one passes on; if one sees oneself in a problematic, ironic relation to that story as its narrator; if one cannot tell the story without disrupting it—then in that case, one's vocation is at once more difficult, more dangerous, and much more interesting.

For me, acting as a voice for Alice Walker and William Shakespeare, for nameless black slaves and white prostitutes, for Annie and Patty and others who "just needed to hear me say it," has been my means of finding my own voice. As often as I give the call and the students respond, the roles are reversed.

Adrienne Rich, remembering teachers who made a difference, speaks of those

> *who gave you the books*
> *who let you know you were not*
> *alone   showed you the twist*
> *of old strands   raffia, hemp or silk*
> *saying: this belongs to you   you have the right*
> *you belong to the song*
> *of your mothers and fathers   You have a people*[12]

A vocation: a song in many voices.

Part Three

FIRST PERSON . . . SINGULAR

As the metaphor of voice has moved to the center of feminist theory in the past decade, so it has moved to the center of my life as a teacher, a learner, and, to my amazement, a public speaker. Coming to terms with my public voice has been both catalyst in and product of my ongoing thinking about women, teaching, writing, and learning. When Carol Gilligan and then, subsequently, the revolutionary Women's Ways of Knowing *described female development in terms of voice, it came to me not as a new perspective but as the confirmation of something I had been discovering on my own, in the classroom, in the office, and in the chapel on Fridays.*

What follows are public words, most of them spoken in front of Stetson Chapel at Kalamazoo College on Friday morning.

*I first took the podium on a morning in July of 1983. I was astonished to be there, recalcitrant as I had been for my first six years at Kalamazoo even to think about myself in the role of "preacher." Thinking back on what brought me there, I realize that I was driven by two forces often cited in accounts of women who have adopted the public voice: First, there was something that wanted voice, rather than an individual desire to speak. And second, I felt I was speaking for others beside myself. I had been hearing voices and was offering myself as a conduit. The voices came, first, from a novel that had taken me by storm—*The Color Purple, *which then was a fairly new phenomenon, unsullied by cinema or charges of male-bashing. Second, the voices came from the classroom in which I had been exploring the book with some fifty students who found themselves as overwhelmed as I by the novel—which is, ultimately, an account of a woman's passage from silence to voice.*

11

A Purple Creature

July 29, 1983

The Invocation

God made a little Gentian—
It tried—to be a Rose—
And failed—and all the Summer laughed—
But just before the Snows
There rose a Purple Creature—
That ravished all the Hill—
And Summer hid her Forehead—
and Mockery—was still—
The Frosts were her condition—
The Tyrian would not come
Until the North—invoke it—
Creator—Shall I—bloom?
                    —Emily Dickinson

You may have heard of the book which lies at the center of my remarks this morning, *The Color Purple*, a novel by Alice Walker. Since it appeared last year, it has been gathering all kinds of kudos, including, most recently, a Pulitzer Prize in fiction. I picked it up at a friend's home in Richmond, Indiana, in February, and it made me a lousy guest. It is one of those books that take one by storm, leaving one transfixed and the world transformed. It is one of those books that remind me why I loved books in the first place and why I chose this profession.

I gather it has had a similar effect on most of my students in Literature of Women this summer. I have detected something of the passionate involvement, the willingness to be moved, in the fullest sense, that warms the cockles of the English teacher's heart. It has been wonderful to watch.

And a little amazing, too. My class consists mostly of white, middle-class Kalamazoo College folks, and *The Color Purple* is the story of what Jesus called "the least of these": a poor, black woman in rural Georgia sometime in the early part of this century. Her name is Celie, and her life is a perfect litany of oppression: illiteracy, rape, brutality, loss after loss, and the terrible numbness that is the human spirit's defense against too much pain. Her abusive husband, Albert, defines what Celie amounts to in the accounts of the world: "Look at you. You black, you pore, you ugly, you a woman. Goddam, . . . you nothing at all."[1]

The novel, written in the form of Celie's letters to God and to her lost sister, Nettie, is the story of Celie's coming to humanity from "nothing at all." In the process, other metamorphoses occur, including that of her monstrous husband. I remember that one day in class I said that the thing I found so moving, so astonishing in the novel was its belief in the human capacity for change. Around me I saw various heads nodding vigorously. I found myself, to my utter surprise, using the word "miracle."

In our discussion groups, from which I am discreetly absent, I gather there was talk of the credibility of the enormous changes of which the characters find themselves capable. But the tone of these discussions seems to have been not the predictable cynicism but rather a sort of wistful hopefulness, a desire to believe. Alice Walker's faith —and I use the word carefully—is contagious, compelling. Literature is like that. We all know it's a pack of lies, and we all believe every word. It's really quite insidious. No wonder various churches have historically condemned it as the devil's work; they know a powerful rival when they see one.

Always ready to leap upon an opportunity, I asked the class, in the form of paper topics and journal assignments, to think about how these changes might be explained, to examine the forces which, according to Walker, seem to catalyze or foster change in people.

I got a wondrous spectrum of answers.

Many said it was love. Celie meets Albert's mistress, the infamous Shug Avery, who is everything Celie is not—beautiful, smart, sexy, talented, and above all powerful. Instead of despising her as a threat, which according to certain hallowed myths about women she really ought to do, Celie falls completely in love. And she is loved in return —for the first time in her life since her sister vanished. And it is quite a love, different from our usual definitions. It is a brave, challenging, supportive love, one which is willing to fight battles, take risks, sacrifice and persist. There is nothing passive about it. Above all, it is a love rooted firmly in the ability to see the heroism, the beauty in the loved one, and dedicated to helping that hidden magnificence find its voice. For those of us who often cannot believe in ourselves, sometimes someone else must do the believing for a while. And that is the love big enough to fuel us to become what we truly are.

Others in the class said it was anger that precipitated change. At a point where Celie has scraped together enough of a self to speak to her husband in her own voice, she delivers a bone-chilling curse: "Until you do right by me, everything you touch will crumble. Until you do right by me, everything you even dream about will fail."[2]. This anger is the very first thing Celie has ever been able to claim as her own, and it is the beginning of everything else. After she curses Albert, he responds with that miserable description of her which I quoted earlier. She muses on it in a letter to her sister: "I'm pore, I'm black, I may be ugly and can't cook, a voice say to everything listening. But I'm here."[3] She has never before known that miraculous fact, that she is here. My students explained to me that to be angry, one must know that there is a self which has been violated. It is a paradox that I think we all mulled over: that anger, which we so often think of as the antithesis and enemy of love, may in fact be its cohort, the second necessary element in the synergy of human change. It is fashionable now to speak very respectfully of anger. Anger is "in." But it seems to me that whenever I see it, it is followed closely by apologies and attempts to explain it away. How much of our power do we diminish when we deny our own anger or another's?

Celie's bitter curse defines yet another point at which change can occur: atonement, the act of reparation, of "doing right by" those who have been wronged. *Atonement* means exactly what it says: the act of making ourselves *at one* with those we have wounded, with ourselves, with the universe. Both Celie and Albert enact this ritual at different points in the novel, and both their miserable lives turn in another direction at that moment.

Albert's son marries an Amazon named Sophia, but having learned from his father's example what a husband is supposed to be to a wife, Harpo attempts to turn Sophia into a copy of Celie—doglike and dumb. When Sophia fights back, he asks Celie for help, and she, in a moment of terrible capitulation to the tyranny of the way things are, advises him to beat her. For a while afterward, she cannot sleep, her soul cannot rest. Then Sophia turns up at her door, demanding an explanation of this betrayal. Why did Celie say such a thing? And Celie suddenly understands: "I say it cause I'm a fool," she says. "I say it cause I'm jealous of you. I say it cause you do what I can't." "What that?" asks Sophia, and Celie answers: "Fight."[4] At that moment the overlay of false enmity between the two women dissipates and their natural alliance emerges. Having said that she wishes she could fight, Celie begins then to know the fighter in herself. But first comes the act of atonement, a long talk with Harpo about the insanity of beating the woman whom, in fact, he married for her strength and spirit.

Albert makes a similar atonement. For decades he keeps from Celie the letters from her sister, attempting to break the only human bond in Celie's life. This ultimate violation precipitates Celie's flight with Shug. Alone now, Albert has no one to abuse but himself. He undergoes a dark night of the soul, in which we recall Shug's response when Celie asks her what causes people to find God: "Sorrow, Lord. Feelin' like shit."[5] It is that nadir at which a spirit either succumbs finally, or turns upward. When Celie returns, Albert is cleaning his house, planting flowers, being kind to people. Amazed, she asks Sophia, "What make him pull through?" Sophia recounts the story, including a night when Albert was discovered sleeping in the arms of his estranged son, Harpo, another of his victims. So love and terrible aloneness, ironic partners, have worked their changes on Albert. But atonement, says Sophia, was the real turning point: "Harpo made him send you the rest of your sister's letters. Right after that he start to improve. You know meanness kill . . ."[6]

If meanness kills—that is, if there are modes of action and feeling which dehumanize and diminish us — then there are others which rehumanize and augment us, making us more than we thought we could be. Some of my students—perhaps with some small prompting from me—saw the source of change in the novel in the variegated forms of creativity which the characters discover. At the dramatic moment when Celie finds herself standing behind Albert's chair with an open razor in her hand, Shug convinces her to start sewing, using a sharp implement creatively rather than destructively. Celie begins making pants, slowly at first, then furiously, passionately, in wild colors, including, of course, purple. As for the other characters: Shug is a singer, and her art is essential to the spirit she sustains. So is Harpo's lover, known as Squeak, and as she finds her own voice, she demands her own name, Mary Agnes. Meanwhile, Harpo at long last grows comfortable with his love of cooking and stops beating women. Albert has his flowers and finally allows Celie to teach him to sew, whereupon he begins to make shirts to match her pants. And, as I pointed out to the class, the book itself is presented as Celie's creation, consisting as it does of her letters. They are the desperate yearnings of a spirit for its own expression, though she doesn't know that for a long time. Celie is literally creating herself with these letters, which evolve from brief, halting, inarticulate scraps to poetic, feisty, stylish, ruminative documents as she, like Mary Agnes, gains her voice. Celie is literally creating herself with these letters.

Ultimately most of my students saw the real point of change in the novel in the dialogue where Shug tells Celie about God. The Color Purple, they told me, is the most powerful force for change. So what's the Color Purple? I queried, and the answers are still coming in. The consensus seems to be that it represents a nexus of love and creativity. I would say that these two are nearly identical in Walker's vision. In the transformed universe to which Shug gives Celie the key—an act of love in itself—everything and everybody is enmeshed in a tense, vital web of existence, created with love by a spirit whom it is our proper destiny to imitate in its loving creativity, its creative love. God is fundamentally an artist, and so is each of us. That God creates a purple flower for no utilitarian purpose at all is a sign of the artist at work, and a signal to the rest of us to get busy with our own pallettes, in devout imitation. Whatever Creation is for us—writing, singing, cooking, planting flowers, sewing, playing soccer, dancing, counseling, teaching, carpentry, cutting hair, maybe even conversing with a computer—it is our fundamental human act: the immensely powerful act of ordering and interpreting the often chaotic and painful data of our world. It is the activity in which we work on and with the world and are no longer simply acted upon by it—which is why it makes all the difference for Celie. It is the act in which we become subjects rather than objects, seeing ourselves as raw materials in our own hands. It is our eternal *lux esto*[7] and our declaration of independence in interdependence; it is the moment when we say, with Celie, "But I'm here," realizing simultaneously that others are here too. The radical transformation of the universe in *The Color Purple* from one of atomized, alienated, objectified and objectifying beings to one of collaborative mutual creation in which the aliveness of self and other are absolutely interdependent—this is the real miracle of this novel.

Is it important, one of my students asked, that Sophia, jailed and beaten by the white sheriff, is covered with purple bruises? You bet, I say, never missing a trick: The Color Purple is pain and anger, too, the pain that says, "I am human, I suffer," and the anger that says, "But I'm here." I suspect that it is this hue on the purple spectrum which Emily Dickinson had in view when she described bleak, unpromising landscape out of which "There comes a Purple Creature," the beautiful, lonely gentian. Out of our suffering and the often incomprehensible cruelty around us come astonishing—no, miraculous—heroism and beauty. I learn this every day. In fact, this very course of mine this summer is a continuing reeducation for me in the heroism that weaves itself through the common fabric of our lives. In the students' journals, in the original poetry they have read to the class, in my office, I hear stories that might justify all manner of bitterness, depravity, hardness. It's amazing to me what one can suffer by the age of twenty. And instead I mostly see people ready to trust life a little, ready to turn clear, sympathetic eyes upon those very nightmares and old ghosts, incorporating them into the novels of their own lives—recreating themselves. Think about people you know who have managed—miraculously?—to come out of abuse and loss and injustice with whole souls and loving hearts. Think about how you have done it yourselves. It's there; our job is to learn to see and celebrate and foster it, for if we miss it, God is indeed probably pissed off.

The Color Purple is this regality apparent in the mundane, the eternal in the transient, the world seen in a grain of sand, according to William Blake, the vision Dickinson saw daily from her upstairs corner window, where she communed steadily with Eternity as if it were her best friend. The Color Purple is the awareness that the earth is not data, but a poem; that its details, human and otherwise, are organically related and therefore charged with meaning and value. It is, to switch to my other course this summer, what Robert Browning meant when he had his worldly artist, Fra Lippo Lippi, say:

> This world's no blot for us,
> Nor blank; it means intensely, and means good;
> To find its meaning is my meat and drink.

To see the Color Purple is to be joyfully, fearfully aware that our every action entails a reaction; that when we strike out, something bleeds; that when we soothe, something purrs; that when we nurture and love, something grows, if only in ourselves. It is what Jesus meant when he said, "Inasmuch as ye have done it unto the least of these, ye have done it unto me." And it is what Celie means when she tells Albert that what he does to her will rebound against himself.

Albert discovers the blessing hidden in that curse, however. As one student so beautifully explained it, he, the victimizer, has also been "nothing at all," like Celie, another victim in the network of abuse. But when he takes responsibility for the anguish he has caused, he gets his own humanity in return: He sees himself for the first time as an actor in a living universe in which he has choices and power, real power. As Celie tells him, "If you know your heart sorry, that mean it not quite as spoilt as you think."[8]

Albert knows that somehow, through his tunnel of remorse and aloneness, he has been reborn into a different world. He tells Celie, "I'm satisfied this the first time I ever lived on Earth as a natural man."[9] This rebirth, he says, began with questions:

> You know how it is. You ast yourself one question, it lead to fifteen. I start to wonder why us need love. Why us suffer. Why us black. Why us men and women. Where do children really come from. It didn't take long to realize I didn't hardly know nothing. And that if you ast yourself why you black or a man or a woman or a bush it don't mean nothing if you don't ast why you here, period.

So Celie asks him that big question, and he responds:

> I think us here to wonder, myself. To wonder. To ast. And that in wondering about the big things, and asting about the big things, you learn about the little ones, almost by accident. But you never know nothing more about the big things than you start out with. The more I wonder . . . the more I love. [10]

"And peoples start to love you back, I bet," Celie adds. And Albert responds with surprise, "They do."

Only one of my students talked in her paper about the lovely double meaning of Albert's key word, "wonder": the wonder that is questioning, and the wonder that is pure awe, that admiration that Shug says God craves as much as we do. It is this wonder that the Color Purple is really all about, that humility in the fact of a mysterious and beautiful, outrageous and painful universe that enables us to become natural women and men, seeing and loving the little scraps of purple in each other and ourselves. And that wonder empowers us to make the most miraculous changes, alongside which water-into-wine looks almost like child's play.

The Benediction

Me, change! Me, alter!
Then I will, when on the Everlasting Hill
A Smaller Purple grows—

At sunset, or a lesser glow
Flickers upon Cordillera—
At Day's superior close!

. . .

In the name of the Bee—
And of the Butterfly—
And of the Breeze—Amen!

—Emily Dickinson

In the fall of 1984, I was asked to open the fall Chapel series, so I thought I'd better try for something that would address itself primarily to incoming new students. This time the germ of my talk was a perplexing, disturbing experience in a Shakespeare course over the preceding summer. It had driven me back to my basic assumptions about literature and made me articulate them to myself for perhaps the first time. This was one of the first occasions when I realized that I was not necessarily going to find myself in ready spiritual intimacy with the generation of the eighties, and that the teacher who ignores what the students bring into the classroom with them is talking to the wind.

Rereading my words, I still marvel that I attempted to combine Shakespeare, the poetry of my colleague Conrad Hilberry, the poetry of Keats, the life of a Nobel Laureate in medicine, the concept of Biblical knowledge, and my own theories of education into a coherent stew, and I'm still not sure I did it. But the fact that I tried testifies to the influence of Kalamazoo College in moving me over the years away from the narrow graduate-school path toward a much bigger intellectual world.

12

No Abstract Fires

A New Year's Message

October 5, 1984

Wise Man

I

No one here is old enough. The father,
if that's what he is, stands awkward as a stork.
The mother does not know whether to smile
or cry, her face beautiful but ill-defined
as faces of the young are. Even the ass
is a yearling and the sheep mutter like children.
To whom shall I hand this myrrh that has trailed
a bitter breath after it over the desert?

I am tired of mothers and their milky ways,
of babies sticky as figs. I have left a kingdom
of them. There must be some truth beyond
this sucking and growing and wasting away.
A star should lead an old man, you would think,
to some geometry, some right triangle
whose legs never slip or warp or aspire
to become the hypotenuse. Instead, this star
wandering out of the ecliptic has led us
to dry straw, a stable, oil burning in
a lamp, a mother nursing another mouth.

II

Creation, then, is the only axiom—
and it declines to spell itself across

the sky in Roman letters. Some events
are worth a journey, but there are no
abstract fires or vague births. Each fire
gnaws its own sticks; the welter of what is
conspires in this, a creation you can hold
in your hands, a child. A definite baby
squalls into life, skids out between the legs
of a definite woman, bedded in straw, on the longest
night of the year. And a certain star burns.

— *Conrad Hilberry*[1]

"Season of mists and mellow fruitfulness," John Keats called this time of the year. For me it is a peculiarly intense, wrenching time, where past and future intersect with a particular poignancy. Autumn always carries in its wind some longing for lost possibilities, for which Nature conveniently invented the metaphor of falling yellow leaves. (Forgive me; I'm teaching poetry this quarter.) But for those of us who somewhere along the way got academe so deeply into our blood that we couldn't shake it—rather like malaria—autumn is psychologically and emotionally the start of a new year. I have always thought that Judaism has the right idea: New Year's Day ought to be moved closer to Labor Day. Who wants to start anything in January anyway? There is solid Biblical precedent for my revised calendar: After all, human history really begins with the Fall.

By the beginning of October, summer suddenly seems very far away. I watched it go by the northern shore of Lake Michigan, where I wrote most of these remarks staring out sliding glass doors across miles and miles of blue water to South Manitou Island. Words came slowly, like the great freighters pulling across my horizon toward Mackinac. It was sunny and still quite warm, but the air had changed in that subtle way that tells you that summer is over. The golden light was September, not July. I had come up to recuperate from summer quarter before pushing off into another new year, another entering class. Many of you here, particularly my war-weary colleagues, spent the summer as I did, dodging sprinklers and tennis brats[2], watching the long shadows on the quad, wondering what ever happened to the semester system and why Kalamazoo College has this penchant for idiosyncracies like summer quarter. Others of you—returning sophomores, incoming members of the class of 1988, transfer students, deviants of all flavors[3]—doubtless passed the long summer days in romantic locales in the company of romantic companions—the kind of summer I know only from Beach Boys songs. I, however, spent the summer with William Shakespeare.

As my colleague Walter Waring used to say, "That Shakespeare; he's got everything." And so he does. He is a formidable summer companion. As a teacher of literature, one gets used to the company of greatness, but not in his case. I never get over how good he is. Every once in a while it occurs to me that maybe he really understood everything he was doing in those plays, really knew what he seems to know about art and human nature and suffering and redemption. I sensed that some of my students were impressed by the realization that this provincial sixteenth-century Englishman could know what it meant to be Jewish in a hard Christian world, or to be an African general married to the daughter of a rich white man, or how a smart, wealthy woman who's been a good daughter all her life could suddenly find such delicious freedom in donning men's clothes and crashing a courtroom to set the stupid guys straight about their bonds and their pounds of flesh. In my efforts to show my students the dazzling array of possible perspectives on each play, I dizzied myself. Age cannot wither, nor custom stale, his infinite variety.

Which brings me to *Antony and Cleopatra*, from which that line comes, slightly altered. And a suitable play it is for this season, since it is often said to belong to Shakespeare's "autumn." Indeed, when I dragged out my graduate school notes on the play, there it was, the word *autumnal*, highlighted in yellow as if it were the key to everything, as undoubtedly I thought it was when some eminence at the University of Virginia uttered it. Anyway, *Antony and Cleopatra* is indeed autumnal, not only in being written at the beginning of the end of Shakespeare's career, but also in its golden-brown, bittersweet atmosphere of mellow fruitfulness before the fall. It is a grand love story, a sort of anti-*Romeo and Juliet*—a play most definitely not about kids and virgin passion. Its lovers are aging, battle-scarred warriors with established reputations, a lot of history between and behind them, and many other loves. Instead of charming balcony scenes there are harrowing screaming matches, rage and petulance, passionate reconciliations. Most of you probably know the story. If you don't know Shakespeare's version, you remember Liz and Dick.

Antony and Cleopatra has always been my favorite Shakespeare play, partially because it *is* about very fallible grownups, but also because its two reprobate heroes enact a powerful psychodrama in which the dynamics of gender play a central role. Cleopatra is nothing short of a composite of every single archetype I know of the Bad Woman, the Eve figure who permeates our literature, right down to all the snake imagery surrounding her. In the course of the play, Antony has two proper Roman wives, both stunning contrasts to their Egyptian antithesis, the perfect (and perfectly impossible) Mistress. And Cleopatra, instead of wisely perceiving their superiority and adopting a more ladylike demeanor, perversely insists upon being her infuriating self. Antony, meanwhile, is the legendary hero, the warrior every Roman boy wanted to be, the walking definition of manhood who suddenly blows it, finding himself incapable of disentangling from the Serpent of Old Nile and getting himself back to Rome to pursue the requisite manly political and military activities. The play is peppered with laments for Antony's lost masculinity, including wonderfully Freudian references to his being robbed of his sword. He is torn between his manhood and his humanity, in fact, unable to enact a limited version of himself: warrior or lover, stoic or sensualist, Roman or Egyptian, public or private, male or female. The play describes a classic clash of male and female worlds, in which two hopelessly human beings act themselves out.

Now, I warned my class in advance that *Antony and Cleopatra* was being saved for the end of the course, and that it was my favorite play, and that I would tolerate no tenth-week slumps. So they were prepared for the frenzy into which I wrought myself as August drew to a close. As it happened, about two-thirds of the class of fifty were submitting extra-credit discussion questions each time we began a new play. On the night before we started *Antony and Cleopatra,* then, I was looking over the stack of questions. Thirty seconds into the pile, my mouth went dry. The questions fell (with a large thud) into two general categories, roughly paraphrased as follows: "How can he love that woman when she's so BAD and NASTY and VILE?" and "WHY is he such a WIMP?"

I'm accustomed to jarring discoveries of the gap between my understanding of a literary work and that of my class, but this was more serious. Let's face it: If the audience has no comprehension of or sympathy for the heroes, the play is lost on them. The class response raised a fundamental issue in literary interpretation: What makes a hero heroic? And what if the author's and readers' assumptions differ on that question? A few moments' thought reminded me that on one level the students were perfectly correct: By almost any generally accepted rational standards, Antony and Cleopatra are failures— moral, political, and emotional. He's a lousy man and she's a terrible woman. Their "reputations are shot," as the Everly Brothers used to say. Their "love" makes J. R. and Suellen look like Ozzie and Harriet. They lose their war against Caesar and thereby their kingdoms. And they're both dead at the end, though Antony cannot even manage to fall on his sword correctly and makes rather a bloody mess of it. So how are they heroes? What's to admire or lament? We know about tragic flaws, said my students, but this is ridiculous.

The problem is that Shakespeare clearly disagreed, didn't he? And it is the nature of this disagreement that I set out to try to convey to the class. I fear I was mostly unsuccessful. One student swore that as time went on she was learning to love "Tony and Cleo," but I think she believed, rather touchingly, that if she loved them enough, her C+ would mystically transmute into a B-. Enhancing the confusion in class was my own sudden lack of clarity about the play, precipitated by my students' questions. In the course of the next two weeks they forced me to confront the experience of literature as I had not done for some time, and in the process, I came to some understandings of love, heroism, and most importantly, knowledge. And that, after this unforgivable preamble, is my actual subject today.

❦

I fought on, feeling less like the priest interpreting divine mystery to the faithful (a nice fantasy teachers entertain) than like a mediator between sixteenth-century Management and a disgruntled twentieth-century Labor Force. And like all good mediators, I first had to arrive at a clear definition of the impasse for myself. I knew that Shakespeare disagreed with my students; his love for his incorrigible heroes is palpable. But I also knew that his disagreement was not that Antony and Cleopatra are admirable, "good" characters misunderstood by the world and meant to be applauded by the audience. Nor was it even that they are terribly flawed people who are to be admired despite their shortcomings. It is a more radical play than that. I submit that Shakespeare actually demands that we *love* (not admire) Antony and Cleopatra, not despite but *because* of what they are. How positively amoral can you get? After all, what would happen if we responded to real people that way?

It became apparent to me, then, that *love* was the critical missing element in most of the students' understandings of the play. As I considered standing down on that silly platform in 103 Dewing Hall begging a roomful of people to love Marc Antony and Queen Cleopatra, I realized that I would get strange evaluations. In the questions I read, however, and in the subsequent discussions, I was hearing a lot of judgments, quite legitimate, as I said before, according to objective, abstract, traditional standards. But ironically, those are the very standards represented in the play by the insufferable prig Octavius Caesar and his stoic and very boring Roman legions. My students were reacting like perfect Romans! Judgment, but very little sympathy—and of course the insidious thing about literature is that it demands sympathy with all sorts of eccentrics and deviants. Now "sympathy" means "feeling with"; it implies intimacy. Judgment, on the other hand, is reserved for God, Sandra Day O'Connor, and a bunch of people in the front row at the Miss America Pageant. Most of us believe it not only implies but requires distance and separation. So what I really want, I said to myself, is for these students to "come on down," as they say on "The Price is Right," to get closer to the play.

This all remained inarticulate for me until I found the words in another source altogether. Toward the end of the summer, I read Dr. Evelyn Fox Keller's biography of the geneticist Barbara McClintock, published serendipitously just a few months before McClintock received the Nobel Prize for her work with the transposition of genes in maize. Her lonely, isolated decades at her Cold Spring Harbor laboratory in New York have contributed mightily to our present understanding of the mechanism of inheritance, yet until very recently her work was ignored, suspected, even ridiculed by her colleagues. The biography is entitled, significantly, *A Feeling for the Organism*. As Keller explains it, McClintock, like most certifiable geniuses, has a different kind of vision from most of us: She simply sees more deeply than others do, a capacity which is likely to lead as often to ridicule and ostracism as to insight and discovery. One of her colleagues, Marcus Rhoades, recalls saying to her, "I've often marvelled that you can look at a cell under a microscope and can see so much!" McClintock responded, "Well, you know, when I look at a cell, I get down in that cell and look around."[4]

Can you see the lightbulb flashing over my head? As soon as I read that line, and read it again, I knew I had my answer. The majority of my students had read the play, "understood" it, and judged it according to a very respectable set of standards and wholly unexamined assumptions which are theirs by right of inheritance from their culture. "Tacit assumptions," McClintock calls them when she sees her scientific colleagues bringing them into the laboratory. Keller defines McClintock's resistance to "an implicit adherence to models that prevents people from looking at data with a fresh mind. These tacit assumptions impose unconscious boundaries between what is thinkable and what is not."[5] McClintock's account of dealing with this breed of scientist struck a very sympathetic chord in me: "They didn't know they were bound to a model, and you couldn't show them . . . even if you made an effort."[6] Yes, I thought, yes: Tacit. Boundaries between what is thinkable and what is not. This is why the dissonance between *Antony and Cleopatra* as read by my class and the play as read by me felt not like disagreement but like something more profound. The mental inhibitions that impede science are precisely those that keep a committee paralyzed in a task, or keep someone from recognizing the racism in a joke, or keep people from seeing another version of a relationship beyond inherited, constructed roles, or keep a class from really understanding a 350-year-old play.

McClintock reports wishing to say to scientists afflicted with tacit assumptions, "If you'd only just let the material tell you."[7] And this was precisely the line for which I was fumbling with my class. Without this willingness to allow the subject matter to speak—whether it be genes on a chromosome or Cleopatra on a barge—there is only knowledge without insight. Most of my students either had not been willing or had not known how to take the enormous risk of getting down into that play and looking around. So they missed what McClintock defines as her single greatest strength as a scientist: "A feeling for the organism."[8]

If this "feeling" is the secret of brilliant science, it is also not a bad prerequisite to decent literary criticism—which makes me think that it might be the key to a lot of different kinds of learning. I think it is not far from what my ever-wise colleague John Spencer meant when he told students that to understand a writer, they must first spend some time sitting at that writer's feet, not in adoration or abasement, but in submission to another reality. If Marigene Arnold were here, I'm sure she would tell you how much of good anthropology depends on the observer's willingness to yield to an alien culture, to become a participant. And she ought to know, having munched goat testicles in Mexico.

✻ঞ্জ✻

It seems to me that all of us who would truly *know* something or someone must become anthropologists, not merely studying but entering our subjects, minds and senses as open as we can get them. This requires the willed fortitude of the traveller who resists the temptation to sit in the bar with other Americans and instead ventures out into the wilderness of unknown streets and a cumbersome foreign tongue. It requires also the cultivated looseness of the actor foraying into another self, not in order to evaluate or even, strictly speaking, to understand the role so much as to become it. One reason I love having theatre

majors in English classes is that they generally grasp literature im-
aginatively instead of merely cerebrally. They see people moving and
speaking, and they imagine playing the roles—instant "sympathy."
The result is a knowledge from the inside. This kind of knowing tends
to resist easy abstraction, for it is concrete and detailed by definition.
It tends to defy stereotypes because it is empathic by definition. After
all, we abstract and stereotype the experience of everyone except
ourselves and those we love; the latter we consider real, for we have
known it intimately.

This is the poet's way of knowing, too. As the eighteenth century
melted into the nineteenth, the English Romantic poets regenerated
their literature by this means, reacting against the smug rationalism of
the preceding age. We can see it in Keats' portrait of autumn, in the
profusion of concrete detail which is the poet's raw material. His
autumn is seen and felt at its core; he has surely got down into autumn
and looked around. In the process he sees Autumn more clearly
perhaps than it has been seen before or since—so clearly, in fact, that
it appears before him, and us, in the flesh, sprawled happily on the
granary floor, hair waving in the wind. His vision, like McClintock's,
is that which renders the abstract or obscure clear and concrete by
entering bravely into what Conrad Hilberry's Wise Man calls "the
welter of what is." Like the Wise Man, we yearn for the restful refuge
of abstraction, "some geometry, some triangle," "some truth be-
yond/this sucking and growing and wasting away" that comprises life
in all its messiness. But the Wise Man enters into a very particular
stable and looks around, only to find—not God, not an abstraction, but
a "definite baby"; and therein, of course, lies the miracle.

This revelation, this concrete, intimate knowledge from the inside,
is another version of Barbara McClintock's feeling for the organism.
You know about this kind of knowledge if you have ever become
proficient at riding a horse or sailing a boat: There is a feeling for the
laws and motion of your vehicle that no amount of instruction, no
number of handbooks could ever give you. It comes with time and
experience and the willing ability to dissolve a little into the horse's
magnificent musculature or to feel the wind in you as the sail feels it.
It occurs to me that I chose these two examples as the two activities in
which, as a kid, I felt most powerful, but the power came not from
controlling something but from becoming something, joining a force
of which I was a part, but not the whole, and of which I was never
wholly in control.

This way of knowing is so little respected or understood in our
culture that I had come to see it as the province of the arts and

humanities, also little respected or understood. This is why the McClintock biography was such a revelation to me, scientifically illiterate as I am. Unfortunately, we at this college are products of a culture that, for the most part, likes to see the individual as discrete and sacrosanct, mounting the marble steps of Reason to worship the chilly deity of Objectivity. This alternate knowledge comes to us mostly through Eastern philosophy and our few mad geniusses like McClintock and Keats. As we slog on through the eighties, our "rationalism" moving us ever closer to unthinkable annihilation, it seems to me that we who are educators must fight harder and harder to give this other way of knowing at least equal time, not as a sentimental or mystical activity that is good for the soul, but as an intellectual skill that is critical to academic, professional, and personal success, not to mention to the survival of the species and the planet. Learning too often takes either the form of conquering an object, dominating the material, or the equally dangerous form of arrogating the material into one's own subjectivity, so that *it* becomes *me*. Both of these perversions, you might notice, can be inflicted upon people as well as upon biology or Spanish—or Shakespeare. And both boil down to egoism, individualism run amock. The capacity to feel for the organism is perhaps becoming as obsolete as the ability to write. Maybe we should make it a graduation requirement and administer placement tests to incoming students.

Our resistance to this other way of knowing comes from a number of fears, I think. In the first place, it calls not only upon what we know but upon what we *are*. In the second, it introduces into academe uncomfortable concepts like *spirit* and *feeling* and *intuition*, and with them the whole realm of the non-rational which we are never sure we want mucking up our classrooms. In the third place, it asks what is for us Westerners a supreme sacrifice. Barbara McClintock herself describes it: "As you look as these things" under the microscope, "they become part of you. And you forget yourself. The main thing about it is that you forget yourself." Keller continues:

> Throughout history, artists and poets, lovers and mystics, have known and written about the 'knowing' that comes from loss of self—from the state of subjective fusion with the object of knowledge. Scientists have known it too. Einstein once wrote: "The state of feeling which makes one capable of such achievements is akin to that of the religious worshipper or of one who is in love." Scientists often pride themselves on their capacities to distance subject from object, but much of their richest lore comes from a joining of one to the other, from a turning of subject into object.[9]

Einstein? Yes, in fact he regarded a feeling for the organism as essential to profound scientific discoveries: "To these," he wrote, "there leads no logical path, but only intuition, supported by being sympathetically in touch with experience."[10] And intuition requires effort that "comes from no deliberate intention or program, but straight from the heart."[11] Einstein understood what intuition really is: no mystical power that comes as a freebie with ovaries, but simply a clarity and depth of vision one develops by observing and identifying with the object until it becomes subject and is thus known from the inside, in the context of its own reality. His analogies to religious and amorous experience are apt, for both are terrifying as well as exhilarating. And both recall what I remember of the horse and the sailboat: that unearthly power one draws from joining a force larger than oneself.

※⟨⟩⟩⟨⟩⟨

The paradox, as McClintock says, is that in becoming part of the material, you make the material part of you, understood so profoundly that you are changed, enlarged by it. Those "tacit assumptions" you were leaning against may not be quite so comfy anymore. I don't know, of course, but maybe after you've walked around in a microscopic cell for a while, the tree outside the lab window doesn't look the same. I'm surer about what happens after you've got down inside Cleopatra's Egypt and looked around. You see things through her eyes, and Antony's, and most of all, Shakespeare's. You find that it is rather more difficult to shut her up in a tidy moral or sexual category, given the sheer expanse of her passion, her experience, her guts, her monumental selfhood. Similarly, you find, instead of a wimp suckered by a devious dame, a man brave enough to love, to suffer, to confront his humanity, and to explore its farther corners in the face of the world's opprobrium. You discover, in fact, that "greatness," for Shakespeare, consists not in success or even in virtue but simply in the dimensions of one's humanity.

In these altered judgements, Einstein's analogy between *knowing* and *loving* suggests itself: We find it difficult to pass simple "objective" judgments upon something or someone we have known with the imagination and heart as well as with the brain and senses. The Other's experience is too much our own, too real. Our "objectivity" is well and truly lost. It confounds me that we speak so highly of objectivity, as if it were one of the Commandments, as if the more we could remove personality and experience from the act of knowing (that is, assuming we could do so), the more pristine and clean and therefore reliable our knowing would be, or as if the further away from a thing we could get, the better we could see it. There is genuine, precious insight in intimacy, in *sympathy*, in having walked around inside a cell, or a play, or the life of another person.

Shakespeare, of course, knew this. In the final act of the play, when Antony is pitifully and messily dead, a Roman named Dolabella, a most decent and unimaginative chap, visits Cleopatra in her monument, where she has sought sanctuary from the men who beseige her—from both Antony in his anger and Caesar in his eagerness to carry her to Rome in triumph. Dolabella attempts to discuss a surrender to Caesar, but the queen is lost in an imagined vision of Antony, which she paints in the air before the audience, almost as if to counteract our final, debased image of the sorry hero:

> I dreamt there was an Emperor Antony.
> O, such another sleep, that I might see
> But such another man . . .
> His face was as the heav'ns, and therein stuck
> A sun and moon, which kept their course and lighted
> The little O, the earth. . .
> His legs bestrid the ocean: his reared arms
> Crested the world: his voice was propertied
> As all the tuned spheres, and that to friends;
> But when he meant to quail and shake the orb,
> He was as rattling thunder. For his bounty,
> There was no winter in't: an autumn 'twas
> That grew the more by reaping: his delights
> Were dolphin-like, they showed his back above
> The element he lived in: in his livery
> Walked crowns and crownets: realms and islands
> As plates dropped from his pocket.
>
> (V, ii, 77-92)

"Think you there ever was such a man?" asks the queen plaintively, and poor, rational, truthful Dolabella, of course, answers, "No, my Queen." Whereupon the Serpent hisses back at him: "You lie, up to the hearing of the Gods." Now, Dolabella is not lying. Antony's legs never bestrid any oceans. But Cleopatra is also right: Antony *was* bigger than other men. That's Shakespeare's whole point. And her retort to Dolabella is his challenge to the audience: What she affirms is the truth of the heart's imagination, the truth that intimacy and sympathy can see but that the naked eye and the objective Roman mind must always miss.

We like to keep knowing and loving separate, as if one violated the other somehow. We think knowledge will destroy the "illusion" of love (which phrase in itself speaks volumes about us). And we think love will, in turn, destroy the objectivity necessary to knowledge. But maybe we're wrong. Perhaps the two intersect more often than not. In any real act of knowing, defined as a feeling for the organism, there is a movement of the mind and the imagination into another reality that surely resembles loving. And in the act of loving there is the intimacy, the bridging of the gulf between self and other that characterizes knowledge. Perhaps this is what is meant by "knowing in the Biblical sense."

It all reminds me of a story: about a GodFather who so loved the world that he gave his only begotten son—that is, he made himself concrete. An abstract Word was made flesh and dwelt among us. A removed Authority who specialized in carving rigid principles in stone decided to get down off the mountain into this little cell and look around, to develop some feeling for the organism by becoming one. In the sad thirty-three-year process, he discovered that the stone tablets weren't enough, that we were in need of another, greater rule. Perhaps when he told us to love our neighbor as we love ourselves, he had in mind this proximity of loving and knowing. Maybe we are supposed to try to know each other's realities as we know and respect our own. Maybe we are to get down into other lives and look around, to try to develop some feeling for the miraculous organisms walking around brushing shoulders with us, locked in their mysterious Otherness. We work with them, talk and laugh with them, marry them, eat and sleep with them, and they are foreigners. Similarly, we study a subject for ten weeks, write about it, emerge with an honorable B, and it's foreign, as foreign as I fear *Antony and Cleopatra* remains to most of my summer crew because I had not the microscope to let them in. Perhaps we could resolve to begin to change that, as part of our New Year's celebration in this season of mists and mellow fruitfulness. Perhaps we could resolve not to be quite at ease with something or someone until we have beamed ourselves down and looked around and achieved some kind of feeling for the organism. I wish this particularly for the class of 1988, by way of welcome to our little microcosm on a hill, which may occasionally feel like a cell of some sort. See what you can do about using these next very expensive years not to "get" something but to know, to love, and to become something, and to move somewhere else. Think of the Wise Man, yearning for geometrical perfection, who discovers that there are "No abstract fires, no vague births." Fire and birth ought to be what your next four years are about. Strength is indeed required for your journey, carrying your six-pack of myrrh, following whatever star it is you're eyeing; but strength is wasted if when you approach knowledge you have not cultivated the courage, or wisdom, or imagination, or whatever it takes to step into that particular stable, where the miracle is waiting.

Try it, OK?

Happy New Year.

The next fall it was finally time to speak about speaking. I had just begun to explore the history of the female voice, in light of my ongoing observations of my own voice and the voices of my students. This was my first attempt to pull it all together.

My title comes from Marge Piercy's wonderful poem of the same name, combined with Paul Laurence Dunbar via Maya Angelou, whose autobiography—yet another saga of emerging and embattled voice—I had just been studying with a class of first-year students.

13

Unlearning to Not Speak

or

Why the Caged Bird Sings

November 22, 1985

In [the] spring of 1873, I delivered my first lecture. It was delivered to no one, queer as that may sound . . . And indeed, it was queer altogether. I was learning to play the organ, and was in the habit of practising in the church by myself. . . One day, being securely locked in, I thought I would like to try how "it felt" to speak from the pulpit. Some vague fancies were stirring in me, that I *could* speak if I had the chance; very vague they were, for the notion that I might ever speak on the platform had never dawned on me; only the longing to find outlet in words was in me; the feeling that I had something to say, and the yearning to say it. So, queer as it may seem, I ascended the pulpit in the big, empty, lonely church, and there and then I delivered my first lecture! I shall never forget the feeling of power and of delight which came upon me as my voice rolled down the aisles, and the passion in me broke into balanced sentences, and never paused for rhythmical expression, while I felt that all I wanted was to see the church full of upturned faces, instead of the emptiness of the silent pews. And as though in a dream the solitude became peopled, and I saw the listening faces and the eager eyes, and as the sentences came unbidden from my lips, and my own tones echoed back to me from the pillars of the ancient church, I knew of a verity that the gift of speech was mine, and that if ever—and it seemed then so impossible—if ever the chance came to me of public work, that at least this power of melodious utterance should win hearing for my message I had to bring.

But that knowledge remained a secret all to my own self for many a long month, for I quickly felt ashamed of that foolish speechifying in an empty church, and I only recall it now because, in trying to trace out one's mental growth, it is only fair to notice the first silly striving after that expression in spoken words, which, later, has become to me one of the deepest delights of life.

— Annie Besant, 1885[1]

I know precisely how Annie Besant felt. In fact, this account parallels frighteningly closely my own first time at this lectern (with the single exception that the pews *were* full of upturned faces). Besant was among the first generation of women to attempt public speaking. It was one of the great revelations to my life as a scholar to learn that the public furor over the early suffragists had less to do with the radicalism of their cause than with the fact that these women travelled about, sans male escort, *speaking publicly*. That was the great offense. For Besant to do so, and to do so from that bastion of patriarchal authority, the pulpit, was a major act of courage, even if the church was empty. When I first read her story, what moved me was the tension in the passage between her shining memory of the glorious power she felt as her newborn voice took over, and the self-abnegating, ladylike disclaimer at the end, where the whole wonderful episode becomes "foolish speechifying." Even after a lifetime of public speaking, which she calls "one of the deepest delights of life," there is enough residual shame at that unmaidenly self-exposure to cause her to refer to her magnificent "striving after expression in spoken words" as "silly."

You heard a few minutes ago what was always, for me as a child, the most beautiful of black American songs. It was not until many years after I'd sung it in choir that I learned the truth about "Steal Away": that going home to Jesus was only the song's literal message. It is not another piece of evidence, as we are often told, for black people's passivity under slavery, their resignation to a better world beyond. It is one of the many songs that functioned as a critical form of political communique between black people who could not speak openly to one another. "I ain't got long to stay here" signalled that a break for freedom was imminent. Like "Wade in the Water" and so many other songs, it carried a subtext of life-and-death urgency. Music became the language which broke the slavery of silence, creating a network of which the white masters remained ignorant.

In 1893, Elizabeth Hyde Botume recorded the reminiscences of black women who had grown up in slavery. She captured for posterity some astonishing accounts of the devices employed to penetrate this terrible silence. One of these stories in particular has lodged itself in my memory permanently:

I couldn't read, but my uncle could. I was waiting maid, an' used to help missis to dress in the morning. If massa wanted to tell her something he didn't want me to know, he used to spell it out. I could remember the letters, an' as soon as I got away I ran to uncle an' spelled them over to him, an' he told me what they meant.[2]

Think about this: A little girl with a veritably prodigious memory carries the individual letters, meaningless to her—and carries them in the correct order—home to her uncle, who harbors the dangerous weapon of literacy and who can thread them together into words, translating critical news, often about the war, to the family and thus to the community. A collaborative voice speaks where individually there was silence and isolation, two of the primary components of power-lessness.

❦

When I was a child, I had a recurring nightmare in which I was in some situation of peril and would try to scream, straining my throat to its limits and producing only silence. The scream stayed within me, like a caged animal. What was this terror of speech, this dumb demon no one could exorcise? When I had anything important to say, I usually wrote it. I left notes to my mother when I felt misunderstood, which was often. On paper I always found my voice waiting, ready, willing, and able, fluid and gymnastic, saying what the baby of the family always wanted to say but nobody ever understood. My spoken voice, though, was traitorous and alien. On Thanksgiving and Christmas my mother would drag out the huge old purple reel-to-reel tape recorder, which weighed about fifty pounds. In the early fifties, there was a jazzy and faintly suggestive popular song called "Green Door," of which I could do a particularly hot version, and without fail I was bidden to warble it into the microphone. I remember the horror of listening to my voice played back, always lower than any good little girl's voice had a right to be, clumsy and thick, awkward, like me.

I sang in choirs constantly from eight to eighteen, though. There I learned about the collaborative voice—the surge of power when your voice melts into the others, your alto holding up the harmony and sustaining the soprano melody, creating something much bigger than yourself. Then, in eighth grade, I was given a solo. I always had a good choral voice, in no way a solo voice, but in the eighth grade such subtleties are irrelevant. But in the middle of one choral piece was an alto solo, with one vicious high note. In the shower, for a full month before the concert, it sounded magnificent. On the night of the performance, with the gym of Bloomfield Hills Junior High packed with parents, I went for the sixth note, the high one, and heard that terrifying silence from my old dream. The rest of my solo sounded pale, thin, weak, weak, weak. It was not my voice at all. Some stranger was squeaking in front of all these people.

Thus I comprehend the anxiety of my students about speaking in class. For me, good classes were places of impossible tension. On the one hand, I *always* had something to say, something urgent. I always knew what everybody else was stupidly missing and needed desperately to hear. But on the other hand, there was that silence, a great heavy hand squeezing my throat, compressing my lungs. An idea, an insight would fill me, and then the thought of my lone, naked voice would chase it back to its dark corner. So when paralyzed, I reverted to that old reliable written voice: I wrote out the comment I wished to make, quickly memorized it, and shot my hand into the air. The only drawback of this method was that by the time I spoke, my comment was usually irrelevant.

I have also confessed to entirely too many people around here that my real secret dream, deeper even than becoming the Charlotte Bronte of my age, was to act. Yet I never brought myself near a stage, except for one brief, shining hour (and about three brief, shining lines) as Eliza Doolittle's stepmother in the 1968 Ann Arbor High School production of *My Fair Lady*. To walk out onto a stage and face that darkness full of ears without the reliable written word in front of me, and to let my voice go—that was unimaginable. My alternative, apparently from a very young age, my mother tells me, was to assume the voices of other people. This dubious talent has made me a sort of party game here at Kalamazoo. Speaking as somebody else is not quite so difficult as speaking for yourself.

So I went to graduate school to study the written word, my old friend. But those who enter graduate English departments in order to read and write tend to come out the other end, to their astonishment, expected to teach, which is quite a different matter. There was simply no alternative to making friends with my spoken voice. It was not easy. To speak as the teacher means not only to speak before a small crowd, but to speak with authority—to speak, in fact, as the God of that little microcosmos, the classroom. Your voice suddenly acquires a power that still shocks me: When you speak, people shut up (sometimes). People scribble your words in notebooks (that is, if you've just been remarkably eloquent and memorable or have just made reference to "the exam"). Other opinions and perspectives evaporate into deferential, deadly silence. It's terrifying.

But not so terrifying as Kalamazoo College's own particular form of torture, speaking in chapel. I resisted "the call" for six full years, no longer because of my fear of my spoken voice, but because of my doubt of it. To speak in chapel, I thought, surely implies an authority, a legitimacy, a right to be at the front of a *church*, for heaven's sake, sermonizing others. A lecture on the semicolon I can manage, but not this. And then one day, I simply wanted to speak. It was not that I convinced myself of my authority to do so; it was simply that I had something that needed to be said, and it took precedence over my terror and self-doubt and dubious religious belief. I didn't want to speak; I had to speak. When I remember the episode in those terms, I recall what Betty Adcock said repeatedly about poetry when she was writer-in-residence here a few summers ago: A good poem, she said, has a necessity about it; it tells a reader that it *had* to be written. I think also of the Quaker tradition of speaking from the silence. There is no sermon, so single authoritative voice. Instead, members of the meeting rise and speak when something in them wishes to be said. And finally, oddly enough, I think of the climactic scene in *The Miracle Worker*, where Helen Keller drags Annie Sullivan's hand back to the pump handle. She must feel the water again, cold and hard as possible, in order to pull from the well of her memory the one syllable that holds the key to the entire universe for her. King Lear's speech in the storm may be more eloquent, but there was surely no more powerful word ever spoken than Helen Keller's single "WA."

Speaking is now for me, as for Annie Besant, "one of the deepest delights of life." But the ghost of that terrible silence in my dream still haunts me. I think it may well be the one that haunted Annie, and all the other women who would speak but could not, gagged by a culture that dictated that they were, like children and other inferior beings, to be seen and not heard. My silent ghost resembles those I have seen hovering around so many other women who open their mouths to utter a good idea and instantly wrap its nakedness in qualifiers, disclaimers, and apologies, which are the tools of the Powers of Silence. In effect, we beg pardon for the heresy of speech, the affrontery and aggression of utterance, just as we heard Besant apologize and rationalize. A few months ago, a friend and I were discussing the tendency of female students to do this verbal self-effacement. I was telling him about the research on female speech patterns, in which he showed admirable interest. Soon afterward, we were seated together on a table at the rear of the room during a faculty meeting. Some hot discussion was in progress, and the spirit moved me to enlighten my assembled colleagues as to the error of their thinking. I raised my hand, was called upon, and what came out went something like this: "Um, maybe I'm wrong about this or not understanding what's been said, and I don't want to disagree with some of the points that have been made, which were really good, but, um, it really seems to me, I mean, don't you think that . . ." By this time the raging spirit that had moved me had flown out the window and across the quad, and my friend was laughing so hard that it was all I could do to finish the sentence without strangling.

Oh, the traitorous voice. My life, it seems, will always be a pitched battle between that awful, deathly silence I used to dream, that ingrained urge to "stifle," as Archie Bunker used to command Edith, and another drive, deeper, I think, certainly truer: the profound human need to express—or, as George Eliot put it, the "urge to utter." Reading a senior project on Margaret Chase Smith last year, I noted with a flash of recognition her account of rising to speak as the first woman in the United States Senate, which is even worse than a faculty meeting: "I didn't believe that as a woman, I should be dictating . . . until I got on to my feet."[3]

We are terrified by the audacity of our voices—until we lose them, until they are snatched away by some awful powers-that-be, within us or without. Early this quarter I had my Expository Prose class write about their most difficult transition into college life. One of the students described finding herself at college with severe laryngitis. It has never occurred to me how serious a handicap this might be: You can't identify yourself in all the ways that new students do; you can't get to know your roommate; you can't brag about your high school; you can't make yourself known to your new professors; you can't ask the questions puzzling you; others avoid talking to you because they know you can't respond. To be in a new context without a voice is to be a sort of non-person.

⁂

Today so much of my teaching consists of encouraging, pushing, pulling, manipulating, inciting, and inspiring students to find their voices, oral and written. For me, one of the manifold burdens of teaching Expository Prose is the sadness I feel for students who do not have the trust and love for the written voice that sustained me through those years of public silence. Some want to express themselves but can't. Just a few weeks ago I asked a student what a particularly baffling passage in his paper really meant, and he responded, in despair and frustration, "I don't know what I mean!" Yes, I said to myself, and when you do, you'll be able to write it. But others, to my horror, don't seem to feel the crying need to put life into words. I confess that I am confounded by indifference to the written voice.

Writing badly or writing in a self-denying attempt to assume someone else's voice are, of course, forms of silence, throttling oneself and one's message. But every teacher's nightmare is the time when that silence on paper spreads over a classroom like a miasma. For silence speaks all too loudly, but in a cryptic tongue which the teacher must decipher. A stretch of silence may mean any number of things. It may mean "We have no idea, as we have not yet even glimpsed the frontispiece of this text." Or "You appear to be operating under the naive delusion that we care." Or "I will never drink orange vodka again." Or "If she doesn't call me tonight I will throw myself off the chapel tower." Or "If you'd just break down and tell us the answer, we could all go home and sleep." Very often it means "I am a cretin in a classroom of geniuses." But teachers, often bad translators, usually interpret it as follows: "We despise and loathe you. We have lengthy dinner conversations about what kind of god could preside over a universe in which you are allowed to impersonate a teacher."

Lately, though, I have begun watching students' individual struggles with their spoken voices. As the inherent power of the voice at once fires and stifles them, the voice becomes, I think, a metaphor for coming of age. Last year a senior whose severely nasal speaking voice had impeded her for years told me she wished to confront this problem. I suggested that she enroll in "Voice and Diction," and she did me one better by signing up for private singing lessons as well. As the spring progressed, she gave me periodical updates—in a steadily deepening, opening voice. But the real fascination for us both was that as she found another voice, she felt it as her true one. The strained, unnaturally high voice belonged to a certain version of herself, she said, that was self-doubting and diminishing. At this I smiled, having listened for years as my own low voice shot up the register in situations where I was ill at ease or subconsciously wishing to make myself more feminine and acceptable.

Another vocal transformation occurred in New York last year, where two of our students were studying acting in the Arts Program. I received letters from both of them the same day, recounting exactly the same story: They had done a difficult scene in class, and when they finished, the instructor had said, "You know, you two usually use little-girl voices. But there in that scene, toward the end, when you got so intense, you sounded like real women." The point, of course, is that in acting and speaking as real women, they discovered that they were.

In assuming the mask of a role, their customary vocal disguise dropped away and the truth spoke.

※\(ʊʊ\)⁂

This quarter in my freshman seminar, "Coming of Age," we read Maya Angelou's autobiography, *I Know Why the Caged Bird Sings*. In one of its pivotal episodes, Maya, aged eight, is raped by her mother's boyfriend. She tells her brother what has happened, and the rapist is killed by her uncles. Maya's response to the situation has a disturbing logic in its understanding of the terrible power of the voice: "If I talked to anyone else that person might die too. Just my breath, carrying my words out, might poison people and they'd curl up and die . . ."[4] So Maya retreats into silence for the next few years of her life. And then along comes Mrs. Flowers, whom Angelou remembers as "the aristocrat of Black Stamps[, Arkansas]" and "the lady who threw me my first life line."[5] Mrs. Flowers, elegant and educated, takes Maya on. First she tells her, "Words mean more than what is set down on paper. It takes the human voice to infuse them with the shades of deeper meaning."[6] She then recites from Dickens' *A Tale of Two Cities*. The sound is, for Maya, a revelation: "Her voice slid in and curved down through and over the words. She was nearly singing. I wanted to look at the pages. Were they the same that I had read? Or were there notes, music, lined on the pages, as in a hymn book?"[7] Finally Mrs. Flowers loans Maya one of her precious volumes of poetry, instructing her to memorize one for their next meeting. In effect, she hands back to this tormented little girl, possessed by the demon of silence, her own voice. And considering that this is the autobiography of a writer, a story about finding a voice, that is a substantial gift.

So, I asked my seminar when we finished the book, why *does* the caged bird sing? I expected that awful silence again, but an answer came immediately from one student: "What else can it do?" Which is, of course, precisely correct. What else indeed? What Paul Laurence Dunbar meant in his poem, from which Angelou took her title, was that the caged bird knows a pain which *must* be expressed—and also that this expression is liberty. The voices you heard today, retrieved from the last century, all expressed an understanding of the power and value of the voice known only to those who have been denied one. None of us here will ever understand the preciousness of expression as did Annie Besant in her empty church and the little girl who ran home to the slave quarters with a head full of letters.

But there are levels on which we can partially comprehend, if only in that in each of us there is some caged bird waiting to sing, knowing that singing is its birthright, feeling as compelled to utterance as the psalmist who wrote, "I was dumb and silent, I held my peace to no avail; my distress grew worse, my heart became hot within me. As I mused, the fire burned; then I spoke with my tongue" (Psalms 39). We hold our peace to no avail, for we are born singers. Expression is as primal a need, I have come to believe, as food or warmth or even sex—and nearly as thrilling when it's done right. For many of us, it's bloody hard work, claiming that birthright, unlearning to not speak, as Marge Piercy wonderfully phrases it in the title of a poem. For the dumb demon is not merely our fear of the audience—the teacher, the class, the congregation, the faculty meeting; it is our deep and accurate knowledge that to speak is to commit, to assert, to assume the outrageous authority of a self, to announce to the world, "I am here." And that is a song the world waits in silence to hear, a song to delight and redeem the ghosts of Annie Besant and that anonymous enslaved girl, a song that inspires and empowers other singers, a song that slips through the bars of the cage and takes wing.

In the fall of 1987, I had just returned from my first sabbatical. I had spent most of the time at the Institute for Research on Women at Rutgers University, but I had also done two artists'-colony residencies.

In part this chapel talk was for me—I set myself the task of making congruent sense out of my year away. But I wound up going much further back than the previous September and rethinking my evolution as a feminist. To explain this to the diverse group that attends chapel, I had to justify women's studies once more, covering old territory. But that, to me, has always been one of the great challenges of speaking in chapel: One is required to translate private terms into a public language accessible to eighteen-year-old Young Republicans, fifty-year-old full professors, thirty-year-old clerical staff members, seventy-year-old emeritus faculty. It is, as they say in the theatre, a stretch.

14

A Room of One's Own
or
Running Away to New Jersey and Other Holy Places

October 9, 1987

> *There is a solitude of space*
> *A solitude of sea*
> *A solitude of death, but these*
> *Society shall be*
> *Compared with that profounder site*
> *That polar privacy*
> *A soul admitted to itself*
> *Finite Infinity*
> *—Emily Dickinson*

If a woman wrote, she would have to write in the common sitting room. And as [Florence] Nightingale was so vehemently to complain,—"women never have half an hour . . . that they can call their own"—she was constantly interrupted. Jane Austen wrote like that to the end of her days. "How she was able to effect all this," her nephew writes in his Memoir, "is surprising, for she had no separate study to repair to, and most of the work must have been done in the general sitting room, subject to all kinds of casual interruptions. She was careful that her occupation should not be suspected by servants or visitors or any persons beyond her own family party." Jane Austen hid her manuscripts or covered them with a piece of blotting paper. To Jane Austen there was something discreditable in writing *Pride and Prejudice.*

— Virginia Woolf,
A Room Of One's Own, 1928

This talk leaped full-blown into my head one day last fall, as I was jogging around the campus of Douglass College in New Brunswick, New Jersey. The fact that I was writing my homecoming chapel talk barely a month after I'd left Kalamazoo will tell you how homesick I was.

Earlier that week, I sat in my apartment on the edge of the Douglass campus watching "The Cavanaughs," a short-lived sitcom about a three-generation Irish-American family. In the second generation is a woman who misses her career in show biz and chafes at the constraints of domestic life far from the bright lights. In this particular episode, she escaped to a hotel room somewhere in New Jersey to think things over. Her teenaged niece, a strait-laced, good Catholic girl named Mary Margaret, followed her, having decided that she wanted to be more like her wild, reckless aunt. When she showed up at the motel and her aunt asked what she was doing there, the girl said she'd run away. "But Honey," said the aunt, "nobody runs away to New Jersey."

Well, I did. And I sat there laughing in my living room, the laughter of despair. Here I was, finally On Sabbatical. Sabbatical, that mysterious term for the sacred year when the professor makes some pilgrimage to an exotic place to do important research on an arcane subject. The word comes from the Hebrew for "rest" and is thus related to "sabbath." The sabbatical is, then, the academic Sabbath, the year in which the godlike professor rests. Unlike God, however, we rest not *from* the work of creation but *through* it. The sabbatical is "recreation" only in the true sense of "re-creation": creating oneself anew.

This was one lump of clay desperately seeking re-creation. Now, I knew that this was quite normal, for I'd watched my colleagues go through it before me, going to India, Japan, Germany, Mexico, even Florida. I went to New Jersey. "Remember the Sabbatical, to keep it holy," my friends had warned me. It is one of the Academic Commandments. And out of all the intellectual and cultural meccas the world affords, I pick New Jersey. Woody Allen once said that he believes there *is* an "intelligence in the universe, with the exception of parts of New Jersey." I was in one of them: one of the densest patches of crabgrass and stinkweed the Garden State can boast.

But as I ran around the Douglass campus that day, I was thanking heaven for small mercies. Douglass College was originally the New Jersey College for Women. When it merged into Rutgers University it changed its name to honor Mabel Smith Douglass, its previous president, but it retained its identity. And even in 1981, when the independent colleges constituting Rutgers merged administratively, Douglass hung on as a women's institution—in fact, it is the largest women's college in the United States, the largest of a dying breed. Its little campus is also by far the prettiest in the university and the closest thing to verdant to be found anywhere within twenty miles. As I ran through the fall air, I thought about what an oasis Douglass is, physically, within the city and within the monster megaversity. An island of grace and greenery in an urban wasteland.

Naturally, my thoughts turned west. Believe me, New Brunswick makes Kalamazoo look like paradise, but still, this campus of ours, this cozily enclosed quadrangle on our fair Arcadian hill, has a quality of separateness about it, felt by all of us. Many colleges do, and many were built with that ideal in mind: the idea of the academic village on the hill, a place apart, a physical space sanctified to unfettered contemplation and thoughtful discourse. Our campuses are direct descendants of medieval monasteries, as some of us are all too painfully aware. Nowadays, for better or worse, not much remains of that original ideal of quiet separateness but the physical campus itself. Nowadays, unfettered contemplation and thoughtful discourse are but two supplicants waiting their turn in the long line outside my office door.

And that is why there are sabbaticals, I thought, puffing around a corner. Sabbaticals are campuses of the mind and spirit. Sabbaticals are sacred, separate spaces in time, reserved and protected amid the New Brunswick of daily life. A sabbatical is the room of one's own to which one repairs from the common sitting room, as Virginia Woolf put it.

࿇ᏧᏨᎻ࿇

Looking straight down Nichol Avenue, I saw the spire of Voorhees Chapel on the Douglass campus. I am here, I thought, because in the basement of that chapel is housed one of the most extensive, ambitious, prestigious women's studies programs in the world. And one of its components, the Institute for Research on Women, has invited me to be something called an Affiliated Scholar. I am here because there is a book overdue in me, a book that has been whining and demanding to be written for six years, a book about women and teaching. About women teaching. About teaching women. And there has been no space for it at home. No space of time large enough, but also no room private enough, protected enough, where I wouldn't feel I had to hide the manuscript hurriedly when someone came in. So I sought not only a room far away from the crush and clutter of my Kalamazoo life, but a room where I could relax and speak freely, a comfortable room with the right pictures on the walls. That is, I went looking for a room of my own in a house where the talk of women proliferated; where the language of women was spoken fluently and clearly; where the serious study of women was neither ridiculed nor merely tolerated but encouraged and celebrated; where it was not marginal but central; where the other tenants were engaged in similar pursuits so that their work could validate and invigorate my own. I went looking, in fact, for a protected space—not in the sense of its being sheltered from reality, but in the sense of its being free, free of unwarranted, unhealthy impediments to good, hard work. Protected as we protect a child, or a plant, or a relationship, or even a nation, not in order to retard it, but in order that it might grow strong.

This is what Virginia Woolf wanted for Jane Austen and for the other literary foremothers who populate *A Room of One's Own*. Her title refers literally to that physical room that women didn't have in the houses they ran, for want of which their creativity suffered. But that room becomes a powerful, complex metaphor for the separate intellectual space women needed then and still need. Woolf shows how they needed it individually in order to accomplish anything artistic in the midst of lives cramped by oppression and consumed by the demands and needs of others. She leaves it mostly to her readers to make the larger connection, to see how women collectively need a room of their own as well where they can hear themselves speak, unmediated and undistorted by other voices, in order to understand clearly that they have an experience and a tradition of their own. Toward the end of this slim book, which has probably had a greater effect on me than any other, Woolf calls upon her audience—students at Newnham and Girton, the women's colleges at Cambridge and Oxford, in 1928—to direct the newly released light of their energy and creativity toward the vast, profound darkness surrounding women historically. She implores them to use their new intellectual, social, political, and economic freedoms to enlighten themselves and their daughters about themselves. That is, she calls for a serious study of women. Know thyself, she says like Socrates, but to a new audience, which had never had the chance to do so.

It took me years to develop the nerve to disregard the jeering voices within and around me and open that door and step into that room, the women's room. When I did, I was exhilarated—and relieved. First of all, it felt like home. It was *my* room. And second, instead of confinement, I found expansion; instead of limitation, endless possibility; instead of bias, balance; instead of partiality, wholeness; instead of separation, integration and completeness. And the windows in that room! I began to see that a separate room, a protected space, is not a place to hide but a place from which to look out. And whether we realize it or not, none of us is omniscient, none of us is God; all of us, in looking at the world, are looking out from some particular place, limited by who we are, where we've been, what we have, what we know or don't know. Standing in that room I was, as Emily Dickinson puts it, "a soul admitted to itself/Finite Infinity." That is, I began to observe the endlessly opening universe around me from a distinct vantage point called Myself.

One of my side-pilgrimages this year was to Amherst, Massachusetts, where I stood in front of Dickinson's house, looking up to that second-story window on the right side. From this window Dickinson observed the comings and goings of the neighbors from whom she kept her legendary distance. And at this window she wrote the poem you heard earlier and 1774 more, including the one that begins, "The Soul selects her own Society/Then shuts the door." Her famous reclusiveness was traditionally interpreted by stunningly condescending commentators as fearful and neurotic. Only recently have critics suggested that it may instead have been a professional choice and a very wise, brave one at that: the choice of protected space in which the poetic imagination of a Victorian woman could flourish. If "Lawyer Dickinson's half-cracked daughter," as they called her, "retreated" from the world, it was in that special sense of the word "retreat" as not a flight from an enemy but (and I quote again from my faithful Oxford English Dictionary) "a place of seclusion or privacy, a retired place or residence, a private chamber"—that is, a room of her own.

As I stood looking up at the window, my favorite Emily story came back to me: the one where she takes her niece Martha by the hand, pulls her into that room, closes the door, mimes locking it with an invisible key, smiles and whispers, "Matty—here's freedom!" Certainly she was acknowledging that only in that room could she preserve herself from the incessant domestic and social demands that defined female life in Amherst, Massachusetts, in the nineteenth century. But it was more than that. It was a political statement in the deepest sense. And it contained her rich understanding of how the finite can open onto infinity—the same understanding that makes her our premiere poet of interior space and the presence of the infinite in small things.

And I suddenly understood the nature of this sabbatical of mine, as a space set apart in time. I saw that it was not going to be pleasant always, for finding oneself alone in one's own room is not always pleasant. There is much silence and strange shadows move on the wall, and one is tempted to run down to the kitchen, where everybody is drinking coffee and laughing. "One need not be a Chamber— to be Haunted," writes Dickinson:

> *One need not be a House—*
> *The Brain has Corridors—surpassing*
> *Material Place—*
>
> *Far safer, of a Midnight Meeting*
> *External Ghost*
> *Than its interior Confronting—*
> *That Cooler Host*

That Interior Confronting was what my year would be about. Given the prospect of the Exterior world of New Brunswick, New Jersey, I thought the Interior began to look pretty good. So I walked in, locked the door, and whispered, "Griffin—here's freedom!"

✻⧉✻

I did it two more times in the course of my year away, entered two more secluded, sacred spaces, Finite Infinities. They were artists' colonies, places deliberately set apart to allow writers, visual artists, and musicians to work, undistracted and nurtured. One was the Millay Colony, in the Berkshires of far eastern New York State. Originally the home of Edna St. Vincent Millay, it is a collection of white clapboard farm buildings atop a mountain, where the silence becomes a presence. The other was the Ragdale Foundation in Lake Forest, Illinois, thirty miles north of Chicago in one of its posher suburbs. Mr. T lives right down the street. Ragdale was the estate of a nineteenth-century Chicago architect, Charles van Doren Shaw, and it sits amid English gardens, a vast meadow, and a wooded nature preserve. True culture shock after New Jersey, both of these places, and they couldn't have been more different from each other. But the experience was the same: entering a sacred, private room of one's own, enduring that Interior Confronting, feeling deeply both the terror of the blank page and the joy of being in a place where the significance of one's work is assumed and takes priority over all else. A highly unreal world, you might conclude, cloistered and serene, worshipping impractical deities like Poetry. Yet in both places I touched realities in and around me that I hadn't touched in years, or had never seen before.

We have always designated our holy places and made our pilgrimages: Delphi, Mecca, Jerusalem, Canterbury. Nowadays, perhaps, the holy places are not so well marked. Most of us must find or make our own. For me, this chapel has been one of them. But they are all around us, anywhere one finds or claims a room of one's own, where a soul is admitted to itself; anywhere one stumbles or seizes upon a "profounder site," a Finite Infinity. They are everywhere. Even here. Even in New Jersey.

> *The Heart is the Capital of the Mind—*
> *The Mind is a Single State—*
> *Heart and Mind together make*
> *A Single Continent.*
>
> *One is the population*
> *Numerous enough—*
> *This ecstatic Nation*
> *Seek—It is yourself.*
>
> —Emily Dickinson

A few years ago, in an effort to humanize residence halls and to narrow the gap between dorm rooms and classrooms, our Assistant Dean for Residence Life instituted the "Last Lecture" series. The premise goes thus: If you were going to die tomorrow, what would you want to say to the students?

An inspired and engaging idea. But when you actually face the prospect, it turns remarkably intimidating. I'm not certain that what follows amounts to my definitive Final Word, but it's close. For now, I'll let it stand. In my end is my beginning.

15

To the Land of the Dead
And Back Again
My "Last Lecture"

Tuesday, October 17, 1989

DeWaters Hall

Last Friday—the 13th, you'll recall—when those splendid publicity posters hit the campus, advertising Gail Griffin's Last Lecture, I had to explain to my Literary Questing class that, no, I was neither terminally ill nor about to resign my job. However, since the unguarded moment three long weeks ago when I heard myself say those four little words, "Sure, I'd love to," I have had the growing sense that both of those things might turn out to be true. On Friday last, when the Muse had steadfastly refused to get her butt in gear and Inspiration for this talk was nowhere in sight, I happened to read the Daily Bulletin. There was another announcement, which concluded with the words, "FREE FOOD—as if Gail wasn't enough!" At that point, entertaining visions of myself with an apple in my mouth, being dismembered, carved, and devoured, I knew the omens were getting pretty grim.

So Friday night was make-it-or-break-it time. Writing is much like childbirth: Sometimes the thing is all ready and slides right out; sometimes it takes days of labor; and sometimes you finally have to go in after it. I cleared away the dinner dishes, turned off "Cheers," and put on Mozart, my thinking music. A few minutes later I realized that I had chosen his "Requiem." It figured.

Suddenly—I kid you not—fireworks went off outside my house. Homecoming at Western Michigan University, I remembered, moving to the front window to watch. But also another omen: I had found my subject.

Last lectures. Me with an apple in my mouth, being devoured. Mozart mourning his dreadful old father. Friday the thirteenth. This had to add up to something. I suddenly thought of Odysseus, whose long voyage home I had just finished tracing with my Literary Questers. He is told by Circe, a wise and sexy witch, that in order to get home he must descend to the Land of the Dead to be instructed. There he meets the ghosts of his mother, his comrades in the Trojan War, and various others including the prophet Teiresias, who tells him about getting home. In class we had discussed this episode as a common one in quest stories: the necessary descent and symbolic death in order that new energy, renewed vision, and a new identity might be born.

That was it: I had to revisit my own Land of the Dead, and I had to tell you about it. Once I knew that, I understood an even earlier omen that came to me a month ago, when President Bush and company met at the University of Virginia in Charlottesville for the Education Summit. You see, that was my Land of the Dead, unlikely as it may seem: Thomas Jefferson's gorgeous campus at the foot of the Blue Ridge. When I left there to come here in August of 1977, I began devoting a great deal of energy to not thinking about Virginia. Periodically I am forced to go back down there, to talk to the ghosts, to learn again how to get home. Tonight is one of those occasions. I warn you that there is no expressway to the Land of the Dead. This will be a journey full of detours and back roads. But I'll get there—and back again.

To begin at the beginning, our first stop is the Garden of Eden, where another woman stands with an apple in her mouth. Her hunger for that forbidden fruit, you will recall, supposedly brings Death into the world. That is, she leads our descent to the Land of the Dead, better known as the Fall. She and her Significant Other are driven from their nice garden into the wilderness, to suffer and labor and try to "get themselves back to the Garden," as Joni Mitchell once put it. Like Odysseus, they begin the long trip home, back to a good relationship with their God, with themselves, with nature, with each other.

This particular myth has simmered inside me for many years now. I find it compelling for two reasons. One is that one interpretation of the story has provided justification for the oppression of women in the western world. Another is that there are so many other possible interpretations, all of them, to me, terribly relevant to our human experience and especially to the female experience of half of us.

These myths—one Greek, one Hebrew—have some commonalities. Both emphasize the necessity of human suffering. Odysseus just wants to sail home to his wife and son, whom he hasn't seen for twenty years. He's been through hell already. But when told he must make this perilous detour and actually go there in person, he grits his teeth and does it. Eve precipitates human beings from timeless Paradise into the world of time and struggle and loss—that is, the world we really live in. Seen in this light, she is not the Original Sinner but rather the Original Quester, taking us from a protected, childlike existence to the difficult world where we must grow up and "get a life."

Both stories also have to do with dangerous knowledge attained by two brave students. Odysseus follows orders and listens to all that hell has to teach him—and it ain't pretty. Eve, on the contrary, does not follow orders. In essence she's told not to want to know something, for it will make her too powerful. But she's hungry, and innocent, and she reaches up her hand and bites into that knowledge anyway, and like most powerful education, it hurts.

Finally, both myths have to do with exile and getting home—the long way. That is, both have to do with the treacherous voyage of human life, whose ultimate goal is our home port—ourselves, our fullest humanity, our rightful place in the universe. Literature from all ages tells us that there is no getting home without those voyages to the Land of the Dead. The more we try to stay on course by avoiding those dark detours, by buffering ourselves against them, the more we find ourselves lost.

It's from this vantage point that I look back at Virginia and realize what was happening to me, and why it had to happen as it did.

※\(※\)※

"Why did you choose Virginia?" English majors ask me. I've asked myself that question more than once.

I went to Virginia to study English literature, which I loved more than anything in the world. I went to Virginia because it was the best graduate program that had accepted me, and times were getting tough for Ph.D.'s in English. I went to Virginia because I thought the South might be interesting. I went to Virginia because I didn't know what the hell else to do with my life at 21. I went to Virginia because I knew I was a good student and wasn't too sure I was good at much else. I went to Virginia because Jeremy had gone there. He was the vital, vibrant, hairy, corduroy-clad young professor who taught my senior honors seminar in Keats and Shelley. I wanted to be just like him. I also wanted to run away with him, but a doctorate in English was a lot more likely.

I generally loved and adored my professors. Or, if I despised them, I loved despising them and did it with gusto. All of them were men. I had not one female teacher after high school. This was no accident, nor was it a function of the absence of women at Northwestern University. They were there, though in very small and untenured numbers. The sad fact is that I avoided them. When I now look back and ask why, the answer is painfully obvious: I was a good student, as I said, and I had learned my lessons well, and one of the lessons was that male teachers and male books counted. That was where the power lay. They were the real thing. I knew this so well I wasn't aware I knew it.

About a year ago I went into one of my cleaning binges, and the target this time was the storeroom in my basement. Another descent to the Land of the Dead. I came across moldy folders and manila envelopes and boxes crammed with every English paper I wrote in college. I hadn't looked at them for fifteen years. I lugged them upstairs and sat down on the floor of my living room and paged through them in an ecstacy of embarrassment, pride, hilarity, and pity for my eager little literary self. And along the way, I began to notice a certain obscure pattern. There was the paper written for my 18th century literature course on Samuel Richardson's huge novel, *Clarissa*. I had chosen for my topic the villainous character Lovelace and a strange, long fantasy Richardson gives him. It is a fantasy of raping the virginal Clarissa and being carried into the courtroom a hero, to the resounding applause of the crowd. There was also a paper for my American Literature I course on Hawthorne's *Blithedale Romance*. I had chosen for my topic the female characters, and the professor had written at the end that this was the first full treatment of the subject he had ever read—A. I came across my papers for Jeremy's Senior Honors Seminar: One was on Keats' letters to his girlfriend. I analyzed the way in which Keats conceptualized her, turning her into more of a symbolic destructive force than a real woman. The other was on the summer of 1816, when a group of extraordinary English writers of the Romantic period happened to be living in proximity to each other on the shores of Lake Geneva in Switzerland. In the paper I analyzed comparatively the works that emerged from that summer. One of the writers was Byron; another was Shelley. But the third was a young woman, eighteen years old, the daughter of William Godwin, an eminent philosopher, and Mary Wollestonecraft, the mother of feminist theory. Her name was Mary Wollestonecraft Godwin Shelley, and that summer she wrote *Frankenstein*.

Sitting on my living room floor I realized the presence of a ghost. She was someone I had been but had never known: a girl who never would have called herself a feminist and who avoided female professors, but whose imagination apparently kept drifting toward the female side of experience, obviously in search of herself, her own presence in the literature she was studying. In the papers she had become so proficient in churning out, she was accustomed to referring to "the reader" as a "he." But clearly, on some level in her brain, the reader was no such thing. The reader was a She.

And it was She who set off for Virginia in the fall of 1972.

✲❧✦❧✲

There are a million stories in the Land of the Dead. I want to tell you just two of them. Both involve an apple of knowledge, though one is wormy and one is crisp and sweet. Both are dangerous, for they involve a Fall from a what seems a safe, innocent garden into a wilderness. Both involve the death of an old self. New selves were waiting down the line. They always are, if you're willing to go for them. But what nobody ever tells you about this rebirth business is that it hurts. Ask any mother whether birth hurts. If babies could remember and articulate what it was like, they'd tell you how awful it is too. And another thing nobody tells you is that this rebirth takes time, and while it's going on, it mostly feels like dying. Mostly what you feel is the loss. Only years afterward—say, when you're about 39—do you look back and say, "Oh, so that's what I was turning into."

It was November, just two months after my arrival at "Mistuh Jeffuhson's Univuhsity," as they say in Charlottesville. I lived by myself in a nice new apartment about three blocks from campus. One night at about 3 a.m., I woke up. I was fully awake, as you are when you've heard something. What I had heard was my door opening and closing. With a sick flash I remembered that I'd unlocked it to run across the hall to borrow something, and I'd forgotten to relock it. Then I heard footsteps in my living room.

All student communities are targets for rapists. In the past two months, my neighborhood had been the site of several rapes, attributed by the police to one suspect. The one presently exploring my living room.

You always wonder what you'll do, what will go through your mind in a situation of physical danger. My life didn't flash before my eyes, but I did imagine the police or the university calling my mother. I thought very clearly: I thought about my options, which were few.

Realizing immediately that I had no idea whether he was armed, I knew I could not risk confronting him. Or maybe that's what I think I thought. Maybe I just froze. I know that my heart beat so powerfully that I thought I might have a coronary. I know that "time" became a fairly meaningless concept. I know that I prayed—to the man in my living room: Just go. Take my stereo. Take my purse, it's right there on the chair. Just go. But he didn't. I heard him come to the bedroom door, which was open. I opened my eyes a crack and saw his shadow there. I made a meager plan: I will not move unless he touches me. There is always the chance that he will go away.

He finally moved toward the bed. He seemed slow and disoriented; later it occurred to me that he might have been drunk or drugged. He sat on the floor next to my bed, within a foot of me. He sat there, breathing, for a full minute, or twenty, or twenty years. At last he reached up and touched my leg.

All my life I had been plagued by a dream in which I was in great peril and tried to scream, but nothing came out. I used to wonder if I was capable of a scream. When I felt his hand, I shot upright and uttered a truly world-class shriek. He fought with me for a second, or a minute, or an hour, or something, and then he turned and ran.

The police, one of them dusting for fingerprints, the other taking my story. Then the other one making me tell it again, and telling me in an exasperated voice that if he came back I should please try to get a better description. *If he came back?* The neighbors telling me that they had heard something but decided to ignore it. The fellow graduate student who listened and said, "Don't tell anybody. You don't want people here to think you're unstable or something."

And the trek home from campus each night, after I'd put it off as long as I could, knowing that once that door closed behind me, no matter how many times I locked and relocked it, I would not sleep. I would leave the lights on all night again, I would run the dishwasher over and over to drown out sounds I thought I heard, I would check every closet and cupboard over and over again, but I would not sleep. Not for six months.

And the worst of it, which was not the fear but the awareness of how fearful I could be. And the recognition that somehow something had happened to my eyes, because when I looked out my window I saw an entirely different world, as if some hand had drawn away a curtain. And the knowledge that that world was here to stay, that there was no going back, no unknowing what I now knew: that I was something I had never ever believed before that I was—a potential victim. I hated that knowledge. It infuriated me that this stranger could intrude into my reality and alter it permanently. I wanted ignorance like I wanted sleep. That is, I wanted unconsciousness. I wanted not to know this. Eve undoubtedly felt the same way.

Nothing happened, I kept telling people. Nothing happened, I told myself. But something had happened. Something for which I had no language. Something which no one else seemed to take very seriously, which meant that I must be taking it much too seriously myself, so I made light of it by daylight and lived with it sitting on my chest all night, every night.

With the innocence of young people about how life works, I urged myself to "get over" this. I was impatient to digest this experience and put it behind me and get back to being myself and leading my life. But somewhere in me I vaguely sensed the truth: that I would never be that self again. That some experiences are like scars: The wounds heal, but they do not disappear, and they mark you for good. The notion that such a mark might be a distinguishing mark, a mark of identity, never occurred to me.

ᔑᓭᓀᓂᔑ

That story comes from my first months down there in the Land of the Dead. The other one I want to tell you comes from my last months there. But between them is a space of five years, the longest five years of my life. The odd thing was that I was doing fine in my courses, proceeding apace toward the brass ring, the Ph.D. I wasn't the departmental star, but I wasn't struggling either. I learned a great deal about literature, but I learned more about the academic game. One goes to graduate school a bright student, but one leaves an academic, and that's different.

The University of Virginia, a state school, admitted women as undergraduate students in 1969, three years before my arrival. It had admitted black men much earlier. That in itself tells you what they thought of women of any color down there, because believe me, it was no paradise for black men. Only recently had they ceased the singing of "Dixie" at football games, and Confederate nostalgia was everywhere. On the gender front Mr. Jefferson's University was equally neanderthal. Despite sexual integration, the favorite sport for Virginia Gentlemen was "Rolling Down the Road," that is, mounting a caravan of cars to one of the nearby women's colleges to hunt out women. It was more sporting than dating women on campus, I guess. Alcohol (and I mean grain alcohol in tubs) and good-ole-boy behavior was the name of the game. The prestigious English department consisted of some sixty-five faculty members but not one single tenured woman. There was a handful of depressed, frightened, pressured untenured women scurrying around doing the scutwork of the department and trying to get their books published, but generally they were ground up and spit out after three years. I kept my unblemished record by never taking a class from any of them. If the power lines were visible at Northwestern, they were downright obvious at Virginia.

One of these young women was interested in women writers and feminist criticism. She had a small group of adherents, but mostly she was the butt of jokes among the graduate students and certainly the male faculty as well. It never occurred to me to take her courses. One of my fellow students got a graduate women's group going while I was there, and she too was the subject of contempt and ridicule. Contempt and ridicule in which I participated. I remember one standing joke amongst us, regarding Virginia's world-renowned Shakespeare scholar. As the story went, he emerged from the Ph.D. oral exams of a female student and announced to a group of assembled colleagues, "Cupcake's got brains." We roared at that one, over and over again.

It's not easy for me to face these memories. But graduate school was tough enough and the tight job market was closing in on us with each passing year. I wanted to be on the inside, not the outside, not "one of Them." I wanted to be accepted, included, taken seriously. Which meant allegiance to the regime, to the Brotherhood, to the Fathers.

I muddled through. My life was totally insular, centering on The Department and The Dissertation Director and, in general, Them, the men on whose approval my entire future and sense of self rested. But recently a memory that had been submerged for ten years surfaced again: During my last couple years there, I wandered into the campus Rape Crisis Center and volunteered my time, making up information pamphlets and distributing them. What prompted me to make that move I cannot recall at all, but I'm certain that it was more instinct than anything else. I wandered into a place where there were other women who understood. I knew that I was very fortunate not to have been raped or killed, more fortunate than millions of other women; but I also knew I had faced something that I needed to understand better. What this means is that I sensed a commonality with other women that needed expression. And I think that maybe on some level my finest instincts told me that the only possible way to redeem this experience of mine was to turn it to good use for someone else. How strange that for ten years I should repress the memory of such a milestone. For it was surely at the moment that I walked through that door that I began my ascent from the Land of the Dead.

❧

I said that one apple was wormy and the other crisp and sweet. Such is the nature of difficult, dangerous knowledge: Sometimes it tastes awful and makes you sick for days; sometimes it comes like wind on a hot day or spring in Michigan, refreshing and welcome. In this case you discover that you have been in the Land of the Dead and now see light up above. Sometimes, as Odysseus discovered, the Goddess Athena is there to lead you out.

She handed this apple to me during my last year at Virginia, as I was wrestling two hairy monsters worthy of Odysseus himself: the Dissertation and the Job Market. The Golden Delicious took the form of two books that were not on any reading list in the English Department. One was Virginia Woolf's *A Room of One's Own*, originally published in 1928. The other was more recent, a book called *Literary Women*, by the late Ellen Moers. My mother sent it to me for my 26th birthday. It was among the first full-length works of feminist literary criticism, a study of the best known women writers and the commonalities among their lives and work. Woolf's brilliant little book is simply a history of English literature from the point of view of someone asking the forbidden question, "Where are the women?" Its most famous passage is the story of Shakespeare's fictional sister. Both books made me look back, there as I was nearing the end of my formal education, and ask questions I had never thought to ask, questions I had been discouraged from asking.

I remember quite clearly a singular feeling while reading these books: a combination of delight and outrage. The delight was the discovery not so much of individual women writers but of a genuine, bona fide female tradition in literature. The outrage was simple and pure: Why, in nine years of top-notch post-secondary education, had no one told me this? Why had this mother lode which was my heritage been buried and kept from me?

Moers and Woolf discussed all the women writers I loved and some of whom I was ignorant—but they discussed them as *women*. I had learned to think that this somehow diminished them, just as surely as I had learned to think that my femaleness diminished me. Instead, these books made them sisters in a common enterprise. And this, suddenly, was the enterprise I was joining. This world of literature was suddenly one in which I was a citizen, one which was mine to explore and to open to my students.

Sometimes we do not discover what we need until the need is filled. Then we see what has been missing, the unrecognized hunger. The girl who naively concocted woman-centered papers at Northwestern had finally found the teacher she needed to put it all in context, to give it meaning and validity. The girl who wanted to be a female professor but had never experienced one began thinking about what it meant to be a woman at the front of a classroom. The lover of English literature began to think about what she had studied and what she had not studied, about who made the Major Authors List for the Ph.D. oral exams and who did not, about how some writers got to be considered Important while others were abandoned to oblivion or regarded as "minor." The woman who had felt alien and isolated for five years at Mr. Jefferson's University began to understand part of the reason why.

Years later, I read the words of Elizabeth Barrett Browning, writing in the mid-nineteenth century: "I look everywhere for grandmothers, and find none." Measure that against the words of Virginia Woolf: "We think back through our mothers, if we are women." I think this concept may be hard for white men to understand because their education, wherever they go to school, consists precisely of their own tradition, given to them in books and courses and speeches and prizes. I think this may be hard for women to understand because it is a need we often do not know we have, so acculturated are we to the status quo, the prevailing notions of what is important; and so adept do we become at identifying with the male point of view. But without our grandmothers we are adrift on the ocean, thinking that our experience is isolated, unique, private, neurotic. Without our past we are blanks, amnesiacs, lacking identity or purpose. The fundamental goal of education is to give us a usable past, to make us members of the human family. And the human family, like any family, becomes dysfunctional when some of its voices are silenced or unheard.

I plowed ahead with my dissertation on the autobiographies of four Victorian Englishmen. But other voices were in my head.

※⟨⟨⟩⟩※

One day I found myself in my packed-to-the-roof Toyota station wagon in the Blue Ridge, heading north to Kalamazoo, the Land of the Living.

One of my themes seems to be that oftentimes things are working within us which we cannot name or understand. Deep inside me that day was a resolve of which I was unaware until years later—in fact, until the dust cleared after the battle over women's studies here at Kalamazoo. I had resolved, without really knowing it, that now that I was going to be a teacher, it would be part of my job to make sure that no student went hungry as I had done if I could help it; that no student, female or male, who needed mothers and grandmothers would go orphaned.

Those of you who have visited my office know that I have the primo office door at Kalamazoo College. It is a point of real pride. Above the doorknob there is a brown and white sticker that reads, "Feminism Spoken Here." I remember quite clearly the day I stuck it on there, along about my fourth or fifth year at K. I deliberated nervously for a long time before doing it. The "F-word" frightened me as much as it probably frightens many of you. What would it do to my reputation to advertise myself as One of Those? Believe me, I found out. Yet something in me knew that sticker had to go there, to let people know that if they want to venture into the forbidden tongue, I will speak it with them; that if they are coming to realizations for which there is no other language, my office is a place where they can try to describe them.

A year ago a reporter from the *Index* came to interview me. He waited outside my office while I finished a conference with another student, and like most of my waiting clients, he read my door. When I ushered him in, he began his interview with a question that stopped me cold: "'Feminism Spoken Here.' Do you then consider feminism to be a language?"

I heard myself say yes, realizing how absolutely accurate it was. Yes, indeed, that is precisely what feminism is to me, I said: a language. A way of speaking about experience. Like most languages, when you enter into it, you see things differently; a new reality emerges, full of possibilities.

That sticker has brought into my office the most significant discussions I have had at Kalamazoo College. By no means are they all pleasant, or easy, or gratifying. In fact, most of them are not. Over twelve years I have listened to tales of rape, abortion, and sexual harassment that have sent me home at night in despair. On those days I am in the Land of the Dead once more. But I am never sorry that I have been there to hear them, and I am grateful daily for the other people on this campus who, in their own ways, advertise to students that they will listen too. That sticker has also elicited the conversations that can singlehandedly make my day and justify my professional life, where young women and men tell me things that actually make me believe the human race might be worth fighting for.

Using that language, I can now describe meaningfully the two experiences in the Land of the Dead that I have shared with you. The first, the experience of the stranger who entered my life in November of 1972, was my poisoned apple, my descent into the aspect of female existence that is terrorized, victimized, and oppressed. According to statistics, the reality of sexual abuse is shared by one-fourth of women by the time they are eighteen years old. The odds are that one-third of women in the United States will be raped. A rape occurs every seven seconds in this country. What happened to me is utterly trivial compared to what happens to other women daily, hourly. But it did serve to allow me access to the world of those women, to understand, if only minimally, their experience, and through that, our mutual danger as women and the critical need for us not to let each other be alone.

The second episode, involving the other strangers, who entered into my life in the summer of 1976, is my golden apple, the other side of female being. It is the pride, the dignity, the accomplishment and perseverance against unfathomable odds. It is the great gift of being able to think back through my mothers. It is the presence of grand-mothers, gathered around me, welcoming me. But it too has its dangers. My point—and, I think, the point in Genesis—is that all apples do. The danger of the golden apple is that, as with the poisoned apple, your vision is changed forever. The world does not look the same to you as it does to the majority of your fellow human beings, and you are regarded as at least strange, at most deviant, dangerous, or crazy. You live always on the margins of the institutions to which you belong—even beloved institutions, like this one. Once you have eaten the apple, you often feel lonely and isolated, often angry, sometimes paranoid. But you do feel real. Somewhere in this apple is a core that tells you who you are, and seeds, too, that promise something new and wonderful.

Both apples have left me with a single legacy, again a piece of knowledge: the knowledge that whatever I do, whatever I become, I am standing on the shoulders of those who went before, women who struggled and achieved, women who suffered and died, literally or figuratively. Queens and slaves, mothers and madwomen, poets and prostitutes— all of them are there. We live in a culture centered on the individual in many ways. One thing the language of feminism has taught me is how narrow, how partial this view is. I have come to the point where I garner more strength from being part of a force larger than myself than from the notion that I am unique, separate, and capable of achieving everything on my own. I think this is a dangerous delusion, a fallacy in western thought, in fact. Women have always been more collective beings than men, and this truth, reflected in feminist thought, has been a salvation for me. In the aftermath of the first apple, the poisoned, wormy one, the ultimate power of the experience came through only when I connected it with the experience of other women. In digesting the second apple, the sweet and golden one, I essentially joined a historical community of women. There are stories of women that I carry with me in everything I do—women I've known, women I've read about; women I've taught, women who've taught me; those who inspire me through their achievement, those who inspire me through their suffering. Their pain and their triumph are equally valuable to me. And both are within me, parts of me. Both guide me on my way through the wilderness, assuring me that exile is the human condition and apples the human food; and that if my mother Eve could forge her way into the unknown, so can I. I see her not as the perpetrator of sin and death, but as the archetypal pioneer, moving through the Land of the Dead to a new world, as Linda Pastan suggests in one of my all-time favorite poems, "Aspects of Eve"[1]:

> To have been one
> of many ribs
> and to be chosen.
> To grow into something
> quite different
> knocking finally
> as a bone knocks
> on the closed gates of the garden—
> which unexpectedly
> open.

Notes

PART ONE: THE FORTUNATE FALL

Chapter One—THE FORTUNATE FALL

1. *Two-Headed Woman* (Amherst: U. Mass., 1980), p. 53.
2. Ibid., 47.
3. Quoted in *Root of Bitterness: Documents of the Social History of American Women*, ed. Nancy F. Cott (N.Y.: Dutton, 1972), pp. 227-28.
4. Quoted in *Black Women Writers at Work*, ed. Claudia Tate (Harpenden, Hertfordshire: Oldcastle, 1985), pp. 114-15.
5. Ibid., 34.

Chapter Two—FAIR ARCADIAN HILL or "YES, THERE REALLY IS..."

1. "Alma Mater," R.F. Holden and W.F. Dunbar.
2. Charles T. Goodsell and Willis F. Dunbar, *Centennial History of Kalamazoo College* (Kalamazoo: 1933), p. 29.
3. *Century of Struggle: The Woman's Rights Movement in the United States* (N.Y.: Athenaeum, 1972), p. 122.
4. For an analysis of the role of the midwest in the spread of coeducation, see my article "Emancipated Spirits: Women's Education and the American Midwest," *Change* 16:1 (January/February 1984), 32-40.
5. Quoted in Belle M. Perry, *Lucinda Stone, Her Life and Reminiscences* (Detroit: Blinn Publishing Co., 1902), p. 309.
6. Quoted in Perry, pp. 115-16.
7. *Signs* 3:4 (1978), 759-773.

Chapter Three—ALMA MATER

1. Julia Gilbert Elder, ed., *Reunion of Former Pupils of Rev. J.A.B. Stone, D.D., and Mrs. L.H. Stone* (Kalamazoo Publishing Co., 1886), p. 55.
2. Ibid., 56.
3. Ibid., 54.
4. Ibid., 46.
5. Ibid., 57.

6. *Kalamazoo Gazette*, March 15, 1900.
7. Quoted in Belle M. Perry, *Lucinda Stone, Her Life and Reminiscences* (Detroit: Blinn Publishing Co., 1902), p. 59.
8. Elder, 35.
9. Quoted in Perry, 341.
10. Quoted in Mary Field Belenky et al, *Women's Ways of Knowing* (N.Y.: Basic, 1986), p. 214.
11. "February 13, 1980," *Two-Headed Woman* (Amherst: U. Mass., 1980), p. 15.

Chapter Four—A RITE OF PASSAGE

1. Lewis Carroll, *Alice's Adventures in Wonderland* (N.Y.: Harper, 1901), pp. 93-94.
2. Ibid., 94-95.
3. Ibid., 95.
4. Ibid., 59-60.
5. Ibid., 108-09.
6. Ibid., 109.

PART TWO: VOCATION

Chapter Six—A GOOD AND WORTHY VOICE

1. "Voices," *The Five Stages of Grief* (N.Y.: Norton, 1976), p. 7.
2. Quoted in *Black Women Writers at Work*, ed. Claudia Tate (Harpenden, Hertfordshire: Oldcastle, 1985), p. 78.
3. "friends come," *Two-Headed Woman* (Amherst: U. Mass., 1980), p. 56.
4. *Joan of Arc: The Image of Female Heroism* (N.Y.: Vintage, 1982).
5. Ibid., 22.
6. Ibid., 22.
7. Ibid., 23.
8. Ibid., 21.
9. Ibid., 132-36.
10. Ibid., 134.
11. Ibid., 122.
12. Ibid., 121.
13. Ibid., 123.
14. In *On Lies, Secrets, and Silence: Selected Prose 1966-1978* (N.Y.: Norton, 1979), pp. 157-183.
15. *Stealing the Language: The Emergence of Women's Poetry in America* (Boston: Beacon, 1986), pp. 40-41.

16. Cambridge: Harvard, 1982.
17. "The Willing Suspension of Disbelief: Conflicts of Female Adolescence," working paper, Laurie Chair Seminar in Female Adolescence, Douglass College, Rutgers University, fall, 1986, pp. 2-3.
18. Gilligan, "The Willing Suspension of Disbelief," 20.
19. "to joan," *Two-Headed Woman*, 57.
20. Charlotte Bronte, *Jane Eyre* (N.Y.: Norton, 1971), p. 8. All subsequent page citations refer to this edition.
21. Acceptance Speech, 1974 National Book Awards, on behalf of herself, Audre Lorde, and Alice Walker.
22. Quoted in Miriam Gurko, *The Ladies of Seneca Falls: The Birth of the Women's Rights Movement* (N.Y.: Schocken, 1976), p. 10.
23. Quoted in *Black Women in White America: A Documentary History*, ed. Gerda Lerner (N.Y.: Vintage, 1973), p. 564.
24. Quoted in *Strong-Minded Women and Other Lost Voices from Nineteenth-Century England*, ed. Janet Murray (N.Y.: Pantheon, 1982), pp. 215-16.
25. *A Room of One's Own* (N.Y.: Harcourt Brace, 1929), p. 51.
26. Quoted in Murray, 205.
27. *Two-Headed Woman*, 60.
28. Quoted in *Black Women Writers*, 78.
29. *No More Masks! An Anthology of Poems by Women* (Garden City, N.Y.: Anchor, 1973).

Chapter Seven—MAN HATING: VOICES IN THE DARK

1. "The Contemporary Emergency and the Quantum Leap," *On Lies, Secrets, and Silence* (N.Y.: Norton, 1979), p. 264.

Chapter Nine—ORPHANS OF THE STORM: THE F-WORD AND THE POST-FEMINIST GENERATION

1. Foreword, *On Lies, Secrets, and Silence* (N.Y.: Norton, 1979), pp. 11-12.
2. Reverend Al Sharpton, Radio Interview, March, 1987.

Chapter Ten—VOCATION

1. Mary Field Belenky et al, *Women's Ways of Knowing* (N.Y.: Basic, 1986), p. 217.
2. "Bryn Mawr Commencement Address (1986)," *Dancing at the Edge of the World: Thoughts on Words, Women, Places* (N.Y.: Grove, 1988), pp. 148-49.

3. Ibid., 149.
4. Ibid., 150.
5. "Thoughts on Writing: A Diary," *The Writer On Her Work*, ed. Janet Sternburg (N.Y.: Norton, 1980), p. 112.
6. "Woman/Wilderness," *Dancing at the Edge of the World*, 162.
7. *In Search of Our Mothers' Gardens* (N.Y.: Harcourt Brace, 1983), pp. 155-160.
8. *The Color Purple* (N.Y.: Washington Square, 1982), p. 253.
9. Newspaper interview, 1989.
10. *On Lies, Secrets, and Silence* (N.Y.: Norton, 1979), p. 67.
11. *The Color Purple*, 247.
12. "Poetry: II, Chicago," *Your Native Land, Your Life* (N.Y.: Norton, 1986), p. 67.

PART THREE: FIRST PERSON... SINGULAR

Chapter Eleven—A PURPLE CREATURE

1. Alice Walker, *The Color Purple* (N.Y.: Washington Square, 1982), p. 187.
2. Ibid., 187.
3. Ibid., 187.
4. Ibid., 46.
5. Ibid., 177.
6. Ibid., 201.
7. The motto of Kalamazoo College, "Let there be light."
8. Walker, 247.
9. Ibid., 230.
10. Ibid., 247.

Chapter Twelve: NO ABSTRACT FIRES: A NEW YEAR'S MESSAGE

1. *The Moon as a Slice of Pineapple* (Athens: U. of Georgia Press, 1984), pp. 24-25.
2. The Kalamazoo student body's term for the players who descend upon the College each August for the United States Tennis Association's Junior Nationals tournament.
3. "Deviant" is no term of opprobrium at Kalamazoo. It simply refers to the large number of students who formally deviate from the official Kalamazoo Plan.

4. Quoted in Evelyn Fox Keller, *A Feeling for the Organism: The Life and Work of Barbara McClintock* (San Francisco: Freeman, 1983), p. 69.
5. Ibid., 178.
6. Ibid., 178.
7. Ibid., 179.
8. Ibid., 198.
9. Ibid., 118.
10. Quoted in Gerald Holton, *Thematic Origins of Scientific Thought* (Cambridge: Harvard, 1973), p. 357.
11. Quoted in Banesh Hoffman and Helen Dukes, *Albert Einstein, Creator and Rebel* (N.Y.: New American Library, 1973), p. 222.

Chapter Thirteen—UNLEARNING TO NOT SPEAK or WHY THE CAGED BIRD SINGS

1. Quoted in *Strong-Minded Women and Other Lost Voices from 19th-Century England,* ed. Janet Murray (N.Y.: Pantheon, 1982), p. 294.
2. Quoted in *Black Women in White America: A Documentary History,* ed. Gerda Lerner (N.Y.: Random House, 1972), pp. 29-30.
3. Quoted in a Senior Individualized Project by Jane S. Field, Kalamazoo College, 1985.
4. Maya Angelou, *I Know Why the Caged Bird Sings* (N.Y.: Bantam, 1971), p. 73.
5. Ibid., 77.
6. Ibid., 82.
7. Ibid., 84.

Chapter Fifteen—TO THE LAND OF THE DEAD AND BACK AGAIN: MY LAST LECTURE

1. *AM/PM: New and Selected Poems* (N.Y.: Norton, 1982), p. 53.

DATE DUE

11-9-94			
MAY 2 7 1995			
JUN 0 9 1995			
GAYLORD			PRINTED IN U.S.A.